NEW HISTORY IN CONTEXT 2

M.E. Collins

Peter Gallagher

Jim Byrne

John Keogh

General Editor: M.E. Collins

THE EDUCATIONAL COMPANY

First published 1996

The Educational Company of Ireland

Ballymount Road

Walkinstown

Dublin 12

Design and artwork: Design Image

Cover: Design Image

Origination: Impress Communications Group

Printed in the Republic of Ireland by Smurfit Web Press

Part No AHI 50725

0123456789

The
paper used in
this book comes
from Managed
Forests in
Northern
Europe
For
every
tree
felled, at
least one new
tree is planted

CONTENTS

Part 3: International Relations in the Twentieth Century

ACKNOWLEDGMENTS

The publishers wish to thank the following for assistance with photographic material and for permission to reproduce copyright material:

John Topham Picture Library, Radio Times Hulton Picture Library, Documentation Francaise Phototheque, Weimar Archive, Rod Tuach, Tom Sheedy and Geraldine Considine of Bunratty Folk Park, Stewart McKee of UCD Library, National Portrait Gallery, Paul Popper Ltd, Keystone Press Agency Ltd, Imperial War Museum, National Library of Ireland, National Gallery of London, National Museum of Ireland, Independent Newspapers Ltd, Irish Times, National Portrait Gallery of London, The Cork Examiner, Mary Evans Picture Library, Folklore Department UCD, Ulster Museum, Ulster Folk and Transport Museum.

PART 1

POLITICAL DEVELOPMENTS IN IRELAND IN THE TWENTIETH CENTURY

CHAPTER 1

Ireland in 1900: Part of the United Kingdom

Then and now

In this section, you will study the great changes which have occurred in Ireland since the beginning of the twentieth century. It will be easier to understand these changes if you look at the two maps below. They show Britain and Ireland as they are today and as they were in 1900. Look at the maps and then answer these questions.

QUESTIONS

1. Which map shows Britain and Ireland today? Which map shows them in 1900?
2. Mention three differences you notice between the two maps.

DID YOU GET THAT RIGHT?

☑ Today, a **border** divides the island of Ireland into two parts, the **Republic of Ireland** and **Northern Ireland**. In 1900, there was no border.

☑ Today, only Northern Ireland is part of the United Kingdom. In 1900, the whole of Ireland was part of the UK.

In this section, you will find out how these changes came about.

IRISH ATTITUDES TO THE UNITED KINGDOM

In 1800, the British parliament passed the **Act of Union**. This act joined Ireland and Britain into "the United Kingdom of Great Britain and Ireland". But by 1900, Irish people were divided in the way they felt about this arrangement.

☑ Some of them thought that union with Britain was good for Ireland. They wanted to keep Ireland within the United Kingdom. They were called **Unionists**.

☑ Some thought that union with Britain was bad for Ireland. They were called **Nationalists** because they believed Ireland was a nation in its own right, not just a part of Britain. They wanted Ireland to have its own government and to run its own affairs.

A

THE UNITED KINGDOM OF GREAT BRITAIN AND IRELAND

B

THE UNITED KINGDOM OF GREAT BRITAIN AND NORTHERN IRELAND

THE REPUBLIC OF IRELAND

Who were Nationalists and who were Unionists?

▟ **Religion** was one answer to this question. Most Irish Catholics were Nationalists. Most Irish Protestants were Unionists.

▟ **Economic conditions** provide a second answer. Most Unionists lived in the north-east of Ireland, around the city of Belfast. Since the Act of Union in 1800, this area had prospered while the rest of Ireland had got poorer.

The map at the right shows where most Unionists lived at that time.

The box below explains the views of Nationalists and Unionists.

☐ Nationalists

■ Unionists

Where Nationalists and Unionists lived in 1900

Nationalists and Unionists lived in every part of Ireland. But as the map shows, Nationalists were in the majority in one area, while Unionists were in a majority in the other.

WHY DID NATIONALISTS NOT WANT TO STAY IN THE UNITED KINGDOM?	WHY DID UNIONISTS WANT TO STAY IN THE UNITED KINGDOM?
▟ 75% of Irish people were Catholic but in Britain most people were Protestant. Catholics felt the British discriminated against them.	▟ Only 25% of Irish people were Protestants. They knew that Irish Catholics would outnumber them in an Irish parliament and they felt safer linked to Britain.
▟ Many Irish Catholics felt they were descended from the Celts who lived in Ireland long ago. They felt this made them different from people in other parts of the UK.	▟ Many Protestants felt they were descended from British settlers who came here in the plantations. They felt **both** Irish **and** British and did not want Ireland to be cut off from Britain.
▟ Most of Ireland got poorer since the Union began in 1800. Nationalists thought an Irish parliament would manage the Irish economy better.	▟ Many Unionists lived in East Ulster where industries had grown since the Union. Unionists feared that they would lose business if Ireland left the UK.

▟ QUESTIONS ▟

1. Trace a map of Ireland into your notebook. On it, mark the areas where: (a) most people were Nationalists; and (b) most people were Unionists.
2. Explain in your own words what a Nationalist was. Give three reasons why Nationalists were dissatisfied with the Union. Which of these do you think was the most important? Explain your choice.
3. Explain in your own words what a Unionist was. Give three reasons why Unionists wanted to stay in the United Kingdom. Which of these seems the most important to you? Explain your choice.

CHAPTER 2

Nationalists and Unionists

Who ruled the United Kingdom?

The head of the United Kingdom was the king or queen. Edward VII became king in 1901. But the king or queen had only a ceremonial position. The real power belonged to the **prime minister**.

The prime minister was elected by the parliament which met in the Palace of Westminster in London. Under the **Act of Union**, Ireland elected 105 **members of parliament (MPs)** to the Westminster parliament. Since there were also 550 British MPs, the Irish were always outnumbered. This is another reason why Irish Nationalists were dissatisfied with being part of the United Kingdom.

The Palace of Westminster, where the United Kingdom parliament still meets. In 1900, 105 Irish MPs attended the House of Commons. Today, 17 MPs represent Northern Ireland at Westminster.

Extreme Nationalists: the Republican tradition

In the 1860s, some Nationalists formed a secret society called the **Irish Republican Brotherhood** (the **IRB**). Its aim was to cut all links with Britain and set up a totally independent Irish republic.

The IRB leaders knew that Britain would never agree to this peacefully. In 1867, they staged a violent rebellion to achieve their aims. It was a complete failure. Most Irish Nationalists did not want violence and the IRB did not get much support.

But the IRB did not give up hope. They remained in the background, waiting for another chance to stage a rebellion.

Moderate Nationalists: the idea of Home Rule

Members of the IRB were Republicans or extreme Nationalists. They wanted to cut all links between Ireland and Britain and to do so by force. But most Nationalists were more moderate. They did not want to use force and were happy to keep some links between Ireland and Britain.

Moderate Nationalists wanted Ireland to have its own parliament which would deal with local Irish issues like health and education. In return, they would accept the British king as king of Ireland and let the Westminster parliament make decisions about important issues such as trade or war and peace. This idea was called **Home Rule**.

The Home Rule Party and the Liberals

In the 1870s, moderate Irish Nationalists set up the **Home Rule Party**. Their main aim was to persuade the British to give Ireland its own parliament.

For thirty years, the Home Rule Party grew. By 1900, over eighty of the 105 Irish MPs in Westminster belonged to it. They managed to win one of the British political parties, the **Liberals**, to their cause. The Liberals promised to give Home Rule to Ireland as soon as they won a general election.

The Unionist Party and the Conservatives

Irish Unionists were frightened by the success of the Home Rule Party. They set up the **Unionist Party** to defend the union with Britain. They also persuaded the other main British political party, the **Conservatives**, to back them. For many years, from 1886 to 1906, the Conservatives won one British election after another. This kept the Unionists safe from Home Rule.

◢ QUESTIONS ◢

1. What was a republican? To which secret society did many republicans belong?
2. What was the Home Rule Party? What was its main aim?
3. Write down two differences between a republican and a Home Ruler.
4. Which British political party: (a) supported Home Rule; (b) supported the Unionists?

CHAPTER 3

Ireland's Cultural Revival

Between 1886 and 1906, the Conservative party kept winning elections, so there was no hope of Home Rule for Ireland.

As a result, a number of new organisations grew up in Ireland which were more concerned with Irish culture and Irish sports than with Irish independence. Young people who were tired of waiting for Home Rule joined them in great numbers.

The decline of Irish culture

Throughout the nineteenth century, Irish people became more and more like the English. They spoke English, not Irish. They read English newspapers and played English games like cricket and soccer. They went to English plays and listened to English music.

Proud to be Irish

Nationalists were worried that the Irish were simply imitating English people. If they continued to do this, how could Ireland claim to be a separate nation, independent of England? They set up new movements to reverse this trend and make Irish people proud of their own culture and traditions.

◪ THE GAELIC ATHLETIC ASSOCIATION (GAA)

The first of these movements was the **Gaelic Athletic Association**. It was set up in 1884 by **Michael Cusack**, a teacher from Clare. The GAA set the rules and organised competitions for Irish games like Gaelic football and hurling.

Membership of the GAA grew quickly. Soon, every parish had its own club. A whole series of matches eventually led to the All-Ireland finals, the first of which was played in 1887.

GAA members elected their own leaders, ran the clubs and organised competitions. This gave many Irish men their first experience of running a democratic movement.

◪ THE GAELIC LEAGUE

By 1890, the Irish language was disappearing fast. Only 14 per cent of people could speak it and most of them were old. When they died, the language would die with them.

Two men who were worried by this were **Douglas Hyde** and **Eoin MacNeill**. In 1893, they founded the **Gaelic League**. The League had the following aims:

- to set up clubs where people could learn Irish
- to print books and newspapers in Irish
- to encourage people to speak Irish.

Douglas Hyde (1860-1949), founder of the Gaelic League and the first president of Ireland

Young men and women were eager to join the Gaelic League so they could learn to speak Irish, dance Irish dances and sing Irish songs. The League's newspaper, *An Claidheamh Soluis*, printed news, poems and stories in Irish. It was edited by **Patrick Pearse**.

Douglas Hyde hoped that Unionists and Nationalists could work together to save the Irish language. But republicans believed that only an independent Irish government could protect it. In 1915, they convinced the Gaelic League to support the idea of an Irish republic. Hyde did not agree with this, so he resigned from the League in protest.

THE ANGLO-IRISH LITERARY MOVEMENT

Not everyone wanted to learn Irish, however. Most people preferred to read stories, plays and poems about Ireland which were written in English. In the 1890s, a group of writers came together to encourage the idea of an Irish literature in English. They formed the **Anglo-Irish Literary Movement**.

W.B. Yeats (1865-1939) as a romantic young poet

William Butler Yeats and **Lady Gregory** were two leaders of this movement. Yeats used Irish names and stories in his poems. Lady Gregory wrote plays based on the stories she heard from old people near her home in Co. Galway. In 1904, Yeats and Lady Gregory founded the **Abbey Theatre** in Dublin to put on plays about Ireland which were written in English.

The most famous Abbey playwright was **John Millington Synge**. Synge went to the Aran Islands to learn Irish there. He listened to the stories which the people told. His most famous play, *The Playboy of the Western World*, is based on a story about a man who killed his father. Nationalists thought this was an insult to the

Irish people and there were riots in the Abbey when the play was put on.

Augusta, Lady Gregory (1852-1932)

Yeats on the stage of the Abbey Theatre defending Synge's 'Playboy of the Western World'. Can you see Lady Gregory in the audience?

▪ QUESTIONS ▪

1. Write a short paragraph about the aims and achievements of the GAA.
2. Who founded the Gaelic League? What were their aims and what did they achieve?
3. Give one important difference between the Gaelic League and the Anglo-Irish Literary Movement.
4. Name two people involved in the Irish Literary Movement.

CHOOSE ONE OF THE PEOPLE YOU NAMED IN QUESTIONS 2 AND 4. USE LIBRARY BOOKS TO FIND OUT MORE ABOUT THAT PERSON AND WRITE A SHORT ESSAY ON HIS OR HER LIFE.

Finding Out

CHAPTER 4

The Revival of Extreme Nationalism

The revival of the IRB

By 1900, some Irish Nationalists had grown tired of waiting for Home Rule. Young Irishmen joined the IRB which began to grow once again.

One of these young men was **Seán McDermott** who thought of a new policy. He encouraged IRB members to join and take over organisations like the GAA and the Gaelic League. In 1915, the IRB got the Gaelic League to support their idea of an Irish republic.

Seán McDermott

Arthur Griffith's plan for Sinn Féin

IRB men also supported a new party called **Sinn Féin**. It was set up in 1905 by a Dublin journalist, **Arthur Griffith**.

Griffith was a republican, but he knew that most Irish people did not like the idea of violence. So he came up with a new plan for winning independence for Ireland.

Arthur Griffith (1871-1922) was a Dublin journalist who founded the Sinn Féin party in 1905.

He proposed that Sinn Féin should campaign to get their own MPs elected. But they would not go to Westminster, like the Home Rule MPs did. Instead, they would stay in Dublin, elect an Irish government and simply ignore the British government. In this way, Griffith thought, it would be possible to win independence for Ireland without using violence.

Home Rule and the decline of Sinn Féin

At first, Sinn Féin did well. But in 1906, the Liberal Party finally won an election in Britain. By 1910, they were ready to give Ireland Home Rule. Excited nationalists flocked back to the Home Rule party and abandoned Sinn Féin.

Griffith refused to give up, however. For the next few years, he worked quietly in the background to keep his ideas alive.

The Home Rule Crisis and World War I

John Redmond

In 1900, **John Redmond** became leader of the Home Rule Party. He was good at negotiating with British politicians and worked closely with the Liberal leader and prime minister, **Herbert Asquith**. Asquith needed the votes of Redmond's party to stay in power, so in 1910 he promised to give Ireland Home Rule. It was to become law in 1914.

▲ *John Redmond led the Home Rule party from 1900 until his death in 1918.*

◄ *Sir James Craig helped Carson to oppose Home Rule and took over as leader of the Unionists in 1921.*

people signed the **Ulster Covenant**, promising to oppose Home Rule.

This is the document they signed. Read it carefully. Can you find three reasons the Unionists gave for not wanting Home Rule?

Edward Carson and James Craig

As we learned on page 5, the Unionists were afraid of Home Rule. In 1910, they elected a lawyer from Dublin, **Edward Carson**, as their leader. His second-in-command was a Belfast businessman, **James Craig**.

◄ *Sir Edward Carson became leader of the Unionist party in 1910 and led it until Northern Ireland was established in 1921, when he resigned.*

The Unionist campaign against Home Rule: 1912-14

Carson was determined to resist Home Rule for Ireland.

▰ He organised massive demonstrations against it. At one of these in September 1912, over 400,000

Ulster's Solemn League and Covenant.

Being convinced in our consciences that Home Rule would be disastrous to the material well-being of Ulster as well as of the whole of Ireland, subversive of our civil and religious freedom, destructive of our citizenship and perilous to the unity of the Empire, we, whose names are underwritten, men of Ulster, loyal subjects of His Gracious Majesty King George V., humbly relying on the God whom our fathers in days of stress and trial confidently trusted, do hereby pledge ourselves in solemn Covenant throughout this our time of threatened calamity to stand by one another in defending for ourselves and our children our cherished position of equal citizenship in the United Kingdom and in using all means which may be found necessary to defeat the present conspiracy to set up a Home Rule Parliament in Ireland. ¶ And in the event of such a Parliament being forced upon us we further solemnly and mutually pledge ourselves to refuse to recognise its authority. ¶ In sure confidence that God will defend the right we hereto subscribe our names. ¶ And further, we individually declare that we have not already signed this Covenant.

The above was signed by me at_____
"Ulster Day." Saturday, 28th September, 1912.

── God Save the King. ──

Carson encouraged Unionists to form armed groups to resist Home Rule by force. They were called the **Ulster Volunteers**. In 1914, they bought guns in Germany and smuggled them into Ireland at Larne in Co. Antrim.

The Irish National Volunteers

Some Nationalists decided to copy the Ulster Volunteers. In 1913, Eoin MacNeill, one of the founders of the Gaelic League, set up the **Irish National Volunteers** and was elected their commander-in-chief.

Unknown to MacNeill, however, many other Volunteer leaders were secretly members of the IRB. They hoped to use the Volunteers to start a war against Britain. In 1914, they smuggled guns into Ireland at Howth, north of Dublin.

Partitioning Ireland

There were now two armed groups in Ireland, the Ulster Volunteers and the Irish National Volunteers. Asquith realised that a civil war could break out between them. He persuaded Redmond to talk to Carson about **partitioning** (dividing) Ireland into two parts.

- The part around Belfast, where most Unionists lived, would stay in the United Kingdom.
- The rest of the country would have Home Rule.

Reluctantly, Redmond agreed to partition. But he and Carson could not agree where the border between the two parts of Ireland should be. Carson wanted to keep six whole counties, but Redmond said he should only have four counties (i.e. those areas where the Unionists were in a majority).

World War I begins: 1914

Redmond and Carson were discussing partition when Germany suddenly invaded Belgium in August 1914. This was the start of **World War I**.

Everyone in Britain and Ireland was shocked by Germany's action. Both Carson and Redmond agreed to postpone Home Rule until the war was over. They called on the two sets of Volunteers to fight against Germany for the freedom of small nations like Belgium.

Irishmen in World War I

During World War I, thousands of Irishmen joined the British army. Ulster Volunteers and National Volunteers, who a short while before were ready to fight each other, now went off together to fight the Germans.

MANY NATIONAL VOLUNTEERS ANSWERED REDMOND'S CALL AND JOINED THE BRITISH ARMY. ONE OF THEM WAS TOM KETTLE. LOOK AT THE REASON HE GAVE AND SAY WHAT YOU THINK OF IT.

"WE STARTED THE NATIONAL VOLUNTEERS TO DEFEND THE LIBERTIES OF IRELAND. WELL, IF YOU ARE ENGAGED IN A WORK OF DEFENCE, YOU MUST CARRY THAT OUT IN THE PROPER PLACE, AND THE PROPER PLACE NOW IS NOT IN IRELAND, BUT ON THE PLAINS OF FRANCE AND FLANDERS (BELGIUM)."

Looking at the evidence

IS **YOUR** HOME WORTH FIGHTING FOR?

IT WILL BE TOO LATE TO FIGHT WHEN THE ENEMY IS AT YOUR DOOR SO **JOIN TO-DAY**

The British government printed posters like this to urge men to join the army.

Looking at the evidence ▼ ▼ ▼ ▼ ▼ ▼ ▼ ▼ ▼ ▼ ▼ ▼ ▼

HERE ARE TWO MORE POSTERS WHICH WERE AIMED AT IRISH MEN AND WOMEN DURING WORLD WAR I. WHAT KINDS OF FEELINGS WERE THEY MEANT TO BRING OUT IN IRISH PEOPLE? IF YOU WERE A YOUNG IRISH PERSON AT THIS TIME, WHAT WOULD YOUR FEELINGS AND OPINIONS HAVE BEEN WHEN YOU SAW THESE POSTERS?

IF YOU ARE AN IRISHMAN YOUR PLACE IS WITH YOUR CHUMS UNDER THE FLAGS.

TO THE YOUNG WOMEN OF IRELAND.

Is your "Best Boy" wearing Khaki? If not don't **you think** he should be?

If he does not think that you and your country are worth fighting for do you think he is **worthy** of you?

Don't pity the girl who is alone her young man is probably a soldier fighting for her and her country and for **you.**

If your young man neglects his duty to Ireland, the time may come when he will **neglect you.**

Think it over then ask your young man to

Join an Irish Regiment TO-DAY.

IRELAND WILL APPRECIATE YOUR HELP.

ALEX. THOM & CO., Ltd., DUBLIN.

In all, about 200,000 Irishmen fought in World War I and about 60,000 of them were killed. Kettle was one of them. He was killed at the Battle of the Somme in 1916.

Activity ▼ ▼ ▼ ▼ ▼ ▼

USING THE INFORMATION IN THIS CHAPTER (AND ANYTHING ELSE YOU MAY HAVE READ ABOUT THE WAR IN OTHER BOOKS), EXPLAIN WHY THOMAS KETTLE AND OTHER NATIONALISTS JOINED THE BRITISH ARMY TO FIGHT GERMANY IN WORLD WAR I. DO YOU THINK THEY WERE RIGHT OR WRONG? EXPLAIN YOUR ANSWER.

◢ QUESTIONS ◣

1. Who was the Home Rule leader in 1910? Who was the British prime minister with whom he had to deal?
2. Who were the Unionist leaders in 1910-14? Mention two ways in which they opposed Home Rule.
3. Who set up the Irish National Volunteers in 1913? To what other organisation did many Volunteer leaders also belong?
4. What plan did the British prime minister propose to deal with the differences between Nationalists and Unionists?
5. World War I broke out in Europe in August 1914. What effect did this have in Ireland?

The Easter Rising: 1916

🏛 The "Sinn Féin" Volunteers

In 1914, most Irish Volunteers followed Redmond's advice to fight for "the freedom of small nations" like Belgium. But some Volunteers, especially those led by Eoin MacNeill, disagreed. They said that Irishmen should not fight for the freedom of any other country until their own was free.

Arthur Griffith supported this idea. As a result, those Volunteers who stayed in Ireland became known as the **"Sinn Féin" Volunteers**, although they had nothing to do with the Sinn Féin party.

Eoin MacNeill, the founder of the Irish Volunteers, speaking at an election meeting

🏛 The IRB sees its chance

By 1916, there were about 11,000 Sinn Féin Volunteers. MacNeill did not want them to fight the British, but unknown to him, IRB leaders like Seán McDermott had very different ideas.

The IRB had a saying: "England's difficulty is Ireland's opportunity". Since England was now in a difficult war with Germany, it seemed like the perfect time to start a rebellion against British rule in Ireland.

As soon as World War I began, McDermott and other IRB leaders set up a military committee to make plans for a rebellion in Ireland. Two other men involved in the plot were **Patrick Pearse** and **James Connolly**.

🏛 PATRICK PEARSE (1879-1916)

Patrick Pearse was born in Dublin, the son of an English stone-mason. In school, he learned to love the Irish language. He joined the Gaelic League and wrote poems and plays in Irish. In 1908, Pearse set up an all-Irish school, St Enda's. But he was not a good businessman and by 1912, he was deeply in debt.

Patrick Pearse (1879-1916). He was an enthusiastic member of the Gaelic League who joined the IRB and led the Sinn Féin Volunteers into the Easter Rising.

🏛 PEARSE AND REVOLUTION

By then, Pearse had found a new interest – politics. He believed that if the Irish language died out, Ireland would have lost its soul. To prevent this from happening, he believed that young men like himself should be ready to die for Ireland. He joined the Volunteers and the IRB and began to plan a revolution.

🏛 JAMES CONNOLLY (1868-1916)

Another of the plotters was James Connolly. He was born in Edinburgh where his family were poor Irish emigrants.

Connolly was a **socialist**. He believed that poor workers were exploited by wealthy people who controlled factories, banks and big businesses. He wanted a revolution to destroy this system and guarantee a decent standard of living for all workers.

CONNOLLY IN IRELAND

Connolly came to Dublin to set up a socialist party here. He was shocked by the terrible living conditions in Dublin and other Irish towns. He thought that the real Irish problem, which the Nationalists did not talk about, was the poverty of the people.

James Connolly (1868-1916)

Countess Markievicz joined the Irish Citizen Army and took part in the Easter Rising. She was sentenced to death but freed in 1917. She was the first woman to be elected to Parliament in either Ireland or Britain.

The 1913 Lock-out

James Larkin (1876-1947)

Connolly helped another socialist, **James Larkin**, to organise a trade union, the **Irish Transport and General Workers Union (ITGWU)**. Many of the poorest workers joined. The employers wanted to destroy the union, so in August 1913, they locked out all ITGWU members from their places of work.

This meant that about 100,000 Dubliners had no jobs and no money. They faced starvation, but help soon came from many sides. British trade unionists sent money and food. In Dublin, people like **Countess Markievicz** set up soup kitchens to feed the strikers' families.

But as the months went by, the strikers' situation got worse. By the spring of 1914, most of them were forced back to work on the employers' terms, which demanded that they leave the ITGWU.

James Larkin and his family during the 1913 Lock-out

The Irish Citizen Army

During the lock-out, Connolly formed the **Irish Citizen Army** to protect the workers from the police. It had about 200 members. When World War I began in 1914, Connolly hoped that workers in other countries would start a socialist revolution. But they did not. In despair, Connolly decided that his Citizen Army should lead a socialist revolution in Ireland.

By the beginning of 1916, the IRB had made its own plans for a rebellion. They then heard about what Connolly intended to do. The IRB leadership was afraid that, if Connolly went ahead, their plans would be ruined. They decided to invite Connolly to join them.

Members of the Irish Citizen Army outside the ITGWU headquarters. The sign shows their attitude to World War I. What does it say?

Plans for the Easter Rising

The plotters first decided to ask Germany, Britain's enemy, for soldiers and arms. The Germans would not send soldiers but early in 1916, they agreed to send a ship-load of arms. This ship, the *Aud*, was to arrive off the Kerry coast on Easter Sunday 1916. Its arrival would be the signal to start the rebellion.

Will MacNeill order the rebellion?

MacNeill did not want the Sinn Féin Volunteers to fight the British, so the IRB plotters had to trick him into ordering them to do so.

On 19 April 1916, the Wednesday before Easter, the plotters showed MacNeill a document. It said that the British planned to arrest him and the other leaders. The document was a forgery, but MacNeill did not know this. He ordered the Volunteers to begin fighting on Easter Sunday before they could all be arrested.

But on Saturday 22 April, word reached Dublin that the British navy had captured the *Aud* with the German arms. MacNeill realised that, without guns, there was no hope of success. He decided to cancel the plans for a rising on Sunday.

The rebellion goes ahead

The IRB plotters met on 23 April, Easter Sunday morning. Because of MacNeill's newspaper notice, their plans were now in ruins. But they decided to make one desperate gesture by calling their men out to fight on Easter Monday. However, MacNeill's cancellation notice meant that only Volunteers in Dublin were aware of the new orders.

Easter Week, 1916

Easter Monday, 24 April 1916, was a sunny bank-holiday morning. Pearse, Connolly and the Volunteers marched to the General Post Office (GPO) which they had chosen as their headquarters. Many of them knew they had no hope of success. As they marched out, Connolly said: "We are going out to be slaughtered."

The tricolour of the Irish Republic was raised over the GPO. Then Pearse, with Connolly beside him, read the **Proclamation of the Republic** to an astonished crowd in Sackville Street (now O'Connell Street).

When the British government learned about the rebellion, they immediately sent reinforcements to Dublin. The fighting lasted for five days. The British knew that most of the leaders of the Rising were in the GPO, so they concentrated their attack on it. They brought a gun-boat up the River Liffey and shelled O'Connell Street, leaving it a smoking ruin.

Other groups of Volunteers took over other buildings around Dublin. You can see where they were on the map on page 14.

Caught between the rebels and the British troops, the people of Dublin suffered badly. About 300 of them were killed and many more were wounded.

When the GPO caught fire, the Volunteers retreated into the streets behind it. There, for the first time, Pearse saw how ordinary people were suffering because of the fighting. He decided to surrender. By Saturday 29 April, the Easter Rising was over.

Looking at the evidence ▼

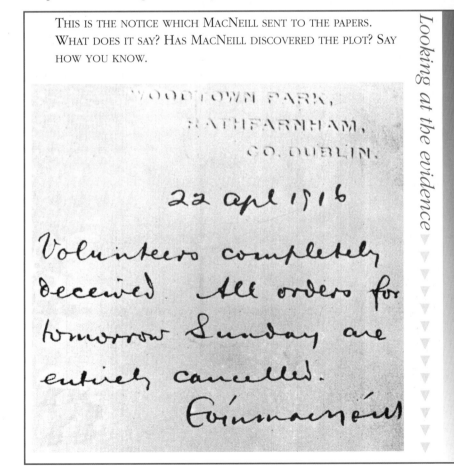

THIS IS THE NOTICE WHICH MACNEILL SENT TO THE PAPERS. WHAT DOES IT SAY? HAS MACNEILL DISCOVERED THE PLOT? SAY HOW YOU KNOW.

WOODTOWN PARK,
RATHFARNHAM,
CO. DUBLIN.

22 apl 1916

Volunteers completely deceived. All orders for tomorrow Sunday are entirely cancelled.

Eoinmacneill

Finding Out

FIND A COPY OF
THE PROCLAMATION
OF THE REPUBLIC.
MAKE A LIST OF
THREE THINGS
WHICH THE PEOPLE
WHO WROTE IT
PROMISED TO DO.

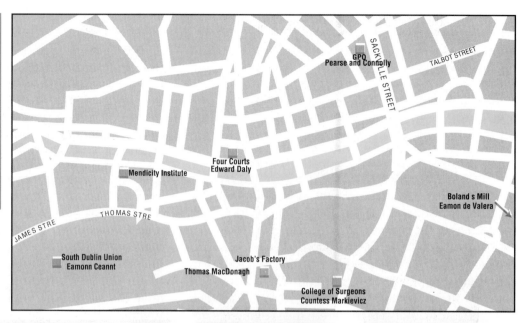

The burnt-out shell of the GPO after Easter week, 1916

Thomas MacDonagh, a poet and teacher, was executed on 3 May 1916.

Éamonn Ceannt, a Gaelic League enthusiast, was executed by firing squad in Kilmainham Jail on 8 May 1916.

Reactions to the Rising

During the Rising, the British army took control of the country. They felt betrayed by the "Sinn Féin" Volunteers who had joined with their German enemy. Three thousand people were rounded up for questioning. About half of them were set free, but the rest were sent to prison camps in Britain. As the Volunteer prisoners were marched to the boats, Dublin crowds jeered at them and pelted them with mud.

The British army set up special courts and tried one hundred of the leaders. They were sentenced to death and the executions began at once. Each day, just before dawn, two or three men were shot. Patrick Pearse and Seán McDermott were among the first to be executed.

As people learned of the executions, their mood changed. They grew more and more angry. John Redmond asked Asquith, the Liberal prime minister, to stop the executions. Reluctantly, Asquith agreed. After fifteen men had been executed, he ordered the army to stop.

James Connolly was the last man to die. He had been wounded in the ankle during the fighting at the GPO and he could not stand. He was tied to a chair and shot. The remaining prisoners were sentenced to life imprisonment.

These executions changed Irish people's views of the Easter Rising. They did not like the violence, but they admired the courage with which the rebels had faced death. Within a few months, people all over Ireland were praising the bravery and self-sacrifice of those involved.

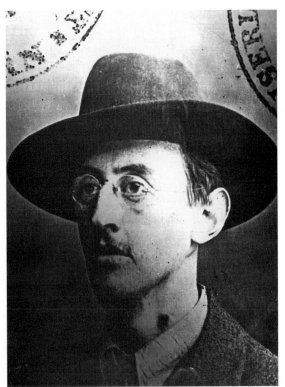

Thomas Clarke, a life-long member of the IRB, was one of the planners of the Easter Rising. He served in the GPO and was executed on 3 May 1916.

Joseph Mary Plunkett drew up the military plan for the Easter Rising. Just before he was executed on 4 May 1916, he married his sweetheart, Grace Gifford, in his cell in Kilmainham Jail.

Looking at the evidence

ONE IRB MAN, MICHAEL COLLINS, WAS IN THE GPO DURING EASTER WEEK 1916. THIS IS WHAT HE WROTE LATER ABOUT PEARSE AND CONNOLLY.

"OF PEARSE AND CONNOLLY, I ADMIRE THE LATTER MOST. CONNOLLY WAS A REALIST. PEARSE THE DIRECT OPPOSITE. THERE WAS AN AIR OF EARTHY DIRECTNESS ABOUT CONNOLLY. IT IMPRESSED ME. I WOULD HAVE FOLLOWED HIM THROUGH HELL HAD SUCH AN ACTION BEEN NECESSARY. BUT I HONESTLY DOUBT VERY MUCH IF I WOULD HAVE FOLLOWED PEARSE – NOT WITHOUT SOME THOUGHT, ANYWAY."

D. RYAN, *THE RISING*

1. WHICH OF THE TWO MEN DID COLLINS ADMIRE MORE? WHAT REASONS DOES HE GIVE FOR THIS?
2. FROM WHAT YOU HAVE READ ABOUT THEM, DO YOU AGREE OR DISAGREE WITH COLLINS'S OPINION OF PEARSE AND CONNOLLY? GIVE REASONS FOR YOUR ANSWER.

◤ QUESTIONS ◥

1. In 1913, Dublin workers were locked out of their places of work. Set out the main events of the lock-out in your own words.
2. What was the Irish Citizen Army? What use did Connolly plan to make of it during World War I?
3. Describe the plan for the Easter Rising. Why did it not take place on Easter Sunday, as the IRB had intended? What did they do then?
4. What steps did the British army take to deal with the Rising? Were they wise to act in this way? Give reasons for your answer.

Finding Out

1. USE LIBRARY BOOKS TO WRITE A PARAGRAPH ABOUT THE MAIN EVENTS OF EASTER WEEK 1916. SAY WHAT EFFECT THE FIGHTING HAD ON ORDINARY DUBLINERS.
2. CHOOSE EITHER PEARSE OR CONNOLLY AND WRITE A SHORT ACCOUNT OF HIS LIFE. YOU CAN FIND OUT MORE ABOUT THEM IN LIBRARY BOOKS.

The Victory of Sinn Féin: 1918

🏛 New leaders

After the Easter Rising, about 1500 Irish people were in jail in Britain. Here are three of the most famous.

◢ **Arthur Griffith** was the founder of the Sinn Féin party. People thought that Sinn Féin had started the Rising, although Griffith knew nothing about it. On Easter Monday, he offered to join the rebels, but Pearse told him to go and write about them instead. When the Easter Rising ended, Griffith was arrested and sent to jail in England.

◢ **Michael Collins** came from Cork. For several years he had worked in London, where he joined the Gaelic League and the IRB. He returned to Ireland in time for the Easter Rising. He fought in the GPO and was sent to a prison camp in Wales.

◢ **Éamon de Valera** was born in New York. After his Spanish father died, his mother sent him to live with her family in Co. Limerick. He became a teacher, joined the Gaelic League and later the Volunteers. During the

Rising, he commanded the Volunteers at Boland's Mills. He was sentenced to death, but the executions ended before he was shot and his sentence was changed to life imprisonment.

🏛 Britain's new leader

David Lloyd George became the British prime minister late in 1916. His main aim was to win World War I, which was then going badly for Britain. He hoped to persuade the Americans to join the war on the British side. To please them, he freed the Irish prisoners. Collins and Griffith were released in December 1916 and de Valera in June 1917.

🏛 Rebuilding the IRB, the Volunteers and Sinn Féin

When Collins returned to Ireland, he took over as leader of the IRB. He also helped to re-start the Volunteers. They behaved like an army, collecting guns and drilling.

Meanwhile, Griffith once again built up the Sinn Féin party (page 7). Its members all worked together to get Sinn Féiners elected as MPs.

WHO IS DE VALERA ?

CLARE - ABU,

AND

DE VALERA ABU.

Of American-Irish Spanish race
DE VALERA spat in England's face,
The gap of danger's still his place
To lead historic Clare's Dragoons.

Viva la for Ireland's wrong !
Viva la for Ireland's right !
Viva la in Sinn Fein throng,
For a Spanish steed and sabre bright !

DE VALERA is 34 years of age. In Rockwell College distinguished as an Athlete and Scholar. Renowned as Professor in Blackrock College. Prominent worker for Irish Language. For further particulars apply to the British Army, which made his acquaintance during Easter Week

UP IRELAND !

Published for the Candidate by his Authorised Election Agent, H. O'B. Moran, Solicitor Limerick, and Printed and Published at the CHAMPION Works, Ennis.

THIS IS A POSTER FROM ONE OF SINN FÉIN'S ELECTION CAMPAIGNS IN 1917. READ IT AND ANSWER THESE QUESTIONS

1. IN WHICH COUNTY WAS THE ELECTION BEING HELD? WHO WAS THE CANDIDATE? WHEN WAS HE BORN?
2. LIST FOUR THINGS THE POSTER TELLS THE VOTERS ABOUT THE CANDIDATE. WHY DO YOU THINK THE PEOPLE WHO WROTE THIS POSTER THOUGHT THESE POINTS WERE IMPORTANT?
3. THE SINN FÉIN CANDIDATE WON THE ELECTION. SET OUT THREE REASONS WHY PEOPLE WOULD HAVE VOTED FOR HIM.

Looking at the evidence ▼

De Valera: leader of Sinn Féin and the Volunteers

Soon after de Valera won the Clare election in June 1917, the Sinn Féin party met. Griffith stepped aside so de Valera could be elected leader. At the same time, the Volunteers also chose him as their leader. This united the political party with the military movement. Both Griffith and Collins also held important positions in these two organisations.

WHAT SINN FÉIN PLANNED TO DO

The Sinn Féin leaders wanted an Irish republic which was completely separate from Britain. They said they could win it peacefully. This was their plan.

- ✓ They would get MPs elected, but these MPs would not go to the Westminster parliament.
- ✓ Instead, they would stay in Ireland and set up an Irish parliament, **Dáil Éireann**.
- ✓ The Dáil would declare Ireland a republic.

The Sinn Féin leaders hoped the Americans would then persuade the British to accept this decision.

In 1917, the United States finally entered World War I. The American president, Woodrow Wilson, said they were fighting for "self-determination for small nations" (letting small countries decide for themselves who should rule them). Sinn Féin thought this included self-determination for Ireland.

The conscription crisis: 1918

At first, many Nationalists were nervous of Sinn Féin. Since it was associated with the Easter Rising, they feared it was planning more violence. But in 1918, an event occurred which won many Nationalists over to Sinn Féin.

World War I was going badly for Britain, and they needed more troops at the Front. The British government decided to **conscript** Irishmen into their army (force them to serve in it). All over Ireland, people protested at this plan. The trade unions held a general strike and the Volunteers said they would fight conscription.

As things turned out, the war ended before Irish troops were needed, so conscription was never imposed. But Sinn Féin and the Volunteers still got the credit for stopping it. The conscription crisis won many new supporters for Sinn Féin.

The 1918 election

World War I ended in November 1918. The prime minister, Lloyd George, immediately called a general election. This was the first election in which Irish women could vote, but they were not yet treated equally. A woman could only vote if she was over thirty, whereas a man could vote when he was twenty-one.

There were three Irish parties in the 1918 election.

In East Ulster, the **Unionists**, still led by Edward Carson, were the main party. They wanted Ireland to remain within the United Kingdom.

In the rest of Ireland, there were now two Nationalist parties: the **Home Rulers** and **Sinn Féin**.

The Home Rule party wanted Ireland to have a limited amount of independence and retain close links with Britain.

The Sinn Féin party wanted Ireland to be a republic, completely cut off from Britain.

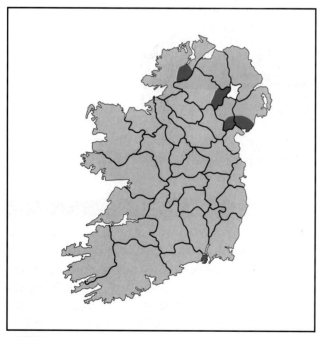

☐ Areas won by Sinn Féin

☐ Areas won by Unionists

☐ Areas won by Home Rulers

◣ *The 1918 election*

Looking at the evidence ▼

THE RESULT OF THE 1918 ELECTION

THIS TABLE SHOWS HOW MANY SEATS EACH PARTY HAD **BEFORE** AND **AFTER** THE 1918 ELECTION. LOOK CLOSELY AT THE TABLE AND AT THE MAP WHICH SHOWS WHERE THE SEATS WERE. THEN ANSWER THE QUESTIONS.

	BEFORE	**AFTER**
UNIONISTS	18	26
HOME RULERS	78	6
SINN FÉIN	7	73

1. BEFORE THE 1918 ELECTION, WHICH WAS THE BIGGEST PARTY IN IRELAND? WHAT DID IT WANT? HOW WELL DID IT DO IN 1918?
2. AFTER THE ELECTION, WHICH WAS THE BIGGEST PARTY? WHO WAS ITS LEADER? WHAT DID IT PLAN TO DO IF IT WON?
3. WHAT DOES THE RESULT OF THIS ELECTION TELL US ABOUT WHAT NATIONALISTS WANTED IN 1918, COMPARED WITH WHAT THEY WANTED BEFORE THE WAR? GIVE TWO REASONS FOR THEIR CHANGE OF OPINION.
4. WHO LED THE UNIONISTS IN 1918? HOW MANY SEATS DID THE UNIONISTS WIN?
5. ACCORDING TO THE MAP, WHERE WERE THE UNIONISTS' SEATS? WHAT DOES THE MAP SUGGEST MIGHT BE THE SOLUTION TO THE QUARREL BETWEEN NATIONALISTS AND UNIONISTS?

◪ QUESTIONS ◪

1. Name the three leaders who emerged after the Easter Rising.
2. What party did these leaders support? List its aims and say how the party planned to achieve them.
3. Some historians say that the 1918 election was the most important election in Irish history. Set down two facts to support that opinion.

The First Dáil and the War of Independence: 1919-21

The First Dáil and the Irish Republic

In December 1918, Sinn Féin won 73 seats in the election. They had promised not to go to Westminster, but to stay in Ireland and form an Irish parliament. On 21 January 1919, they kept that promise and set up **Dáil Éireann**.

THE FIRST DÁIL

▪ declared that Ireland was a **republic**
▪ promised a **democratic programme** of social reforms
▪ picked delegates to go to Paris where a **peace conference** was beginning (pages 80-81). They were to ask the countries meeting there to recognise the Irish Republic.

The first meeting of Dáil Éireann took place in the Mansion House in Dublin.

The Dáil met again on 1 April 1919 and elected a government. Éamon de Valera was president, Arthur Griffith was vice-president, and Michael Collins was Minister of Finance. **Cahal Brugha** was made Minister of Defence, in charge of the Volunteers.

Soon after this, the Volunteers began to call themselves the **Irish Republican Army** (**IRA**).

Cahal Brugha, Minister of Defence in the first Dáil

De Valera in America

Declaring a republic was easy. Now, however, Sinn Féin had to convince the British to accept it. But in Paris, Lloyd George easily persuaded the Americans, French and Italians not to listen to the Irish delegates.

De Valera thought the Irish in America could persuade their government to change its mind. In June 1919, he went to the US where he raised about £1 million for Sinn Féin. But he could not win the approval of the American government. They saw no reason to annoy the British just to help some Irish rebels, especially since they had sided with the Germans in 1916. De Valera returned home in December 1920.

Griffith and the Dáil

While de Valera was away, Griffith acted as president of the Dáil. He believed that independence could be won by peaceful resistance to British rule. He wanted the Dáil government to ignore the British and to run the country itself.

The Dáil government had some success.

- It organised a loan to cover its expenses. People lent it £350,000 (worth about £20 million today). Michael Collins was in charge of this loan.
- It set up Sinn Féin courts to settle disputes and punish criminals. The Volunteers acted as a police force, taking over from the British-run **Royal Irish Constabulary (RIC)**.
- It won the support of county and town councils.

By 1921, there were parts of the country where the Dáil government had more power than the British government. But Griffith's dream of winning independence by peaceful means could not hope to succeed.

- The British refused to accept the Dáil government, even though the majority of Irish people had voted for it. They were determined to put it down by force, if necessary.
- Michael Collins and some of the Volunteers (IRA) had been convinced from the start that the only way to win Irish independence was to fight for it.

Collins's spies

Michael Collins was the Volunteers' Director of Intelligence. He had a network of spies around the country which included post office clerks, railwaymen and even some people in the British headquarters in Dublin Castle. They let him know what the British forces were up to, often before British officials themselves knew. Collins used this information to outwit the British.

Collins was also determined that the British must not discover the Volunteers' plans. He organised a small group, known as "the Squad", whose job was to murder anyone suspected of passing on information to the British. They killed with ruthless efficiency. This worried many Sinn Féiners like Griffith who felt they were dishonouring the Sinn Féin cause.

The IRA's guerrilla war

Collins knew that the British had far more men and weapons than the IRA. Therefore the only way the IRA could hope to win was to fight a **guerrilla war**.

WHAT IS A GUERRILLA WAR?

"Guerrilla" is the Spanish word for "little war". In a guerrilla war, a few soldiers – the guerrillas – attack their enemy using ambushes, bombs and assassinations. Since they do not wear uniforms, the guerrillas can slip away and mingle with ordinary people after an attack. Their enemy has no way of telling who is responsible for the attack and who is just an innocent passer-by. A guerrilla war is often the only way in which a small, poorly-armed force can defeat a large, well-armed one.

SOLOHEADBEG

In 1919, some IRA men began a search for more guns. Their best source was the police, the **Royal Irish Constabulary (RIC)**, who were well armed. On the day on which the Dáil met for the first time, an IRA group in Tipperary ambushed and murdered two policemen and captured guns and dynamite at Soloheadbeg. This was the start of the guerrilla war in Ireland.

◄ *Michael Collins speaking at an election rally after peace was restored. During the War of Independence, he would not let himself be photographed, so the British did not know what he looked like. Sometimes, Collins even wore a disguise to try to hide his identity.*

The IRA campaign

Collins told local IRA units about British plans, but he did not control what they did. Each local IRA commander attacked when and where he wished.

Among the most famous of these IRA leaders were **Liam Lynch** and **Tom Barry** in Cork, **Seán Treacy** in Tipperary and **Seán Mac Eoin** in Longford.

In 1919, the IRA began to kill RIC men and attack RIC barracks. They also ambushed RIC and British army patrols. Gradually, they were able to drive the police out of small towns and villages. At Easter 1920, they burned many RIC barracks around the country.

Lloyd George and the Black and Tans

For most of 1919, the British prime minister, Lloyd George, was in Paris at the peace conference which marked the end of World War I. Only at the end of the year did he turn his attention to Ireland.

Lloyd George thought that the IRA were gangsters and murderers. He was determined to destroy them. He wanted policemen rather than soldiers to do the job, but by now Irishmen were reluctant to join the RIC. So Lloyd George began to recruit men in Britain who would serve as policemen in Ireland.

▲ *Black and Tans searching for arms in Dublin*

Unemployment was high in Britain after the war. Soldiers returning from the war were glad to find any well-paid job, so hundreds joined the RIC. Because there were not enough police uniforms to go round, the new policemen were dressed in a mixture of very dark green RIC uniforms and army khaki. This gave them their nickname, the **Black and Tans**. People soon called them "the Tans".

BLACK AND TANS IN IRELAND

The Black and Tans came to Ireland in the middle of a guerrilla war. Soon, they were being shot at by IRA

men who vanished back into the crowd. In 1920, the IRA killed 182 policemen, many of whom were Black and Tans.

The British government let the Black and Tans hit back ruthlessly. They hoped this would frighten people out of supporting the IRA.

The Black and Tans imposed curfews on towns and cities. Anyone on the streets after 10.00 pm was arrested. They searched houses for arms and suspects. As their lorries thundered down country roads, they fired at people and animals along the way.

▲ *Three Black and Tans*

REPRISALS

Sometimes, after the IRA had killed some Black and Tans, their comrades went on the rampage, burning houses, smashing up towns and killing prisoners.

Sources of The War of Independence

Looking at the evidence

1. This is the report of an English journalist, Hugh Martin. He visited Tubbercurry, Co. Sligo, in November 1920, a few days after the IRA had killed a local policeman, Inspector Brady.

"On Thursday (the night of Brady's death), a lorry full of uniformed men entered Tubbercurry ... The men went straight to Howley's, the principal drinking bar in the town, broke the door open... helped themselves to as much liquor as they could swallow, smashed the windows, wrecked the interior and finally set it on fire. They then went round the village, burning or wrecking shop after shop. As the men worked, they shouted out repeatedly: 'Come out, Sinn Féin' and 'Where are the murderers?'

The surrounding fields were full of terrified women and children, crouching in the wet grass, watching the flames. Two girls fled their homes in their night-dresses only. More women and children had fled earlier in the evening to distant cottages, as soon as they heard of the death of Inspector Brady."

HUGH MARTIN, *IRELAND IN INSURRECTION*

As a result of such events, many Irish people who had disapproved of the actions of the IRA now began to support them against the terror of the Black and Tans.

2. THE IRA'S TERROR TACTICS
The IRA also tried to intimidate people, especially anyone who sympathised with the British. In this letter, the British prime minister, Lloyd George, explains that this is why the Black and Tans acted as they did.

"... A poor woman named Kitty Carroll, the sole support of her aged father and mother and invalid brother, was dragged from her house by a party of masked men who murdered her and attached to her body this legend: 'Spies and informers, beware! Tried, convicted and executed by the IRA ....'

I think it is important for people to realise the character of Sinn Féin policy and the nature of its campaign. ... I should like to repeat that it was not till well over a hundred of their comrades had been cruelly assassinated that the police began to strike a blow in their own defence ..."

C.J.C. STREET, *IRELAND IN 1921*

A family in Balbriggan, Co. Dublin, stands in the ruins of their house which was burnt and destroyed by the Black and Tans.

QUESTIONS

1. Read Hugh Martin's report again. In your own words, describe what happened in Tubbercurry. Do you think Martin approved or disapproved of what the Black and Tans did? Give reasons for your answer.
2. Look at the photograph of the Balbriggan family. Whom do you think they blamed for their plight?
3. Read Lloyd George's letter carefully. What reasons does he give for the behaviour of the Black and Tans? Does this justify what they did in towns like Tubbercurry?
4. Did an event like those described here occur in your area? If so, find out as much as you can about it and write a report based on the evidence.

The War of Independence: the main events

The War of Independence between the IRA and the British forces lasted until July 1921. Here are some of the main events.

1. When the Lord Mayor of Cork, Terence Mac Swiney, was imprisoned, he demanded that the British treat him as a prisoner of war. They refused, so he went on hunger strike. He died after 73 days without food.
2. In an ambush in a Dublin street, a seventeen-year-old British soldier was killed. Kevin Barry, a medical student who had taken part in the ambush, was hanged for his murder. People tried to stop the execution because Barry was so young.
3. Late in 1920, Michael Collins found out that the British were sending spies to Ireland. On Sunday 21 November, members of his "Squad" went to these men's homes in Dublin and shot eleven of them in front of their families.

   Later that day, Black and Tans surrounded Croke Park where a GAA match was being played. They fired into the crowd and twelve people died. That night, three Volunteers were killed in Dublin Castle. It was said they were trying to escape but few Irish people believed this. The day became known as "Bloody Sunday".
4. In December 1920, Black and Tans went on the rampage and burned part of Cork city after an IRA ambush at Kilmichael.

   By the summer of 1921, the country was exhausted and people were longing for peace.

Smoking ruins in part of Cork after the Black and Tans went on the rampage

Activity

READ THE EVENTS OF THE WAR OF INDEPENDENCE NUMBERED 1, 2, 3 AND 4. IN THE CASE OF EACH EVENT, WRITE TWO NEWSPAPER HEADLINES, ONE FROM AN IRISH NEWSPAPER AND ONE FROM A BRITISH NEWSPAPER, DESCRIBING WHAT HAPPENED.

▨ QUESTIONS ▨

1. When did the Dáil first meet in Dublin? List three things it did.
2. Why did de Valera go to America in 1919? Was he successful? Explain your answer.
3. Who acted as president of the Dáil while de Valera was away? How did he hope to win independence?
4. Write a brief account of what Michael Collins did during the War of Independence.
5. What is a guerrilla war? Why did Collins think that a guerrilla war was the best way for the IRA to fight?
6. Who were the Black and Tans? What did they do in Ireland?

CHAPTER 9

Partition, Treaty and Civil War

Lloyd George and Partition

Although Lloyd George sent the Black and Tans to Ireland, he knew that one day he would have to make peace with Sinn Féin. But first he wanted to satisfy the Unionists.

The Unionist leader, Edward Carson, told Lloyd George that they wanted the six north-eastern counties of Ulster. The Sinn Féin leaders were not in Westminster to oppose this, so Lloyd George gave the Unionists what they asked for.

In 1920, Lloyd George drew up the **Government of Ireland Act** which **partitioned** (divided) Ireland into two parts.

- One part had twenty-six counties and was called **Southern Ireland**. It was to have a Home Rule parliament in Dublin.
- One part had six counties and was called **Northern Ireland**. It was to have a Home Rule parliament in Belfast.

The Government of Ireland Act set up Northern Ireland. Edward Carson, who was now old and tired, retired in 1921. The Unionists chose **James Craig** to be their next leader and the first prime minister of Northern Ireland.

A truce in the fighting: July 1921

But the Sinn Féin leaders would not accept Home Rule for "Southern Ireland". The IRA continued to fight until July 1921, when Lloyd George and de Valera agreed to a truce so that they could discuss a peace settlement.

Negotiating a treaty: October to December 1921

In October 1921, de Valera sent Griffith, Collins and three other Irish delegates to London to talk to the British. These men wanted to accomplish the following:

- to have an Irish Republic completely independent of Britain.
- to end partition by bringing the six counties back under Dublin rule.

— The Border

NORTHERN IRELAND

SOUTHERN IRELAND

The Irish delegates during the Treaty negotiations. Arthur Griffith is on the left and Michael Collins is in the centre.

Terms of the treaty

The negotiations lasted until December 1921. Then Lloyd George made his final offer.

1. Ireland would be called the **Irish Free State**.
2. It would have a good deal of independence, including its own army, flag, coins, stamps and passports. It would also be able to protect its industry from British competition.
3. But the Free State would not be a republic. It must still be part of the British empire. **TDs (members of the Dáil)** had to swear an **oath of allegiance** to the British king, who would be head of the Free State.
4. The British navy could continue to use three Irish ports.
5. After the Free State was set up, a **Boundary Commission** of three men would decide where the border between Northern Ireland and the Free State should be. Lloyd George assured Griffith and Collins that the Boundary Commission would give large parts of the six counties back to the Free State.

The Irish delegates said they must go back to Dublin to get de Valera's approval before accepting these terms. But Lloyd George threatened that if they did not sign at once, he would begin an "immediate and terrible war". Reluctantly, on 6 December 1921, Griffith, Collins and the other Irish delegates signed the Treaty.

🚩 *Michael Collins on his way to the Treaty debates*

Debating the Treaty

Irish Nationalists were divided over the Treaty. Many were glad that peace had come at last. But de Valera was angry that the delegates had signed without consulting him. Some IRA leaders also disapproved of the Treaty. They did not want to settle for anything less than a full republic.

When the Dáil met on 14 December 1921, TDs began a long and bitter debate about the Treaty. Here are some of the points made by the two sides.

Arguments for the Treaty put forward by Griffith, Collins and their supporters

1. Ireland would have far more freedom under the Free State than under Home Rule, even if not quite as much as everyone had hoped for.
2. Once the British left, it would be easy to take further steps towards a republic.
3. Ireland at least had peace, which was what most Irish people wanted.

Arguments against the Treaty put forward by de Valera and his supporters

1. The Free State would not be really free because it was still in the British empire and the king was still king of Ireland.
2. TDs had sworn to be loyal to the republic. They would break that oath if they took another oath to the king.
3. The republic had existed since 1916. The IRA must go on fighting until it was fully established.

Both sides ignored partition. They believed the Boundary Commission would destroy Northern Ireland and force the north to re-join the south.

On 7 January 1922, after many days of argument, the Dáil voted on the Treaty.

☑ 64 TDs voted for it.
☑ 57 TDs voted against.

De Valera and those who opposed the Treaty walked out of the Dáil. Griffith was then elected president in his place, with Collins as his second-in-command.

Divisions grow

Outside the Dáil, people also argued about the Treaty. It divided families and friends, with some backing it and others opposing it. In April 1922, IRA leaders who opposed the Treaty seized the Four Courts and other buildings in Dublin. But Collins did not want to fight his friends, so he left them alone. He tried to make a pact with de Valera, but his peace attempt failed.

In June 1922, an election was held. The issue before the people was clear: did they want the Treaty? Here are the results.

The pro-treaty side:	58 TDs
The anti-treaty side:	35 TDs
Other parties & independents:	
(All accepted the Treaty.)	35 TDs

Civil War: 1922-23

The majority of voters had accepted the Treaty. But the IRA, which still held the Four Courts, ignored their decision.

A few days after the election, Collins attacked the Four Courts. At once, de Valera went to join the IRA.

These actions started a civil war which lasted for almost a year. The IRA were soon driven out of Dublin. They held out a little longer in Munster but by August, Collins had defeated them there as well.

After that, the civil war became a guerrilla campaign with ambushes and atrocities on both sides. Michael Collins was killed in an ambush in Co. Cork on 22 August 1922. A week earlier, Arthur Griffith had died suddenly.

After this double loss, William T. Cosgrave became head of the Free State government. He took a tough line against the IRA, who continued their campaign of burning, murder and ambush. Many IRA leaders were executed.

The IRA had not consulted de Valera about the war. When he saw their cause was hopeless, he tried to get them to stop fighting. At last, in May 1923, they listened to him and put aside their arms. Ireland's civil war was over.

QUESTIONS

1. What Act partitioned Ireland? What did it call the two Irish states which it set up?
2. Which Sinn Féin leaders went to London to talk to Lloyd George in October 1921? What did they want? What did Lloyd George offer them?
3. Write a paragraph on what happened at the end of the negotiations.
4. Read the terms of the Treaty on page 25. In your opinion, which was most likely to encourage Irish people to accept it? Explain your opinion. Which would Irish people find most objectionable? Explain your opinion.
5. Read the arguments for and against the Treaty put forward by each side in the Dáil debate (page 25). Which argument on the pro-Treaty side do you find most convincing? Explain why. Which argument on the anti-Treaty side do you find most convincing? Explain why. What was the result of the vote on the Treaty in the Dáil?
6. Divisions over the Treaty developed into a civil war. Write an essay about the main events of the civil war. Find out more by consulting books in the library.

Michael Collins's body lying in state

The ruins of the Four Courts during the Civil War. Many of Ireland's priceless historical records were destroyed in this fire.

SECTION 2

IRELAND SINCE 1922: FREE STATE AND REPUBLIC

CHAPTER 1: THE CUMANN NA NGAEDHEAL YEARS: 1922-32

CHAPTER 2: THE DE VALERA YEARS: 1932-48

CHAPTER 3: A TIME OF CHANGE: 1948-66

CHAPTER 4: A NEW IRELAND: 1966-94

CHAPTER 1

The Cumann na nGaedheal Years: 1922-32

Setting up the Free State

In the 1921 Treaty, twenty-six Irish counties became independent of British rule. They were called the **Irish Free State**. In this section, you shall see how the Free State developed to become the country we know today.

WHERE OUR POLITICAL PARTIES COME FROM

In 1922, the main Irish party was Sinn Féin. The Treaty split it in two.

The two main political parties in Ireland today are **Fine Gael** and **Fianna Fáil**. The diagram shows how they came to be formed.

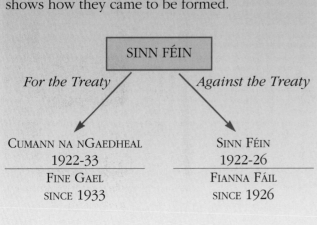

SINN FÉIN

For the Treaty — *Against the Treaty*

CUMANN NA NGAEDHEAL 1922-33	SINN FÉIN 1922-26
FINE GAEL SINCE 1933	FIANNA FÁIL SINCE 1926

The Cumann na nGaedheal government

From 1922 to 1932, the Free State was governed by the **Cumann na nGaedheal** party. Its leaders were **W.T. Cosgrave** and **Kevin O'Higgins**.

W.T. COSGRAVE

Cosgrave was head of the Free State government. He was a good leader who restored order after the civil war.

KEVIN O'HIGGINS

O'Higgins was Minister for Justice. He took a tough line against the IRA and was responsible for several executions. The IRA murdered him in 1927.

The first task of the Cumann na nGaedheal government was to set up the new state. These are some of the things they did.

- They drew up a democratic **constitution** (set of rules) for the **Irish Free State**. It gave all Irish men and women the right to elect their government.
- They set up a civil service, an army, an unarmed police force (the Garda Síochána) and a system of law courts.
- They brought in separate Irish coins and notes.
- They wanted to revive the Irish language, so they ordered schools to teach Irish. But outside school, people did not speak Irish, so this policy failed.

CUMANN NA NGAEDHEAL AND THE ECONOMY

The Free State's main industry was farming. Cosgrave's government encouraged farmers to increase their production. Taxes were kept low to please the bigger farmers.

They built a big hydro-electric plant on the Shannon and started the Electricity Supply Board (**ESB**). This sent electric power throughout the country.

These policies helped the richer people but did nothing for poor farmers or townspeople. In fact, Cosgrave's government cut old-age pensions to keep the taxes low.

The Boundary Commission

The Treaty had said that a Boundary Commission of three men would decide on the location of the boundary between the Free State and Northern Ireland. When these men met, they visited areas around the border and spoke to the local people. In 1925, they decided to make only minor changes but to give some areas in the Free State to the North.

This dismayed Cosgrave, who persuaded the British to drop the Commission's proposals and leave the border unchanged, from what it had been in 1920.

DE VALERA AND THE BOUNDARY COMMISSION

De Valera was the leader of the anti-Treaty Sinn Féin. In an election in 1923, his party won forty-four seats. But its TDs would not take the oath of allegiance to the British king. As a result, they were not allowed into the Dáil.

De Valera was very angry at the Boundary Commission. But because his party was outside the Dáil, there was nothing he could do about it.

De Valera sets up Fianna Fáil

De Valera then decided to bring his TDs into the Dáil. In 1926, he left Sinn Féin and set up a new party called **Fianna Fáil**. It began to campaign to have the oath to the king removed.

But shortly after this, the IRA murdered Kevin O'Higgins. Cosgrave brought in a law which said that all TDs must take the oath or give up their seats. De Valera decided it was better to swallow his pride and take the oath. Fianna Fáil entered the Dáil in 1927.

De Valera leading the Fianna Fáil TDs into Dáil Éireann.

Fianna Fáil's economic policies

De Valera wanted to win the next election. One of his followers, **Seán Lemass**, was appointed to draw up plans to improve the Irish economy and make the country more prosperous. Here are Lemass's main suggestions.

- The Free State sent £5 million to Britain each year to repay the loans given to Irish farmers which helped them buy their farms from the landlords. These payments were called **annuities**. Lemass stated that Fianna Fáil would keep these annuities and use the money to create jobs in Ireland.
- Fianna Fáil would put taxes (**tariffs**) on imports from other countries. This would make them dearer and encourage Irish businessmen to set up their own factories in Ireland. This was called **protection**. Lemass said that protection would create jobs.
- Fianna Fáil said it would give better pensions to the poor and build decent houses for people living in the slums.

The Depression hits Ireland

In 1930, a great economic **depression** swept the world. Everywhere prices fell and people were thrown out of work. Many countries began to protect their industries with tariffs.

Ireland suffered from these problems too, but Cosgrave's government had no idea of how to solve the difficulties caused by the Depression.

This cartoon shows de Valera in the 1930s.

Fianna Fáil wins the 1932 election

The Depression made Fianna Fáil's policies attractive to voters. When Cosgrave called a general election in 1932, Fianna Fáil won the biggest number of seats.

Cumann na nGaedheal hands over to Fianna Fáil

In a democracy, the people can vote to change their government. But in the 1920s and 1930s, democracy was disappearing all over Europe. Dictators like Mussolini, Stalin and Hitler were seizing power and setting up police states.

After Fianna Fáil won the 1932 election, people feared this could happen in Ireland too. They asked:

- Would Cosgrave give up power to de Valera, a man whom he had fought against in a bloody civil war only ten years before?
- If de Valera took over, would he protect democracy or would he set up a dictatorship?

Fortunately for Ireland, both men were democrats. After he lost the 1932 election, Cosgrave quietly handed over power to de Valera. And in turn, de Valera did not take revenge on those who had fought against him in the civil war.

These actions guaranteed that the Free State would remain a democracy. But for several years, the two sides continued to be suspicious of one another.

◢ QUESTIONS ◢

1. Draw a chart showing the origin of Ireland's two main political parties.
2. Name two leaders of the Free State government. What party did they belong to? List four things they did to set up the Free State.
3. Explain in your own words how de Valera entered the Dáil in 1927.
4. After he entered the Dáil, de Valera got Seán Lemass to draw up an economic plan. What were the main points of that plan? Why did voters find them attractive in 1932?
5. "The events of 1932 show that Irish leaders were democrats." Do you think this statement is correct? Give reasons for your answer.

The de Valera Years: 1932-48

Mutual distrust

In 1932, de Valera became the head of the Free State government. But he and Cosgrave still distrusted each other. Each feared that the other planned to overthrow democracy in Ireland.

The Blueshirts

Fianna Fáil had close ties with the IRA. Cosgrave feared this was a threat to his party, so he formed links with a group of ex-soldiers called the **Army Comrades Association**. In 1933, the ACA chose a new leader, **Eoin O'Duffy**. He dressed his men in a uniform of blue shirts. Fianna Fáil called them the **Blueshirts** and said they were fascists, like Mussolini's "Blackshirts" (page 93). When they planned a march near the Dáil, de Valera banned it.

 Eoin O'Duffy helped to set up the Garda Síochána. He was Garda Commissioner until de Valera dismissed him in 1933.

Fine Gael

Cosgrave thought that this showed de Valera was about to become a dictator. To prevent this, he united his Cumann na nGaedheal party with O'Duffy's followers to form a new party called **Fine Gael**.

 A group of O'Duffy's Blueshirts

O'Duffy was the first leader of the new party, but he was a disaster. He let the Blueshirts get into riots with the gardaí. This embarrassed Cosgrave, who had always opposed violence. Within a year, Cosgrave got rid of O'Duffy and became leader of Fine Gael himself.

De Valera and the IRA

Soon after this, de Valera split with the IRA. They had committed several murders which shocked people. Losing patience, de Valera banned the IRA and imprisoned its leaders.

In 1939, some IRA men set off bombs in England, killing many passers-by. De Valera got the Dáil to pass the **Offences against the State Act** which allowed him to imprison (**intern**) IRA members without trial. During World War II, many IRA men were interned, some were executed and others died on hunger strike.

De Valera and the Economic War

Fianna Fáil won the 1932 election because it promised to protect Irish industries. De Valera appointed Seán Lemass as Minister for Industry and

Commerce to do this job. Lemass put **tariffs** (taxes) on imports, most of which came from Britain. De Valera also stopped paying the £5 million annuities to Britain.

These actions angered the British, who retaliated with a tax on Irish cattle going into Britain. Lemass then put a tax on British coal entering Ireland. This exchange of taxes is called the **economic war**.

The economic war damaged farming, Ireland's biggest industry. Prices for cattle fell and farmers were badly off. Manufacturing industry did better, however. Lemass encouraged businessmen to set up new Irish-owned industries, making things like cutlery, shoes, furniture and clothing. These industries created many jobs but they were small and inefficient.

Destroying the Treaty

When he was elected in 1932, de Valera also promised to destroy the Treaty with Britain. He got the Dáil to remove the oath to the king and in 1936, he removed the king as head of the Free State.

A new constitution

These changes meant that the old Free State Constitution was now out of date. So in 1937, de Valera brought in a new Constitution, ***Bunreacht na hÉireann***. These were some of its main points.

- The name of the country was to be Ireland (or Éire in Irish, which was to be the "first official language").
- Articles 2 and 3 of the Constitution claimed control over the whole island of Ireland, not just the twenty-six counties.
- The head of the state was to be the president, elected by all citizens. (This meant that the country was really a republic but de Valera did not use the word as he did not want to offend the Unionists in Northern Ireland.) The first president was **Douglas Hyde**, the founder of the Gaelic League.
- The Dáil was to elect the leader of the government who would be called the **Taoiseach**.
- All religions were guaranteed freedom, but the Roman Catholic Church was to have a special position because the majority of the people belonged to it. After a referendum in 1972, however, the people voted to remove this article from the Constitution.

Reconciliation with Britain

In 1938, the British prime minister was **Neville Chamberlain**. He feared that Hitler was planning a war in Europe. Chamberlain decided to make a generous deal with de Valera in the hope that, if war came, Ireland would side with Britain against Germany.

Neville Chamberlain, photographed on the day on which he became prime minister of Britain

THE 1938 ANGLO-IRISH AGREEMENTS

In 1938, Chamberlain and de Valera signed the **Anglo-Irish Agreements**. These agreements:
- settled the annuities problem with a once-off payment of £10 million to Britain.
- ended the economic war by reducing the taxes which each country put on the other's goods.
- gave the Irish government the three ports which the British navy had held since the Treaty.

Chamberlain hoped that a grateful de Valera would let the British navy use them in the war.

Ireland during World War II

NEUTRALITY AND THE "EMERGENCY"

In September 1939, Hitler invaded Poland. In reply, Britain and France declared war on Germany. World War II had begun. At once, de Valera announced that Ireland would stay out of the fighting and remain **neutral**.

The government declared that the war was an **emergency** and gave itself special powers to deal with it. These included:
- power to censor all newspapers and letters
- power to order farmers to grow crops
- power to imprison people who endangered neutrality.

FEEDING THE PEOPLE

Food and raw materials like rubber and oil were hard to get during the Emergency. De Valera appointed Seán Lemass as Minister of Supplies to deal with this. Lemass brought in **rationing** and ordered farmers to grow more food.

Seán Lemass was Minister of Supplies during the Emergency. Here, he sets a good example by cycling to work.

To make sure food was not wasted, Lemass ordered that bread must be made from the whole of the wheat grain. This produced brown flour and bread. For many people, eating brown bread rather than white is their worst memory of the war.

Petrol and oil were hard to come by. People could not use their cars and bus services were cut in half. Very little coal was imported and most of it was kept to generate electricity and gas.

The caption for this cartoon says "Rationing, glimmermen, shortages - agh... agh...!"

SHIPPING

But many things which people needed were not available in Ireland. Before the war, these goods were carried here in British ships. Now, however, Britain needed her ships for her own imports. Lemass bought a few old ships and set up a company called **Irish Shipping**. Brave sailors sailed these ships through submarine infested waters to carry a thin trickle of imports to Ireland.

SHORTAGES AND RATIONING

In spite of the efforts of Irish Shipping, many goods were scarce. Fruits like oranges and bananas disappeared from the shops. Sugar and tea were in short supply. The weekly ration per person was half an ounce of tea and three-quarters of a pound of sugar.

Electricity could only be used for cooking or light and people could only use gas for a few hours a day. An official called the **glimmer man** went around to see that they obeyed this rule. If he saw the glimmer of a gas flame, or if he felt the cooker and it was warm, he knew that people had been using the gas illegally. People could be fined by the dreaded glimmer man.

Turf became the main fuel for cooking and heating. Townspeople often went out to the bog to cut their own or bought it from dealers. The turf they got was often wet and difficult to light.

People laughed at cartoons like this during the Emergency. The caption reads: "I wish you would hurry with that puncture, Daddy. You know how George hates to be kept waiting!"

Activities

1. WEIGH OUT HALF AN OUNCE OF TEA AND THREE-QUARTERS OF A POUND OF SUGAR. WHAT DO YOU DISCOVER? TALK ABOUT HOW YOU WOULD GET ALONG ON SO LITTLE EACH WEEK.
2. MANY IRISH PEOPLE STILL REMEMBER THEIR EXPERIENCES DURING THE EMERGENCY. SPEAK TO A FRIEND OR RELATIVE WHO REMEMBERS WHAT THINGS WERE LIKE. INTERVIEW THAT PERSON AND WRITE UP YOUR INTERVIEW FOR THE CLASS.

BOMBS IN IRELAND

The country did not escape the war completely. Bombs fell in various places. The worst came in May 1941 when German planes bombed the North Strand in Dublin. Three hundred houses were damaged or destroyed and thirty-four people were killed.

Bomb damage in Dublin in 1941

THE DEFENCE FORCES

During World War II, many countries which had at first been neutral were attacked and forced into the fighting. Ireland was one of the lucky few that were still neutral by the time the war ended in 1945. This was not because the country was very strong, however. During the 1930s, de Valera had neglected the army. By 1939, Ireland's army had only 7700 men and few modern weapons.

However, when the war began, many men joined the defence forces. By September 1940, they numbered 37,000. About 250,000 also served as part-time soldiers in the **Local Defence Force**. De Valera tried to buy more weapons from the US but they would not let him have very many.

THE GERMAN THREAT OF INVASION

The defence forces would have had little hope of success if an enemy had tried to invade Ireland. Fortunately, no one did.

Hitler considered an invasion but decided it was too difficult. Britain stood between Ireland and the Continent, and the distance was too great for the kind of planes he had.

DE VALERA'S PRO-BRITISH POLICY

The British could have invaded Ireland easily. But they did not need to do so because de Valera followed a very pro-British policy.

- He allowed Irish people to work in Britain and to join the British armed forces.
- He arranged secret talks between the British and Irish armies about what to do if the Germans invaded.
- The Irish passed on any information they had to Britain. Irish diplomats in Europe also passed on information to Britain and America. But at the time, Irish people did not know about this. Officially, de Valera remained strictly neutral right to the end.

World War II brought great suffering to the world. At least forty million people died between 1939 and 1945 and many millions more lost their families, their homes and their countries. Compared with them, Irish people had an easy time. Their greatest hardship during the Emergency was the shortage of food and consumer goods.

QUESTIONS

1. Write a short paragraph on the Blueshirts.
2. What was the economic war? How did the Irish economy do during the 1930s?
3. What were the Anglo-Irish Agreements of 1938?
4. In 1939, de Valera declared that Ireland would remain neutral. Explain in your own words what this means.
5. Shortages of food and fuel were the main problems for Irish people in the war. Who was the man appointed to deal with this? List three things which he did.
6. Was Ireland really neutral in the war? Give reasons for your answer.

A Time of Change: 1948-66

The first Coalition government

The war damaged the Irish economy. Factories closed and there was not enough food or fuel. Even when peace came in 1945, food and fuel were still rationed. To add to people's misery, the winter of 1946-47 was the coldest in the twentieth century.

People blamed de Valera and Fianna Fáil who had been in power since 1932. In the 1948 general election, Fianna Fáil lost several seats. Fine Gael, Labour and a new party called **Clan na Poblachta** saw their chance to get rid of de Valera. They joined together to form a **coalition government** with **John A. Costello** of Fine Gael as Taoiseach.

John A. Costello (1891-1976) was a lawyer and politician who led two coalition governments— 1948-51 and 1954-57.

WHAT IS A COALITION?

A **coalition government** is formed when two or more political parties join together. Coalition governments are common in many European countries. In Britain, however, single-party governments (with just one party in control) are more usual.

After 1922, Ireland too had single-party governments: Cumann na nGaedheal (1922 to 1932) and Fianna Fáil (1932 to 1948), until the first Coalition was formed in 1948. Many people thought that it would soon break up, but it lasted until 1951. Since then, Ireland has had many coalition governments.

THE POLICIES OF THE FIRST COALITION

The coalition government made several important decisions.

- In 1949, they finally cut all ties with Britain and declared that the country was a **republic**.
- When the Cold War began (page127), the Coalition refused to join the **North Atlantic Treaty Organisation** (**NATO**) which the Americans had formed in 1949 to resist Stalin. This decision continued Ireland's policy of neutrality which had begun with the war.
- The disease TB (tuberculosis) killed 3000 young Irish people every year during the 1940s. The Minister for Health, Noel Browne, built new hospitals and used new drugs to wipe out TB. Later, he tried to improve conditions for mothers and children, many of whom died young. The doctors and the Catholic bishops opposed him, however. They said his **Mother and Child Scheme** was too much like communism. An angry Dr Browne resigned in 1951.

Dr Noel Browne was Minister for Health in the first coalition government. Since several members of his family had died of TB, he wanted to wipe out the disease.

The economy in trouble

IMPORTS AND EXPORTS

In the 1951 election, the Coalition lost a number of seats and de Valera became Taoiseach again. His government faced a major economic crisis.

Ireland has always had to import many things which we do not produce ourselves: food items like tea, oranges and rice; raw materials for industries like steel or cotton; luxuries like cars. We pay for these goods with money we earn by exporting the things we grow and make. For centuries, Ireland's main exports were farm products like beef, butter, bacon, poultry and eggs.

BALANCE OF PAYMENTS CRISIS

In the 1940s, over 90 per cent of our exports went to Britain. But after the war, the British government gave grants to its farmers to grow more food. This meant that Britain no longer needed Irish eggs, poultry or bacon. By 1951, Ireland was not earning enough from exports to pay for its imports. This led to a **balance of payments crisis** which lasted throughout the 1950s.

Exports   **Imports**

The Balance of Payments Crisis

EMIGRATION

During this crisis, factories closed down and the number of jobs declined. At the same time, farmers could not sell their poultry or pigs. In despair, many of them left the land. Since there were no jobs for them in Ireland, many of them **emigrated**.

Here are two sources which tell us something about the effect of the crisis.

SOURCE A

THESE FIGURES SHOW THE NUMBER OF PEOPLE WHO LEFT THE TWENTY-SIX COUNTIES IN THE YEARS AFTER THE COUNTRY GAINED ITS INDEPENDENCE:

1926 - 36	166,751
1936 - 46	187,111
1946 - 51	119,568
1951 - 56	196,568
1956 - 61	212,003
1961 - 66	80,605

Looking at the evidence

SOURCE B

DONALL MAC AMHLAIGH, A YOUNG MAN FROM CO. KILKENNY, WROTE THIS IN 1951.

"THE MOTHER SAW AN AD IN THE PAPER: 'STOKERS WANTED; LIVE IN. APPLY MATRON, HARBOROUGH RD. HOSPITAL, NORTHAMPTON'.

'YOU COULD GIVE IT A CHANCE,' SHE SAID, 'FOR SURELY GOD PUT IT IN YOUR WAY.'

I HAD BEEN IDLE FOR THREE MONTHS SINCE LEAVING THE ARMY ... I WROTE MY LETTER AND OFF IT WENT ... THE MOTHER AND MYSELF WATCHED EVERY POST, OUR HEARTS IN OUR MOUTHS, HOPING FOR GOOD NEWS. AS SOON AS THE ANSWER CAME, HOWEVER, BOTH OF US WERE MELANCHOLY, THINKING HOW I WAS LEAVING AND GOING FOREIGN ...
AS THE TIME FOR LEAVING DREW NEARER, I COULD FEEL THE COLD TALONS OF DESPAIR TWINING AND UNTWINING INSIDE ME. I KNEW THAT I'D MISS THE SMALL, ORDINARY THINGS I'D BEEN USED TO FOR SO LONG ... NOW ABOVE ALL, I FELT LIKE STAYING AT HOME FOREVER, IF ONLY I COULD HAVE FOUND ANYTHING TO DO; BUT I HADN'T THE LUCK. I WAS GETTING TWENTY-TWO AND SIXPENCE ($£1.12\frac{1}{2}$P) FROM THE LABOUR EXCHANGE AND THAT WASN'T ENOUGH TO KEEP ANYBODY ..."
DONALL MAC AMHLAIGH, *AN IRISH NAVVY*,
TRANSLATED FROM THE IRISH
BY VALENTINE IREMONGER

Looking at the evidence

◪ QUESTIONS ◪

1. Use the figures in Source A to make a graph showing how the rate of emigration changed between 1926 and 1966. How many people left Ireland altogether in these years?
2. Does the evidence in these two sources confirm or undermine the opinion that "Ireland suffered an economic crisis in the 1950s"?
3. What reasons does Donall Mac Amhlaigh give for deciding to emigrate?
4. Did he want to emigrate or not? Pick out and write down the sentences in Source B which support your answer.

Dealing with a crisis

Irish people had always blamed Britain for problems like emigration. But by the 1950s, that excuse no longer made sense. For thirty years, Irish people had run the country and still it could not provide work for its people.

Seán Lemass and the Programme for Economic Development

Some people realised that the only solution to Ireland's economic problems was to find new things to export which would replace the farm produce the British no longer wanted to buy. New exports would pay for our imports, create jobs for Irish people and stop emigration.

T.K. Whitaker was responsible for the first Programme for Economic Development.

In 1958, a civil servant, **T. K. Whitaker**, drew up an economic plan called the **Programme for Economic Development**. It said that the government must do a number of things:

◪ give **grants** and **tax relief** to foreign firms which would encourage them to set up in Ireland. These firms would export their products and provide jobs.

◪ give **grants to Irish firms** to help them become more efficient and better able to export their goods.

Lemass persuaded de Valera to accept Whitaker's programme. In 1959, when de Valera at last retired, Lemass became Taoiseach and held that position until 1966. He continued the new policy and the economy began to improve. Firms from the United States, Germany and Japan set up factories in Ireland. They gave work to Irish people and the goods they produced were exported.

Seán Lemass encouraged de Valera to listen to T.K. Whitaker.

◪ QUESTIONS ◪

1. Explain in your own words what a **coalition government** is. Who led the first Coalition?
2. Write a paragraph about the first Coalition.
3. In the 1950s, Ireland suffered an economic crisis. What caused it? What was the main result of this crisis?
4. Who wrote the Programme for Economic Development? What did it propose? Who put it into force?
5. Did this programme work? Before you answer, look back to Source A (page 35). Is there any evidence there that you could use to answer this question?

A New Ireland: 1966-94

Seán Lemass retired in 1966. Since then, these six men have held the office of Taoiseach.

Jack Lynch became Taoiseach after Lemass. He led a Fianna Fáil government from 1966 to 1973 and again from 1977 to 1979. He took Ireland into the European Union.

Liam Cosgrave was leader of Fine Gael and Taoiseach of a coalition government from 1973 to 1977.

Charles Haughey took over from Jack Lynch as the leader of Fianna Fáil in 1979. He was Taoiseach several times in the 1980s, and in 1989 he formed the first Fianna Fáil-led coalition. He negotiated the Maastricht Treaty with other EU members (page 156) and retired from politics in 1992.

Garret FitzGerald, a member of Fine Gael, led two coalitions with the Labour Party in the 1980s. In 1985, he signed the **Anglo-Irish Agreement** (page 50) with the British prime minister, Margaret Thatcher. This helped to improve relations between Britain and Ireland on the issue of the North.

Albert Reynolds succeeded Charles Haughey as leader of Fianna Fáil and Taoiseach in 1992. He negotiated an IRA ceasefire in Northern Ireland in August 1994 but fell from office in December.

John Bruton, the leader of Fine Gael, became Taoiseach as leader of a coalition government in December 1994.

Old ways

Up to the 1950s, Ireland had been an old-fashioned country.

- Most people were content with the old ways of doing things. They seldom considered new ideas or questioned the way in which politicians ran the country.
- Catholic bishops and priests had a lot of power. Politicians and ordinary people seldom dared to argue with them. The fate of Noel Browne and his Mother and Child Scheme (page 34) showed what could happen to a politician who tried to defy them.
- Books, magazines and films were censored if they had any reference to sex. Many of the best books by Irish writers were banned and could not be sold in Ireland.

In the 1960s, however, all this began to change. Here are some of the reasons.

Television

On 1 January 1961, **Radio Telefís Éireann (RTÉ)** broadcast its first programme. By 1970, over half of Irish homes had a TV set. Television opened a whole new world to Irish people. They watched British and American programmes which showed lives and values which were very different from their own.

On Irish-made programmes like "The Late Late Show", they heard discussions about violence or contraception or poverty. Up to then, people had not talked openly about these issues. Bishops and politicians were asked about their policies and often they were not very good at explaining them.

Television influenced the books people read, the songs they sang and way they furnished their houses. It made Irish people more like the Americans, the British and the Europeans.

All of this encouraged people to ask questions and make up their minds for themselves. Censorship of books and films eased because it was pointless when people could see so much on their own TV screens.

Changes in the Catholic Church

The Catholic Church also changed in the 1960s. In 1962, **Pope John XXIII** called the **Second Vatican Council**. For the first time, Catholics heard bishops arguing about various issues. The council introduced many new rules for Catholics. One important one said that English or Irish could be used in church services instead of Latin, which had been used for hundreds of years.

JOHN XXIII

Although Pope John XXIII (23rd) was an old man when he became pope in 1958, he brought about many changes in the Church during his short reign.

Pope John disliked the religious quarrels which had divided Christians in Europe since the Reformation. He encouraged the **ecumenical movement**. This aimed at uniting Christians by stressing the things they had in common rather than the things which divided them.

In Ireland, where religion had been the main dividing line between Unionists (mostly Protestants) and Nationalists (mostly Catholics), this was important. Catholics and Protestants met to discuss religious issues and to pray together. In the Republic, religious differences no longer mattered very much by the 1960s. Unfortunately, this was not true of Northern Ireland.

Education

By the 1960s, Irish education was very out of date. A report in 1965 discovered some disturbing things.

- Over 50 per cent of pupils left before they had even finished primary school.
- Secondary schools charged a fee which many students could not afford to pay. As a result, only 30 per cent of students went to secondary school and most left without even doing the Intermediate (Junior) examination.
- Few students studied science or a modern continental language.
- Only a tiny minority got a third-level education.

Lemass knew that if Ireland wanted to become a modern country with modern industries, this would have to change. He appointed young, active ministers to take charge of education. The most famous of them was **Donough O'Malley**.

In 1966, O'Malley announced that he was going to bring in free secondary education for all students and free transport for students living far away from a school. As a result, many more students stayed on in secondary school and went on to get a third-level qualification.

Donough O'Malley brought in free secondary education.

Foreign policy

Ireland had been neutral in World War II. This cut the country off from contact with other nations. This began to change in the 1950s.

PEACE-KEEPING WITH THE UNITED NATIONS

In 1955, Ireland was admitted to the **United Nations**. In 1960, Irish soldiers were asked to take part in a UN peace-keeping mission in the Congo (now called Zaire) where there had been a civil war. Unfortunately, ten Irish soldiers were killed there.

Since then, Irish soldiers and gardaí have earned a fine reputation for their work on peace missions in Cyprus, Lebanon, Afghanistan, Somalia, Bosnia and other places.

1973: Joining the European Economic Community

In 1972, Ireland and Britain applied to join the **European Economic Community** (now called the **European Union** or **EU**). In a referendum, the Irish people agreed to accept the terms that Jack Lynch had negotiated. Ireland became a full member of the EEC on 1 January 1973.

An Irish soldier wearing a United Nations' armband and beret. Since 1960, soldiers like this have served the cause of peace in many countries.

Since then, Irish civil servants and politicians have gone to Brussels to negotiate on Ireland's behalf with the other community members. Irish businessmen and farmers have had to get used to the European way of doing business.

EU membership has led to much more trade between Ireland and other EU members. Irish farmers have received many grants under the EU's **Common Agricultural Policy** (**CAP**). The Irish government has also received a great deal of money from the community's **Social Fund** which has been used to modernise the country.

Since the 1970s, many American and Japanese firms have set up factories in Ireland because they can send their goods directly into the EU. As a result, Ireland's exports now include computers, chemicals and machinery as well as beef and butter.

A new economic crisis

Up to the mid-1970s, the Irish economy did well. Employment increased and some emigrants returned home. But in 1973 and 1979, the price of oil shot up because of wars in the Middle East. Irish governments were forced to borrow money to try to keep the economy going, but this proved disastrous.

Taxes went up to pay back these loans. Many jobs disappeared. In the mid-1980s, emigration increased again as many young people left to look for work abroad. The situation began to improve slowly from the late 1980s.

The Republic and Northern Ireland

Apart from the economy, the biggest issue in Irish history since the 1960s has been Northern Ireland. We will look at this when we have seen how Northern Ireland developed after it was set up in 1920.

HOW HAS THE EU AFFECTED IRELAND? FIND OUT ABOUT ONE OF THE FOLLOWING AND WRITE AN ESSAY ON IT: THE EUROPEAN COURT OF JUSTICE; THE EUROPEAN COMMISSION; THE EUROPEAN PARLIAMENT.

Finding Out

◢ QUESTIONS ◣

1. Name the men who have been Taoiseach since 1966. Which of them: (a) brought Ireland into the EU? (b) signed the Anglo-Irish Agreement with Margaret Thatcher? (c) formed the first Fianna Fáil-led coalition? (d) negotiated the IRA ceasefire in Northern Ireland?
2. When did RTÉ start broadcasting? List three ways in which it helped to change Irish people's attitudes.
3. What was the Second Vatican Council? Who called it? The same man also encouraged the ecumenical movement. Explain what this is in your own words. Which of these changes do you think was most important in Ireland? Give reasons for your answer.
4. Who modernised Irish education in the 1960s? List three ways in which he did this.
5. When did Ireland become a member of the United Nations? How has this country contributed to UN work since then?
6. Ireland is a member of the European Union. When did Ireland join? Write down three changes which have occurred here as a result. Which of these do you consider the most important? Explain the reasons for your choice.

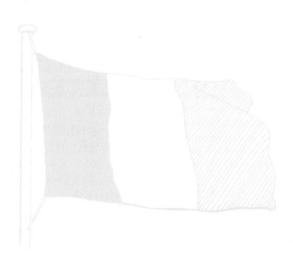

SECTION 3

NORTHERN IRELAND

CHAPTER 1: SETTING UP NORTHERN IRELAND
CHAPTER 2: NORTHERN IRELAND: 1920-63
CHAPTER 3: TROUBLED YEARS IN NORTHERN IRELAND: 1963-95

CHAPTER 1

Setting up Northern Ireland

The Government of Ireland Act: 1920

You have read that the Government of Ireland Act partitioned Ireland in 1920 (page 24).

This Act created two Irish states: "Southern Ireland" with twenty-six counties and "Northern Ireland" with six counties.

The Nationalists in "Southern Ireland" rejected the Act and gained their independence in the Treaty of 1921.

But the Unionists in Northern Ireland accepted the Government of Ireland Act. They now had their own parliament in Belfast to run Northern Irish affairs. However, foreign policy, trade and most taxes were still dealt with by the United Kingdom parliament in London. In this way, Northern Ireland remained part of the UK.

Electing a Northern Irish government

In 1921, the voters of Northern Ireland elected fifty-two MPs to sit in the Northern Ireland parliament. Because two-thirds of the people in the six counties were Unionists, forty out of the fifty-two MPs were Unionists.

The Unionist MPs formed a Unionist government and their leader, Sir James Craig, became the first prime minister of Northern Ireland.

A bad start

About a third of the people in Northern Ireland were Catholics and Nationalists. They felt betrayed when Northern Ireland was set up. No one had asked them if they wanted to be ruled by a Protestant, Unionist parliament.

The IRA refused to accept the new state. Even after the Treaty was signed, they continued to fight the Northern Irish police, the **Royal Ulster Constabulary** (**RUC**), and the British army.

Craig was determined to hold on to Northern Ireland. He enrolled many of the former Ulster Volunteers (page 9) as Special Constables to fight the IRA and convinced the Northern Ireland parliament to pass the **Special Powers Act**. This allowed the RUC and the Special Constables to search people's houses and to arrest and imprison them without trial (**internment**).

TWO HOSTILE COMMUNITIES

These measures worked and by 1923, Northern Ireland was at peace. But it was a sullen peace. Nationalists still resented the new state. Their MPs refused to sit in the Northern parliament. They knew they were always going to be in a minority and that they could never persuade the Unionist government to listen to them.

Unionists resented the Nationalists' attitude. They thought that Catholics could not be trusted. They knew that Catholics were a majority in the whole of Ireland and were always afraid that some day, Catholics from the North and the South would join against them and force Northern Ireland into a Dublin government.

Therefore Unionists never let Catholics take any part in the government of Northern Ireland. For fifty years, the Unionists controlled the North. In all that time, no Catholic was ever allowed to become a Unionist MP or a government minister. They could not hold an important post in the police or civil service.

LIVING APART

This distrust led to Catholics and Protestants living apart. They studied in different schools and prayed in different churches. Catholics shopped in Catholic shops, and Protestants in Protestant shops. Most Catholics played hurling and Gaelic football, while most Protestants played rugby and soccer.

QUESTIONS

1. Look back at pages 2-5. Who were the Unionists and why did they oppose Home Rule?
2. Trace a map of Ireland. On it, draw the border between the Irish Free State and Northern Ireland which was established in 1920.
3. What proportion of the people of Northern Ireland were Catholics? What did they feel when Northern Ireland was set up?
4. Northern Protestants and Catholics distrusted one another. Write down two things which led each community to distrust the other.

CHAPTER 2

Northern Ireland: 1920-63

The prime ministers of Northern Ireland

The Northern Ireland government built a fine parliament building at Stormont Castle. From there, the Unionist party ruled the six counties. Between 1921 and 1969, there were four Unionist prime ministers at Stormont.

◤ Stormont Castle, the seat of the Unionist government

- **Sir James Craig**, who later became Lord Craigavon, was prime minister from 1921 until 1940. He set up Northern Ireland but did little to solve the religious, social and economic problems it faced. He died in 1940.
- **J.M. Andrews** then became prime minister. World War II was in progress and the German bombing of Belfast in 1941 showed how little the government had done to protect the city. Discontented Unionists forced him to resign in 1943.
- **Sir Basil Brooke**, who was later given the title of Lord Brookeborough, was prime minister from 1943 to 1963. He reluctantly brought in the welfare state (page 44) in the 1940s. But he was unable to solve the North's economic problems as old industries like shipbuilding and linen declined.
- **Terence O'Neill** became prime minister in 1963. He began to improve the economy, encouraging overseas firms to set up factories. He also tried to improve relations with the Dublin government and with Northern Catholics.

◩ QUESTION ◩

Name the four prime ministers of Northern Ireland between 1921 and 1969. What party did each belong to?

Hard Times in the 1930s

UNEMPLOYMENT

Before partition, the North was prosperous. Its two big industries, shipbuilding and linen-making, created many jobs. But in the 1920s and 1930s, these industries declined. As a result, jobs disappeared.

At that time, there was little state aid for the unemployed. Housing was bad and many people were hungry. In 1932, unemployed workers in Belfast, both Catholic and Protestant, joined together to demand better conditions. When the RUC tried to stop a march, there was a riot.

The Harland and Wolff shipyard in Belfast suffered during the Depression of the 1930s but recovered during World War II when it built many mine-sweepers for the Royal Navy.

THE UNIONIST GOVERNMENT'S RESPONSE

This alarmed the Unionist government. If Protestant and Catholic workers joined together to demand their rights, it could mean the end of Unionist rule. They were determined to prevent this from happening.

The government ordered the RUC to use guns against the rioters in Catholic areas but to use only batons in Protestant areas. They organised public works where workers could earn money but were careful that few Catholics were employed in these works. Several Unionist leaders made speeches like this.

> *"It is time Protestant employers realised that, whenever a Roman Catholic is brought into their employment, it means one Protestant less. It is our duty to pass the word along and I suggest the slogan should be 'Protestant employ Protestant'."*
>
> quoted by Paddy Devlin in
> *Yes we have no bananas*

These tactics worked. The unity between Protestant and Catholic workers ended. When there were more riots in 1935, Catholic and Protestant workers were again on opposite sides.

◩ QUESTIONS ◩

1. Unemployment was high in Belfast in the 1920s and 1930s. What happened to unemployed workers? How did they respond?
2. List three things the Unionist government did when the workers protested. Which do you think was their main aim: (a) to make life better for all workers; or (b) to prevent the Catholics and Protestants from joining together? Give reasons for your opinion.

Northern Ireland in World War II

Northern Ireland was part of the United Kingdom, so when Britain declared war on Germany in 1939, Northerners were involved too.

Northern Ireland was very useful to Britain in its fight against Germany. From bases along the northern coast, the British navy and air force patrolled the Atlantic, looking for German warships and submarines. When the US entered the war in 1941, many American troops were stationed and trained in the North.

PROSPERITY

The war brought prosperity to Northern Ireland. Linen factories made uniforms, parachutes and tents. In Belfast, the shipyards were busy building ships to replace those lost to German submarines. The new Shorts Aircraft Company produced many planes for the Royal Air Force (RAF).

BOMBING BELFAST

But there was a high price to be paid. People believed Northern Ireland was too far from Germany to be bombed, but they were wrong. In April 1941, 150 German planes bombed Belfast. The government had provided no anti-aircraft cover, so there was nothing to stop them.

The Germans were probably aiming at the shipyards but they hit houses, schools and hospitals. In a night of fire and terror, 747 people were killed and about 1500 injured. Thousands of houses were destroyed. De Valera sent fire brigades from the south to help fight the fires.

After this raid, 100,000 people fled from the city, seeking shelter in country places rather than risk another night of horror. In May, the bombers returned but they did less damage this time. After that, the worst was over.

▟ QUESTIONS ▟

1. "Northern Ireland helped Britain in the fight against Germany." Set out four facts which support this opinion.
2. How did the war bring prosperity to Northern Ireland?
3. When was Belfast bombed? How many people were killed? Why was there no anti-aircraft defence for the city?

Northern Ireland and the welfare state

World War II ended in 1945. In Britain, there was a general election which the Labour party won. Labour then set up what is now called the **welfare state**.
- ▟ It gave better payments to the unemployed.
- ▟ There were better pensions for the old and ill.
- ▟ A free health service was set up.
- ▟ There would be free second-level education for all and good grants for those who wanted to go to university.

THE EFFECT OF THE WELFARE STATE

The Unionists did not want the welfare state but they agreed to set it up, provided the British government paid most of the cost. The welfare state made a tremendous difference to many people in Northern Ireland. For the first time, those who were old, ill or unemployed could have a decent standard of living.

A BETTER START IN LIFE

To youngsters from poor families, free education provided a better chance in life. Any boy or girl who passed an examination at the age of eleven (the "eleven-plus") got a free place in a grammar school and a chance to go to university.

The eleven-plus began in 1948. At that time in Derry, John Hume was ten years old. His father was an unemployed Catholic whose dole amounted to £1.50 a week. He could not afford a good education for his son. The eleven-plus changed that.

John Hume was drawn into politics by the Civil Rights Movement. He helped establish the Social Democratic and Labour Party (SDLP) in 1970 and became its leader in 1979.

Looking at the evidence

"HE (JOHN) SAT AN EXAMINATION ONE COLD JANUARY MORNING, THINKING IT WAS JUST ANOTHER CLASS TEST. HE DID NOT KNOW, UNTIL HE WAS TOLD HE HAD PASSED, THAT IT WAS PROBABLY THE MOST IMPORTANT EXAMINATION IN HIS WHOLE LIFE – THE FIRST ELEVEN-PLUS TEST ... FOR JOHN HUME IT OPENED UP A WORLD OF SCHOLARSHIP UNDREAMED OF BY HIS FOREBEARS. THE USUAL FEE FOR ST COLUMB'S, THE LOCAL CATHOLIC BOYS' GRAMMAR SCHOOL, WAS £7 A YEAR AND ... IT WOULD HAVE BEEN IMPOSSIBLE FOR THE HUMES TO RAISE SUCH A SUM ... IF JOHN HUME HAD BEEN BORN A YEAR EARLIER, HE COULD HAVE BEEN DESTINED TO FOLLOW IN HIS FATHER'S FOOTSTEPS."

BARRY WHITE, *JOHN HUME*

WHAT EXAMINATION DID JOHN HUME SIT IN 1948? THE WRITER SAYS IT WAS "PROBABLY THE MOST IMPORTANT EXAMINATION IN HIS WHOLE LIFE". WHAT REASONS DOES HE GIVE TO BACK UP THIS OPINION? DO YOU AGREE WITH HIM? EXPLAIN YOUR REASONS.

Like John Hume, thousands of boys and girls in Northern Ireland now got a better education than their parents had. And this, like the other benefits of the welfare state, was open equally to Catholics and Protestants.

▟ QUESTION ▟

After the war in 1945, which party won the British election? That party set up the welfare state. List three things that changed.

Troubled Years in Northern Ireland: 1963-95

Protestant fears

Northern Ireland was set up in 1920 to give a safe home to Unionists, most of whom were Protestants. But in the years that followed, they never felt secure. They were always afraid that one day they would be forced into the Republic, where the majority of the people were Catholics.

WHAT WERE NORTHERN PROTESTANTS AFRAID OF?

Northern Protestants feared being brought into the Republic because they believed it was controlled by the Catholic Church. Here are some of the facts they pointed to which supported that belief.

SOURCE A
1. Divorce and contraception, which Protestants accepted but which the Catholic Church disapproved of, were banned in the Republic.
2. In 1951, when Noel Browne quarrelled with the Catholic bishops over his medical policy, he had to resign (page 34).

Protestants believed that if the Republic took over the North, the same rules would apply to them and they would lose their freedom.

COULD NORTHERN IRELAND BE TAKEN OVER?

Was it possible that Northern Protestants could be forced into the Republic against their will? Many Unionists believed that it was. Here are some of the things that made them think so.

SOURCE B
1. In Articles 2 and 3 of de Valera's 1937 Constitution (page 31), the Republic claimed **jurisdiction** (control) over Northern Ireland.
2. There were three million Catholics in the Republic and only one million Protestants in Northern Ireland, so Protestants were outnumbered on the island of Ireland.
3. In the North, there were only 500,000 Catholics compared with one million Protestants, so there were not enough Catholics to win an election there. But Catholic families were usually bigger than Protestant families. In the 1950s, more than half the children in northern schools were Catholics. Unionists feared that one day, Catholics would outnumber them and vote Northern Ireland into the Republic.
4. Most Catholics voted for the Nationalist party which wanted to reunite Ireland by peaceful means. But some Catholics supported Sinn Féin and the IRA, which were prepared to use force to take over Northern Ireland. Politicians in the Republic condemned the IRA's activities and said they would never force the North into a united Ireland, but Unionists did not believe them.

Looking at the evidence

1. NORTHERN PROTESTANTS WERE AFRAID OF BEING UNITED WITH THE REPUBLIC BECAUSE THEY BELIEVED IT WAS CONTROLLED BY THE CATHOLIC CHURCH. DO YOU THINK THAT THE FACTS IN SOURCE A HELP TO EXPLAIN THEIR FEARS? GIVE REASONS FOR YOUR ANSWER.

2. UNIONISTS WERE AFRAID THAT ONE DAY, THEY MIGHT BE FORCED OUT OF THE UNITED KINGDOM AND INTO THE REPUBLIC AGAINST THEIR WILL. READ THE FACTS LISTED IN SOURCE B. WHICH OF THEM DO YOU THINK WOULD FRIGHTEN THE UNIONISTS MOST? GIVE REASONS FOR YOUR CHOICE.

Discrimination against Catholics

Because Unionists feared Catholics, they were determined to keep them from getting any power in Northern Ireland. As a result, they **discriminated** against Catholics in jobs, housing and government. Sources C and D show how this affected Catholics.

SOURCE C

1. As we saw on page 43, Unionist leaders urged their followers not to give jobs to Catholics. They hoped this would force Catholics to emigrate.

2. Between 1920 and 1972, only one party, the Unionist party, held power in Northern Ireland. No Catholic was ever a Unionist MP or a minister in the Northern government.

Think it Over-

Your Family Allowance in

NORTHERN IRELAND is 8/- weekly
(for each Child after the first)

and in the REPUBLIC OF IRELAND
11/- a month for the second child
and
17/6 a month for each other child

Your Unemployment and Sickness Benefit in

NORTHERN IRELAND is 32/6 (SINGLE MAN)
54/- (man and wife with **10/6** for first child and **2/6** for each other child)

AND IN THE
REPUBLIC of IRELAND is 24/- (SINGLE MAN)
36/- (man and wife with **7/-** for each of the first two children.)

Unionists boasted that their social welfare benefits were better than those in the Republic, as this election poster shows.

SOURCE D

The worst discrimination against Catholics was in **local government**. County and city councils had a lot of power.

- They built and distributed council houses.
- They employed many people.

Unionists made sure that Catholics never got control of local councils, even when there was a Catholic majority in a county or city. This was done in two ways.

1. Only people with property were allowed to vote for local councils. A businessman with several shops could have up to six votes, but a family of six adults living in one house could only have one vote. Since Protestants owned more property than Catholics, they had more votes, though poor Protestants suffered too.

2. Each local area was divided into districts called wards. Each ward elected some local councillors. The lines between these wards were carefully drawn to make sure that more Unionists than Nationalists were elected. This is called **gerrymandering**. Gerrymandering ensured that Unionists won control of local councils. They used their power to give jobs and houses to Protestants rather than to Catholics.

THE EFFECTS OF DISCRIMINATION

Here are some facts showing how discrimination affected Catholics in the 1960s.

SOURCE E

1. Of 319 top jobs in the civil service, Catholics held only twenty-three.

2. Of the 10,000 people employed in the Harland and Wolff shipyard, only 400 were Catholics.

3. Only 12 per cent of the RUC and none of the Special Constables who policed the North were Catholics.

4. In Derry city, 8781 Protestant voters elected twelve Unionist councillors; 14,229 Catholic voters elected just eight Nationalist councillors.

5. In Co. Fermanagh, where a majority of the people were Catholics, the Unionist-controlled council employed 338 Protestants and only thirty-two Catholics.

1. BECAUSE THEY FEARED CATHOLICS, UNIONISTS KEPT THEM FROM HAVING ANY POWER BY DISCRIMINATING AGAINST THEM. READ SOURCES C, D AND E. IN THE CASE OF EACH OF THE FACTS LISTED IN SOURCE E, SAY WHICH OF THE POLICIES LISTED IN SOURCES C AND D WAS RESPONSIBLE FOR IT.

2. IF YOU WERE A YOUNG CATHOLIC IN NORTHERN IRELAND IN THE 1960s, WHICH OF THE FACTS LISTED IN SOURCES C AND D WOULD HAVE ANNOYED YOU MOST? EXPLAIN YOUR CHOICE.

3. YOU HAVE READ ABOUT THE FEARS OF THE UNIONISTS AND THE POLICIES THEY FOLLOWED TOWARDS THE CATHOLICS AS A RESULT. DO YOU THINK THEY WERE WISE OR FOOLISH TO HAVE SUCH POLICIES? WRITE A SHORT PARAGRAPH EXPLAINING YOUR OPINION.

The Civil Rights Campaign

A NEW GENERATION OF CATHOLICS

For a long time, northern Catholics put up with discrimination. Then, in the 1960s, a new generation emerged. Thanks to the welfare state, they were well educated. They knew they would not have been so lucky in the Republic where there was no free education at the time. Some of them felt that if they got fair treatment in Northern Ireland, they would not look for a united Ireland.

This 1965 handshake between Taoiseach Seán Lemass and the Northern Ireland Prime Minister, Terence O'Neill, aroused Unionist fears.

A NEW PRIME MINISTER AND A NEW ATTITUDE

In 1963, Unionists elected a new prime minister, **Terence O'Neill**. He wanted better relations with the Catholics in the North and with the Republic. O'Neill made some friendly speeches, visited a Catholic school, and in 1965 asked the Taoiseach, Seán Lemass, to visit him in Belfast. O'Neill's gestures had two results.

▧ They alarmed some Unionists. **Ian Paisley**, a clergyman who had set up his own Free Presbyterian Church in 1951, held demonstrations against O'Neill's policies. His slogan was "O'Neill must go". Even moderate Unionists worried that O'Neill was doing too much, too quickly.

Ian Paisley was the Unionists' most vocal opponent of any concessions to Catholics in Northern Ireland.

▧ Catholics, on the other hand, thought O'Neill was not doing enough. They demanded real changes, not just words and gestures. In 1967, they formed the **Northern Ireland Civil Rights Association** (**NICRA**). It demanded civil rights for Catholics, especially:
▧ an end to discrimination in houses and jobs
▧ "One man, one vote" in local elections.

CIVIL RIGHTS MARCHES

NICRA organised marches to highlight discrimination. Ian Paisley then organised counter-marches. When the two sides clashed, the RUC often intervened on the side of the Unionists.

THE IMPACT OF TV

This kind of thing had happened many times before in Northern Ireland. But in the 1960s, reporters and TV cameras turned up to see what was going on. Reporters dug out stories of discrimination against

Catholics, and when the RUC attacked civil rights marchers in Derry in 1968, TV pictures of it were broadcast around the world.

Bernadette Devlin, then still a student, addressing a Civil Rights rally. She was later elected an MP.

Early Civil Rights marches were peaceful, but rioting developed after a time.

Reforms at last

When Northern Ireland was set up in 1920, it was still part of the United Kingdom with the British government in charge. But for almost fifty years, the British had let the Unionists do what they liked and ignored Catholic complaints.

Now, the British government was embarrassed by the press and TV reports of violence and discrimination. It forced O'Neill to end gerrymandering and to bring in "one man, one vote" for local councils.

The fall of O'Neill

Some Unionists recognised that reforms were needed, but others were outraged. They voted for Ian Paisley's **Democratic Unionist Party (DUP)** and O'Neill had to resign.

The violence begins

In the summer of 1969, fierce fighting between Protestants and Catholics broke out in Belfast and Derry. The British government sent in the army to separate the two sides. Catholics, who were being driven from their homes, greeted the soldiers with relief.

THE IRA AND THE CIVIL RIGHTS CAMPAIGN

The IRA had played little part in these events up to now. In the 1950s, it had attacked customs posts along the border, but that campaign had been a dismal failure.

By the 1960s, IRA leaders had given up violence and supported the civil rights campaign. When Protestant mobs attacked Catholics in Belfast in 1969, the IRA could do nothing. Belfast Catholics complained that "IRA" stood for "I ran away".

At first, the British army was welcomed, but Northern nationalists soon began to attack it.

The birth of the Provisional IRA

Now, some members of the IRA demanded a new policy. In 1970, the IRA split on the issue. The **Official IRA** still favoured a peaceful policy. The **Provisional IRA** (usually called "the Provos") wanted to use force to achieve a united Ireland.

The Provisionals began to gather guns. Some of them also attacked British soldiers who then searched Catholic homes for arms. As they searched, they tore up floorboards and damaged furniture. This turned the Catholics against the British army, especially in the poorer districts of Belfast and Derry. Many young people joined the Provisional IRA whom they saw as their protectors.

1970-71: More violence

Violence increased. The IRA attacked the RUC and the British army. They, in turn, used rubber bullets and CS gas to put down riots. A Unionist terrorist group, the **Ulster Volunteer Force (UVF)**, killed Catholics.

9 August 1971: Internment

The new Northern prime minister, **Brian Faulkner**, thought that **internment** (imprisonment without trial) would restore peace. In the early hours of 9

August 1971, the British army and the RUC rounded up 337 people. But Catholics noted bitterly that only Nationalists were arrested, even though much of the violence had come from Unionists.

▲ *Brian Faulkner (left), the last Prime Minister of Northern Ireland, with William Whitelaw, who took over as Secretary of State for Northern Ireland in 1972.*

Many more Catholics now joined the Provisional IRA and the violence increased, as these figures for the numbers of people killed show.

1969	13
1970	25
1971 (before 9 August)	30
1971 (after 9 August)	143

Bloody Sunday: January 1972

In 1970, Nationalist politicians had formed a new party, the **Social Democratic and Labour Party (SDLP)**. It was led by **Gerry Fitt** and **John Hume**.

They organised marches and demonstrations against internment. On 30 January 1972, British soldiers opened fire on a march in Derry, killing thirteen unarmed men. This "Bloody Sunday" convinced the British government that they must take control of Northern Ireland.

Gerry Fitt, the first leader of the SDLP

The end of Stormont

On 1 April 1972, the British government abolished the Stormont parliament. **William Whitelaw** was made Secretary of State for Northern Ireland (i.e. the British minister in charge of the North). He tried to win over the Catholics by promising to end internment.

Bloody Friday: July 1972

But the Provisionals thought they were on their way to victory and stepped up their violence. They planted car bombs in towns and villages, often killing innocent passers-by. On 21 July 1972, "Bloody Friday", they set off twenty bombs in Belfast city centre, killing eleven people and injuring 130 others.

The Sunningdale Agreement leads to power-sharing

The British government expected that **direct rule** from London would only last a few months, giving Northern Irish politicians time to work out a new way to run the North. They encouraged the two sides to get together to discuss their differences.

In 1973, the SDLP and some Unionists signed the **Sunningdale Agreement**. This set up a **power-sharing government**. It was led by the Unionist, Brian Faulkner, with Gerry Fitt of the SDLP as his second-in-command. For the first time in the history of Northern Ireland, Unionists and Nationalists worked together to run the state.

Ian Paisley bitterly attacked the power-sharing government. So did the Provisional IRA. When Protestant workers organised a strike against power-sharing, the Sunningdale Agreement collapsed.

Twenty-five troubled years

SEARCHING FOR A SOLUTION

After the collapse of the Sunningdale Agreement, the British continued to rule Northern Ireland directly. Various attempts were made to reach a new agreement but they all failed because of the deep distrust between the two communities.

This was made worse by IRA violence on one side and Loyalist violence on the other. Between 1969 and 1994, over three thousand people were killed in Northern Ireland.

THE REPUBLIC AND NORTHERN IRELAND

The outbreak of violence in the North also affected the Republic. It damaged the economy because foreign firms were nervous of setting up anywhere in Ireland. The government also had to increase spending on the gardaí and the army so that they could patrol the border and search for IRA arms.

THE DEBATE ABOUT THE NORTH

The troubles made people in the Republic re-examine their attitudes to Northern Ireland. Since 1922, political leaders like de Valera spoke constantly about ending partition. They paid no attention to the wishes of the Unionists.

People in the Republic now had to look more closely at the reasons why the Unionists feared joining with them in a united Ireland. They began to ask questions like these.

✓ Would it be right to force the Unionists into the Republic against their will?

✓ Was it right for Articles 2 and 3 of the Irish Constitution to claim the right to rule the North? Should these articles be changed?

✓ Were Northern Protestants right about the Catholic Church controlling life in the Republic?

✓ Should we change the law to allow contraception and divorce?

The Anglo-Irish (Hillsborough) Agreement: 1985

In 1985, the Irish government persuaded the British that co-operation between Britain and the Republic could bring peace to Northern Ireland. The British prime minister, **Margaret Thatcher** and the Taoiseach, **Garret FitzGerald** signed the **Anglo-Irish Agreement** at Hillsborough in Co. Down.

In it, the British promised to consult the Dublin government about affairs in the North. And the Irish government promised that it would not try to end partition without the consent of Northern Unionists.

The agreement did not bring peace to the North, however. The Unionists were not consulted and they rejected it. Both the Provisionals and the UVF continued to use violence. But under the Anglo-Irish Agreement, British and Irish officials met to discuss mutual problems. This helped the two sides to understand the other's points of view better.

The Downing Street Declaration: 1993

In 1993, John Hume persuaded the British and Irish governments to sign the **Downing Street Declaration**. It set out the ideas which each side had about the future of Northern Ireland.

This enabled Hume and the Taoiseach, Albert Reynolds, to persuade the IRA to call a ceasefire in August 1994. This was soon followed by a Loyalist ceasefire. The peace process had begun.

Taoiseach Albert Reynolds (second from left) beside Britain's Prime Minister, John Major, announcing the Downing Street Declaration in December 1993.

LONDON BOMBS: FEBRUARY 1996

For eighteen months, people throughout Ireland hoped that the ceasefire would hold. But in February 1996, the IRA exploded a number of bombs in London. The prospects for peace began to look more gloomy.

Gerry Adams, leader of Sinn Féin, who helped bring about the IRA ceasefire to begin the Northern peace process.

◤ QUESTIONS ◢

1. Write down two ways in which some young Northern Catholics in the 1960s were different from older Catholics. What was their view of the Republic?

2. Who was Terence O'Neill? What was his attitude to Catholics? What did (a) Catholics like John Hume and (b) Protestants like Ian Paisley think of his efforts?

3. Write a short paragraph on each of the following: NICRA, the Provisional IRA, internment, Bloody Sunday, direct rule.

4. What was the Sunningdale Agreement? Why did it fail?

5. Write a sentence on: (a) the Anglo-Irish Agreement; (b) the Downing Street Declaration; (c) the 1994 ceasefire; and (d) the resumption of IRA violence in 1996.

PART 2

CHANGING LIFESTYLES IN IRELAND: 1900-1990

Rural Life: 1900 to 1946

The lifestyle of Irish people has changed more rapidly during the twentieth century than ever before in history.

When the century began, motor cars, telephones and moving pictures had just been invented and few people in Ireland had seen them. Most people could not even imagine things like aeroplanes, radio, television and computers. Houses were lit by candles, oil lamps or gas, and most had neither running water nor indoor toilets.

People made their own entertainment and news of the outside world came slowly through newspapers. In politics, women were not even allowed to vote, much less become prime ministers or presidents.

A rural society

One big difference was where people lived. Today, Ireland is an **urban society** with most people living in towns and cities. But in 1900, Irish society was mainly **rural**. The 1901 census showed that 70% of Irish people lived in small villages or on farms. Most of them were farmers or farm labourers.

Farming

By 1920, most farmers had purchased their farms, so they no longer had to worry about landlords. But farming still involved a lot of hard work.

Although machines like tractors were appearing in some countries, few Irish farmers could afford to buy them. Up to the 1950s, many of them still used horses to plough the land and reap the corn. They still milked their cows by hand and drove the horse (or donkey) and cart to the local creamery every day to deliver the milk.

Farmers helped each other at busy times of the year. Neighbours, men, women and children went from farm to farm, working together to save the hay, reap the corn or thresh the grain. This co-operation was known by the Irish word **meithil**.

Two men who changed the twentieth century: Henry Ford (left) the first man to mass-produce cars and Thomas Edison who invented recording and light-bulbs.

Houses

Here are some of the houses that country people lived in at the start of the twentieth century.

This is the house of a prosperous farmer. It had two storeys, a slate roof and at least five rooms. The owner of a house like this would have a big farm of around fifty acres and a good standard of living. Only about 20% of Irish farmers had this much land.

Around 1900, far more farming families lived in houses like the one above. It probably had three rooms. The kitchen was entered through the **half door**. It had a bedroom on either side of it. The cart suggests that the family was prosperous enough to own a donkey or perhaps a horse, but the children would probably have left school at the age of twelve. Many of them had to **emigrate** to find work.

This picture was taken around 1900. It shows a family which had been **evicted** from their home for not paying the rent. This family was very poor, as you can see from the quality of their clothes. Note that the women and children have no shoes.

HOUSES OF THE POOREST FAMILIES

All over Ireland, the poorest families lived in very harsh conditions. They were frequently hungry and poorly dressed. The children got little schooling and many remained **semi-literate**.

They lived in small cottages. Most cottages were entered through a "half-door". The top half was often left open to let in the light. The bottom half remained closed to keep out the animals. The door led straight into the kitchen.

A painting of a typical poor family's cottage.

In 1900, the one-storey thatched cottage was the most common house in the Irish countryside. Few of them survive today, however, and those that do have changed completely. Now, if we want to see what such houses were like, we have to go to museums or folk parks where these old houses have been reconstructed.

LIGHTING AT NIGHT

Even in the daytime, these houses were dark, with the only light coming from the half-door and the tiny windows. At night, people used oil lamps or candles, but these only gave a dim light, compared with what we are used to in our homes today.

In the evening, neighbours often visited one another. In some parts of the country, this was called **céilí-ing**. Everyone gathered around the kitchen fire to gossip, tell stories and sing songs. Sometimes, the people moved the furniture so they had room to dance in the kitchen.

A painting of a céilí in the Great Blasket Island.

🏠 THE KITCHEN AND THE FIRE

This photograph shows the kitchen in a prosperous farmhouse. The kitchen was the centre of the house and was dominated by the open turf fire at one end of the room.

The fire was kept burning all the time, and gathering turf for it was an important part of the farmer's work. The woman of the house did all her cooking on the open fire and the family ate their meals in the kitchen.

🏠 FURNITURE

Household furniture like the **súgán** chair below was made locally. The seat and back were made of straw ropes.

The basket beside the chair was woven from willow twigs. Baskets like this were made in every district and were used for carrying turf, potatoes and many other things.

A súgán chair.

🏠 HOUSEHOLD EQUIPMENT

This photograph shows the implements which were used in cooking over the open fire. There was the kettle in which water was heated for tea and for washing. There were big iron pots in which potatoes and stews were cooked and a flat griddle on which bread was baked.

The kettle and pots hung on a crane which could be raised or lowered over the fire. Smaller pots, called **pot ovens**, were put directly onto the ashes. These were also used to bake bread.

🏠 THE PARLOUR

Bigger farmhouses often had a "parlour" which had the "best" furniture. The parlour was beside the kitchen but was only used on special occasions such as a funeral or the visit of an important person. Can you see the fine furniture in this parlour?

🏛 BEDROOMS

In bigger farmhouses, the bedrooms were off the kitchen. In some houses, there was also a small room under the thatch where children or servants slept. But many poor families lived in one- or two-roomed cottages. Then, some members of the family had to sleep in the kitchen. Sometimes there was a **settle bed** which served as a fire-side bench during the day and opened down into a bed at night.

🏛 Water

None of these houses had water on tap. Until the 1950s, most country people had to carry every drop of water they used from a well, stream or roadside pump.

Source A shows where people got their water in 1946.

SOURCE A

WATER FOR RURAL HOUSEHOLDS IN 1946	
PIPED WATER	9%
WELLS	44%
ROADSIDE PUMPS	26%
STREAMS	12%
OTHER SOURCES	9%

Lack of water affected **health** and **hygiene**. In 1946, only 5% of rural houses had a fixed bath or an indoor flush lavatory.

🏛 The lives of rural women

The women who kept these houses worked very hard indeed. With none of the labour-saving machines we take for granted today, there was the endless drudgery of cooking, cleaning, washing and ironing – all by hand.

🔺 *A turf fire was central to the household tasks, and often women had to cut and save the turf.*

Looking at the evidence

SOURCES B, C AND D BELOW CONTAIN EVIDENCE ABOUT WOMEN'S LIVES IN THE EARLY PART OF THE TWENTIETH CENTURY. USE THIS INFORMATION TO WRITE AN ESSAY ON "THE LIFE OF IRISH FARMING WOMEN BETWEEN 1900 AND 1945".

IF YOU WISH, YOU COULD ADD YOUR OWN SOURCES TO THE ONES GIVEN HERE BY INTERVIEWING SOME PEOPLE WHO REMEMBER WHAT CONDITIONS WERE LIKE FORTY OR FIFTY YEARS AGO. BE SURE TO INCLUDE PLENTY OF FACTS IN YOUR ESSAY. USE QUOTES FROM YOUR INTERVIEW SOURCES.

🏛 CARRYING WATER

Even a simple task like having enough water for cooking and cleaning involved considerable work. In Source B, one woman remembers what not having piped water was like in the 1950s.

SOURCE B

"We got our water from a well across the field near the house. We children usually had to bring it in after school. The big aluminium buckets were light to carry on the way out, but coming back full, they pulled your arms out and the water slopped over your shoes. In summer, it was best to go barefooted.

I hated that job. It was bad enough in summer, but in winter, when your hands nearly fell off you with the cold and your feet were wet and the mud made you slip – that was terrible. I tell you, we were sparing with the well water. It was kept for cooking and tea. We used rain water for washing."

Some county councils provided district water pumps. The water in these was cleaner than water in wells or streams, but it still had to be carried to the house.

Pumps like this were to be seen on roads all over the country. Have you ever noticed one?

🏠 WASH DAY

Since every drop of water had to be carried to the house, washing was a big chore. Source C is Alice Taylor's description of wash day in her home.

SOURCE C

"Bridgie came every Monday to do the washing ... Early on Monday morning, the big twenty-gallon pot was hung over the fire and filled with water and by the time Bridgie arrived, it was sending steam signals up the chimney ...

She placed two chairs facing each other and put the big timber washing tub on their laps. With a tin gallon, she ladled steaming water from the black pot into an iron bucket which she carried across the kitchen and poured into the tub. She then added cold water which she drew in buckets from the stream at the end of the garden ...

When she was satisfied that the temperature was right, she put on her big apron and set to work on the clothes. She caught up one of the bundles, threw it into the tub and rammed the clothes down under the water with the legs of the timber washboard. Not content merely to wash the clothes, she attacked them, banging them onto the ridged washboard and plastering them with a large block of red or white carbolic soap. Then she scrubbed each offending garment up and down with great ferocity ...

As she washed the clothes, clouds of steam enveloped Bridgie ... She squeezed the clothes by hand, rinsed and squeezed again. Meanwhile the pot was kept full and boiling over the fire as tub after tub of washing was piled high on the table."

Alice Taylor, *Quench the Lamp*

🔺 *These items were needed for washing clothes.*

Activities

1. COMPARE THE WAY IN WHICH THINGS WERE WASHED IN ALICE TAYLOR'S HOUSE WITH THE WAY WASHING IS DONE IN YOUR HOUSE.
2. DRAW A SERIES OF CAPTIONED PICTURES WHICH ILLUSTRATE HOW BRIDGIE DID THE WASHING.

🏠 IRONING

After the washing came the ironing. A piece of metal was put into the fire. When it was red hot, it was lifted out with a tongs and pushed into the iron. Women hated these irons because they often burnt their fingers or left dirty streaks on the clothes.

🔺 *Irons were awkward to heat.*

🏠 CHURNING THE BUTTER

On many farms, women made their own butter. First the cream was separated from the milk and then **churned**. The cream was poured into the barrel of the churn. The stick was then pounded up and down, dashing the cream around until it turned into butter. This could take an hour or more.

Afterwards, the churn and all the other implements had to be thoroughly scrubbed in hot water.

The butter was then shaped into pound rolls. Some was kept for use at home and some was sold in the town.

Working on the farm

As well as rearing children, cooking, washing, ironing and mending, women contributed to the family's income by working on the farm. They milked the cows by hand, made butter, and kept chickens, geese and turkeys. At harvest time, they helped to gather in the crops.

Young women tending potato ridges.

Woman spreading flax in Ulster. Flax would later be made into linen.

Women sold butter, eggs and fowl to the local shopkeepers and used the money they earned to buy clothes and groceries and to meet other expenses. Without the money earned by the women, few small farms would have survived throughout the 1920s, '30s and '40s when prices for farm produce were low.

In Source D, a Dubliner remembers the work of the women he saw in Spiddal in Connemara in the 1920s when he went there to learn Irish.

SOURCE D

"Women lived lives of extraordinary drudgery ... Two pictures stand out in my mind. One is from springtime of a mother of a large family I knew well, coming up from the beach, barefooted and soaked to the skin, carrying on her back a load of seaweed to manure the ground for that year's potatoes. The other is of something that happened as regularly as the clock every Saturday. Women setting out in their heavy shawls and petticoats in the early morning with baskets containing eggs, butter, potatoes and vegetables to be sold in Galway ten miles away. They would walk in their bare feet as far as the suburb of Salthill and there, as a concession to the need to appear respectable as they entered the town, they would put on their boots and stockings."

L. O Broin, *Just like yesterday*

Changes after 1945

Irish rural life changed little between 1900 and the end of World War II in 1945. Then it began to change very rapidly indeed. The main reasons for this change were the spread of electric power to country areas after 1945 (**rural electrification**), a **growing prosperity** which led to better houses and, in the 1970s, the introduction of **piped water supplies**. We will look at these changes in the next chapter.

> *Looking at the evidence*
>
> IN SOURCE D, THE AUTHOR SAYS "WOMEN LIVED LIVES OF EXTRAORDINARY DRUDGERY." (A) EXPLAIN WHAT THAT MEANS IN YOUR OWN WORDS. (B) DO YOU AGREE WITH THE AUTHOR? SELECT THREE POINTS FROM SOURCES B, C AND D TO SUPPORT YOUR ANSWER.

✎ QUESTIONS ✎

1. In 1901, what proportion of Irish people lived in the countryside? How did they make their living?

2. Write a paragraph on farming between 1900 and 1945.

3. What was the most common type of house in the countryside up to 1945? Write a paragraph describing it. Mention the appearance from outside, the door, kitchen, fire, lighting, furniture, work and any other points that seem important.

4. Explain how the lack of a piped water supply would have affected people's standards of health and hygiene.

Rural Life after 1946

Life in the Irish countryside began to change rapidly after World War II ended in 1945. One important reason for this change was the **rural electrification scheme** which was introduced by the government in 1946.

Electric power in Ireland

Electricity was first harnessed to provide power and light in the 1870s. In Ireland, electricity was first generated in Dublin in 1880. By 1916, 7000 houses in the city had electric light. Outside Dublin, many towns set up private electricity companies. Most of the electricity was used for lighting homes. Many of the electrical items which we use today were unknown to most people until the 1940s.

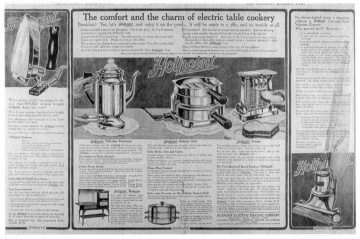

A 1917 advertisement for electrical goods. But few houses had any of these before World War II.

The Shannon Scheme and the ESB

When Ireland became independent in 1922, the new government decided to build a **hydro-electric** (electricity generated by water power) station on the River Shannon. They hoped that cheap electric power would encourage industries to start up. The German firm, Siemens, designed the Shannon scheme which began in 1924. It was the biggest engineering project ever carried out in Ireland.

In 1927, the government set up the **Electricity Supply Board (ESB)** to manage the Shannon station. It took over the small electric companies and set up a national grid to carry electricity around the country. By the time World War II began in 1939, most Irish towns had electricity, but almost two million people, most of them living on farms or in small villages, were not yet connected to the national grid.

After it was set up, the ESB encouraged people to use more electricity. This is a photo of their "ideal kitchen" from the 1920s. How many items can you identify?

The rural electrification scheme

After the war ended in 1945, the government instructed the ESB to bring electricity to the rural areas. They hoped to make farmers more efficient by enabling them to use milking machines, electric pumps, water heaters and other tools which would improve their farming. No one gave much thought to the effect it would have on women's lives.

RESISTANCE TO THE SCHEME

Not everyone welcomed the arrival of electricity, however. Some people were afraid of it. Horror stories went around about electricity setting fire to thatched roofs or leaking out of open sockets. Many poor farmers were afraid that electricity bills would be too high and get them into debt.

THE LOCAL COMMITTEES

In each parish, a committee of local people was set up to overcome these fears. They went from house to house asking people to join the scheme. This is how a woman in Clare felt when they approached her.

SOURCE A

"Two young men descend on us like a heavenly visitation. They are a deputation from the local committee and want to know if we will take the electric! I can hardly believe my ears. What a boon and a solace it would be and how miraculously it would lighten the unrelenting drudgery of a farmhouse. I walk about all day in a dream of immersion heaters, electric irons, churns and incubators as my husband happily contemplates oat-crushers. We hear only one in the district has refused it – a hardy old dame of 85 who says she will not have it and be setting fire to the thatch."

Michael Shiel, *The Quiet Revolution*

Farmers being introduced to an electric pump over tea and biscuits. The ESB held exhibitions like this at creameries to show off their latest labour-saving devices.

Looking at the evidence

STUDY SOURCE A AND ANSWER THESE QUESTIONS.
1. WHO WERE THE TWO YOUNG MEN WHO VISITED THE SPEAKER?
2. DID SHE WELCOME THEM?
3. WHAT DID SHE AND HER HUSBAND DREAM OF AS A RESULT OF THEIR VISIT?
4. FROM THE EVIDENCE OF THIS SOURCE, SUGGEST WHICH PEOPLE WOULD WELCOME ELECTRICITY MOST AND EXPLAIN WHY.

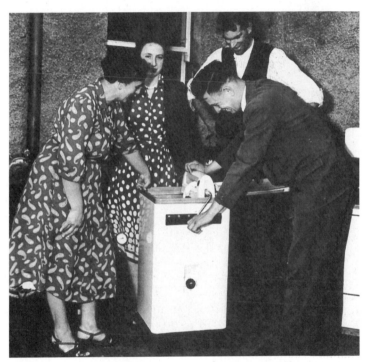

Meanwhile the women were shown washing machines. Many bought them, even before they had piped water, because the machines eased the drudgery of washday.

More "labour-saving devices"

Once enough people had agreed to link into the system, poles were erected and lines connected to the houses. Then came the great day when the light was switched on and the oil lamps and candles were put away. Houses looked strange and unfamiliar in the bright light. People soon began to redecorate their rooms with brighter colours.

The ESB then began to sell electric appliances. Farmers arriving at the local creamery were invited to have a cup of tea and inspect the electric pumps and milking machines while their wives were shown the washing machines and electric irons.

Source B shows the spread of electric appliances in rural homes in the years that followed.

SOURCE B

PERCENTAGE OF RURAL HOMES
WITH ELECTRIC APPLIANCES

	1958	1968	1979
ELECTRIC COOKER	2%	15%	25%
REFRIGERATOR	4%	14%	76%
TV	-	43%	84%
WATER HEATER	4%	8%	24%
IRON	68%	84%	87%
KETTLE	39%	50%	69%
WASHING MACHINE	11%	26%	59%

STUDY SOURCE B AND THEN DO THE FOLLOWING.

1. LIST THE ELECTRICAL APPLIANCES IN ORDER OF THEIR POPULARITY IN 1958.
2. USING WHAT YOU READ IN CHAPTER 1 (PAGES 52-7), EXPLAIN THE POPULARITY OF THE TOP THREE ITEMS.
3. TVS ARE MISSING FROM THE 1958 LIST. WHY IS THAT?
4. NOW LIST THE ITEMS IN ORDER OF THEIR POPULARITY IN 1979. EXPLAIN ANY CHANGES YOU SEE.

Looking at the evidence

The number of milking machines in use in the country increased from 1,000 in 1946 to 10,000 in 1960, and to 60,000 in 1980.

▲ *Milking machines eased the work on dairy farms and allowed farmers to handle more cows at one time.*

Piped water

Electricity provided the power to pump water into people's homes. Starting in the 1960s, people in many rural districts joined together to form district water schemes, digging wells and laying pipes. By 1981, 94% of rural households had a piped water supply.

◄ *Piped water made life easier for people.*

New houses

Since the 1950s, and especially since Ireland joined the European Union in 1973, farmers have become more prosperous. As their incomes improved, many replaced their old farmhouses with modern bungalows. These houses have electricity, running water, central heating and all the modern comforts that were once only enjoyed by townspeople.

▲ *An example of a modern bungalow*

Modern farm machinery

After the war, and especially from the 1960s onwards, farmers began to invest in new machines to help with farming. These included:

- **tractors** which replaced horses almost everywhere
- **combine harvesters** on which one man could do the work formerly done by half a dozen
- **milking machines** which did away with the slow task of hand milking and allowed dairy farmers to keep many more cattle.

But there was loss as well as gain in the spread of machinery. Now that the work of the farm could be done with far less labour, the neighbours no longer gathered to help each other in the *meithil*.

Farming became a more solitary occupation, with just one man and his machines.

By the 1990s tractors and combine harvesters had taken over much of the labour on tillage farms.

The decline of the small farm

Machinery was expensive, so only farmers with big farms could afford it. As a result, it became more and more difficult to make a living on a small farm. Many small farmers gave up this hopeless struggle. In the 1950s, when Ireland suffered from an economic depression and jobs were hard to come by, many of them emigrated.

This situation improved in the 1960s. New factories opened in country towns. Some farmers found jobs in these factories, becoming part-time farmers who supplemented their farm incomes with the wages from their factory jobs. But often, young people did not want the drudgery of farm work, so they sold the farm and moved permanently into the towns and cities. This helped to change the pattern of Irish life from **rural** to **urban**.

Because of these changes, the Irish countryside became a lonelier place at the end of the twentieth century. Fewer people now live in the countryside than in 1900. This has been especially hard on old people who are often left behind when their neighbours and children leave to find a different way of life.

◪ QUESTIONS ◪

1. When and where was electricity first generated in Ireland? Write a paragraph on the spread of electric power in Ireland.
2. What is meant by "rural electrification"? Why did the government begin the rural electrification scheme in 1946?
3. Electricity is one of the main reasons why country people's lifestyles have changed so much since 1945. Compare the information in this chapter with that in Chapter 1 (pages 52-7) and set out some of the main changes in lifestyle caused by electricity.
4. Apart from rural electrification, list three things which changed life in rural Ireland since 1945. In your opinion, which of these was the most important? Explain your answer.

Finding Out

THIS CHAPTER GIVES A SHORT GENERAL ACCOUNT OF THE RURAL ELECTRIFICATION SCHEME, BUT YOU MIGHT LIKE TO DO A SPECIAL STUDY OF THE COMING OF ELECTRICITY TO YOUR AREA.
FIND SOME PEOPLE WHO REMEMBER IT AND INTERVIEW THEM. ASK ABOUT: (A) WHAT LIFE WAS LIKE WITHOUT ELECTRICITY; (B) WHEN THE RURAL ELECTRIFICATION SCHEME REACHED YOUR AREA (THE LOCAL PAPER MIGHT HELP THERE); AND (C) WHAT DIFFERENCE ELECTRICITY MADE IN THEIR DAILY LIVES.
THEN WRITE UP YOUR FINDINGS IN A SPECIAL REPORT.

Irish Towns in the Early Twentieth Century

Towns

In 1901, only 30% of Irish people lived in towns or cities. Most Irish towns were small and built around a long main street.

SOURCE A

Looking at the evidence ▼▼▼

THE PHOTOGRAPHS ON THIS PAGE SHOW ONE TYPICAL TOWN – CLONMEL, CO. TIPPERARY. THE PHOTOGRAPH IN SOURCE A WAS TAKEN AROUND 1900. THE ONE IN SOURCE B WAS TAKEN IN 1991.
1. COMPARE THE TWO PHOTOGRAPHS. LOOK PARTICULARLY AT: (A) FORMS OF TRANSPORT; (B) THE PEOPLE – HOW THEY ARE DRESSED AND WHAT THEY ARE DOING; AND (C) TYPES OF SHOPS AND BUILDINGS.
2. USING THE EVIDENCE IN THE TWO PHOTOGRAPHS, WRITE A SHORT ESSAY COMPARING CLONMEL IN 1900 WITH CLONMEL IN 1991 UNDER THE SAME HEADINGS.

Finding Out ▼▼▼▼▼▼▼▼▼

PHOTOGRAPHS LIKE SOURCE A EXIST FOR MANY IRISH TOWNS. SOME BELONG TO PRIVATE PEOPLE OR TO LOCAL NEWSPAPERS. THE MOST IMPORTANT COLLECTION OF OLD PHOTOGRAPHS IS CALLED THE **LAWRENCE COLLECTION**. IT IS IN THE NATIONAL LIBRARY IN DUBLIN.

TRY TO GET AN OLD PHOTOGRAPH OF YOUR OWN AREA. GO TO THE SAME PLACE AT WHICH THE OLD PHOTOGRAPH WAS TAKEN AND TAKE A PHOTOGRAPH OF IT AS IT IS TODAY. USE THE TWO PHOTOGRAPHS TO DESCRIBE HOW YOUR AREA HAS CHANGED IN THIS CENTURY.

OLDER PEOPLE MAY BE ABLE TO HELP YOU FIND OUT WHEN CERTAIN CHANGES CAME ABOUT.

SOURCE B

Shops and shopping

In 1900, few Irish towns had industries. Their main purpose was as centres for buying and selling. On page 57, you read of country women going to town to sell their vegetables. In the 1900 photograph of Clonmel, you can see people selling their products along the streets. There were also shops but they were very different from today's supermarkets.

In Source C, a man describes his father's village shop in Fermanagh.

SOURCE C

"There is very little comparison between a grocery shop in the 1930s and the modern supermarket. One of the first things which struck one on entering the old-time grocery shop was the smell, which was very pleasant. It came from a mixture of various foods and spices, for most of the supplies came in bulk and were then filled into paper bags as required ...

Our shop was lit by two large brass lamps suspended from the ceiling ... Every morning it was the duty of the shop boys to replenish these with paraffin oil, clean the globes and trim the wicks.

There was a counter which ran the full length of the shop and was used for serving customers and making up orders. Every available square inch of wall was packed to capacity with goods ranging from cornflour to snuff.

My father bought his tea by the chest which contained one hundred and twenty pounds. It was then filled into one-pound, half-pound and quarter-pound paper bags. Filling, weighing and closing 448 quarter-pound bags of tea was a long and tedious job ... The same filling, weighing and closing procedure took place for many other commodities such as sugar, currants, raisins, rice, tapioca, baking soda, flour, oatmeal, porridge meal, barley, washing soda ... All had to be filled by hand or scoop and carefully marked in case a customer got washing soda instead of sugar ... If you spilled or even scattered any on the floor, a sharp slap on the ear was your reward."

William K. Parke, *A Fermanagh Childhood*

SOURCE D

This shop was photographed around 1940. What does it sell? How much did sweets cost?

> **Activity**
>
> COMPARING OLD AND MODERN SHOPS
>
> IN SOURCE C, PARKE SAYS: "THERE IS VERY LITTLE COMPARISON BETWEEN A GROCERY SHOP IN THE 1930S AND THE MODERN SUPERMARKET."
>
> USING THE INFORMATION IN SOURCES C AND D AND YOUR OWN KNOWLEDGE OF A MODERN SUPERMARKET, LIST AND DESCRIBE FIVE WAYS IN WHICH MODERN SHOPS ARE DIFFERENT FROM THOSE EARLIER IN THE CENTURY.

Housing conditions in Irish towns

A COMFORTABLE TOWNHOUSE

Houses in towns have changed less than country houses in the last hundred years. On the outside, they look much the same now as they did then. But inside, there are many differences, as you will see from this description of a Dublin house around 1920.

SOURCE E

"None of the houses in the district had electricity. My mother had a gas stove for cooking; she also used the range. The light was the old gas-mantle type but we used oil lamps too. Candles were used also.

My mother kept our house shining clean. The range gleamed, particularly at night in the gas light. There was a long sofa under the kitchen window and the table stood in the centre ... The sink with one cold tap was in the corner farthest from the front door. In the other corner was the door to the back yard and the toilet ...

One bedroom was over the kitchen; the other over the parlour ... There was no such thing as carpet on the floor. We had linoleum on all of our floors, even on the stairs ...

The parlour was our best room ... Facing the window was a piano which my father often played ... The parlour was our special room for visitors but it was also used by ourselves at Christmas and on special occasions."

Paddy Crosbie, *Your Dinner's Poured Out*

READ SOURCE E CAREFULLY.
1. LIST FIVE THINGS WHICH ARE DIFFERENT FROM A MODERN HOUSE AND FIVE THINGS WHICH ARE THE SAME.
2. WHAT KIND OF FAMILY ENTERTAINMENT IS MENTIONED HERE? WHAT WOULD YOU EXPECT TO FIND TODAY?

Looking at the evidence

Houses like the ones in this photograph can still be seen in most Irish towns. Although they may have been modernised inside, they look much as they did at the start of the century. This is the kind of house that Paddy Crosbie described. They were built from the 1870s onwards and had two bedrooms, a kitchen with a cold water tap and a toilet in the back yard.

The high cost of housing

Although they were not rich, Paddy Crosbie's family was better off than many working people at that time because his father had a regular job. Most working people had part-time jobs and did not earn enough to pay 25p a week to rent a house like that.

SOURCE F

In 1913, a survey of 21,000 Dublin families found that

26% earned 75p per week or less.
42% earned between 75p and £1.00 per week.
21% earned between £1.00 and £1.50 per week.
11% earned over £1.50 per week.

At the time, it was reckoned that a family of five needed at least 70p per week just to buy food. Rent, clothes, fares and other necessities were extra.

READ THE FIGURES IN SOURCE F CAREFULLY. WORK OUT HOW MANY OF THOSE FAMILIES COULD AFFORD A HOUSE LIKE THE CROSBIES HAD.

Looking at the evidence

Dublin tenements

Because people earned so little and because unemployed people got no help from the state in those days, many families had to live in **tenements**.

A hundred years earlier, around 1800, rich people lived in big houses like those in Source G in the centre of Dublin. As fashions changed, they left their old city houses and moved to the suburbs.

SOURCE G

The old houses were then divided up and the rooms were let out to poor families. By 1913, every room from the basement to the top floor contained a family. The better-off could afford two rooms. Most could only afford one. Source H gives the rents they paid.

SOURCE H

Basement 8½p per week
Front parlour 17½p per week
Bedroom 12½p per week

In 1911, 30% of all Dublin families lived in one room in a tenement. In 60% of these families, there were three or more persons per room.

Source I is from the 1901 census. It lists the people living in one tenement room. How many people lived in this room?

SOURCE I

"A widow, her three daughters aged 16 to 24, her sister-in-law aged 56, a nephew aged 26, and two nieces aged 16 and 18. The nephew, one daughter and one niece were employed."

In 1913, the government set up an enquiry into the living conditions of Dublin tenements. Source J comes from this report.

SOURCE J

"There are many tenement houses with 7 or 8 rooms that have a family in each room ... We have visited one house that we found occupied by 98 people, another by 74, a third by 73.

The entrance to all tenement houses is by a common door off a street ... and in most cases the door is never shut, day or night ... Most have yards at the back ... Generally the only water supply is a single tap in the yard. The yard is common (shared) and the closet (toilet) accommodation is to be found there ... The closet is also common, not only to the residents of the house but to anyone who likes to come in off the street and is of course common to both sexes.

The halls and landings, yards and closets were in a filthy condition. At the same time, it is gratifying to find in a number of instances that in spite of the many drawbacks, an effort was made by the occupants to keep their rooms tidy ..."

A second-hand clothes market set up near tenement buildings in Dublin. Slum-dwellers were too poor to buy new clothes.

Slums outside Dublin

Of course Dublin was not the only place with tenements. In most other towns and cities, housing conditions were just as bad for poor families. Even people living in single houses were not much better off.

SOURCE K

This photograph, called "The Turf Sellers" was taken in Foxford, Co. Mayo around 1910. It shows the type of house described in Source L. Houses like this were to be found on the outskirts of most Irish towns. The children here supplemented the family's income by selling turf.

Source L was written by a doctor in Sligo for the 1913 government report.

SOURCE L

"The typical slum dwelling contains two apartments – a kitchen and a room. There is a window in each room, so fixed that they can be neither opened nor closed. The kitchen would measure about 12 feet by 9 feet ... The house is thatched, the floor earthen. Number of inhabitants – man, wife and, say, three children. Rent one shilling and six pence (7½p) per week. The average wage of the bread-winner is twelve shillings (60p) ...

None of the dwellings of the poorer classes may be said to be fit for habitation ... The earthen floor, the sodden thatch, the fixed windows, the lack of proper sanitary accommodation, all conspire against the health and well-being of the unfortunate inhabitants ... There are no suitable dwelling houses in Sligo to let at a rent which the occupants of slum dwellings can afford to pay ..."

A back-lane in Killarney where barrels were made for the local brewery. Small industries like this were common in many towns.

QUESTIONS

1. (a) Explain in your own words what a tenement house was. (b) Use the information in Sources G, H, I and J to write two paragraphs describing life in a Dublin tenement.

2. (a) What proportion of Dublin families lived in these conditions in 1913? (b) Use the information in Sources F and H to explain why they did so.

3. Read Source L. It describes a "typical slum dwelling" in Sligo. (a) List two ways in which it was different from the Dublin tenement. (b) According to the author, why were poor people in Sligo living in these conditions?

CHAPTER 4

How towns have changed since the 1930s

Slow to improve

Tenement houses were very unhealthy. People living in them easily caught TB, typhoid and others diseases which spread outwards from the tenements to infect better-off people. When governments realised this, they began to try to improve housing conditions for the poorest people. But change came very slowly.

Building council houses

From the 1880s, the British government gave Irish local councils the power to build decent houses for the poor. The councils were reluctant to do so, however. New houses were expensive and councillors did not want to increase the local taxes (the **rates**) to pay for them. Rate-payers, after all, were the voters who elected the councillors. This attitude continued in the first years of the Irish Free State.

But in the 1930s, the Fianna Fáil government began to give better grants to pay for council housing. Slowly, more houses were built, the slums cleared and the people re-housed.

In Source A, Kathleen Behan tells how her family got a council house in Crumlin in the 1930s.

SOURCE A

"We had gone down, year in, year out, to the Housing Department of the Corporation. We should have had a house years before that, with nine of us living in two rooms. But there were people even worse off than us and the ones who got the houses first were the ones with TB. Well, one day I went down and Mr Marks in the office told me: 'Good news, Mrs Behan. You have a house if you want it' ...

I dragged Da out to look at the house on the Sunday before we moved ... It was miles away. I nearly died. I thought we were going to Siberia. Crumlin, you know, is right out of the city on the slopes of the Dublin Mountains. It would put your heart crossways, just looking at the miles and miles of new roads. No lights. It was like the Wild West. Da cursed and swore about leaving his old pub and being miles away from his work but I didn't care. He didn't have to put up with one lavatory used by seven families ...

At last we reached Kildare Road. The little house was lovely ... I wouldn't call the Queen my aunt just to be there. Is there anything better than the smell of fresh paint? ... Tiny it was, with a little front parlour and two little bedrooms, but that was still better than all of us stuck in two rooms."

Kathleen Behan, *Mother of All the Behans*

▲ *Terraced houses, built by local councils, like the one described by Kathleen Behan, were a huge improvement on the slum dwellings of earlier years.*

◢ QUESTIONS ◣

1. Why did local councils take so long to build decent houses for the people?
2. (a) Why did the Behan family want to be rehoused? (b) Who got houses ahead of them?
3. In your own words, describe Kathleen Behan's reaction to her new house.
4. From Source A, can you see any disadvantages which a new housing estate might have for the people moving to it?

Improved housing

Since the end of World War II, councils all over Ireland have tried to solve the housing problems by building decent, affordable houses for the poorest people. These pictures show some of the solutions which councils have adopted.

In the 1960s, many councils in Europe saw high **tower blocks** of flats as an ideal solution to the housing shortage. They were not popular with Irish families, especially those with young children. Only one big flat development was carried out in Ireland – at Ballymun, north of Dublin.

A tower-block in Ballymun

Because Ireland's population is small, councils had room to build new houses on the outskirts of towns. The aerial photograph of Athlone below shows clearly how this changed our towns. The old town centre is around the bridge and dates back to the Middle Ages. Near it, the streets are narrow and winding and the houses are crammed together. But on the outskirts, there are modern **housing estates** and factories. In these estates, each house has its own garden.

Not all housing estates were built by the councils. Many were built by private developers for middle class people (shopkeepers, office workers, doctors, solicitors). Up to the 1920s, people like these had usually rented their houses. Since then, most of them have borrowed money from a **building society** to buy their own houses on a **mortgage**. Middle-class houses were usually **detached** or **semi-detached** with at least three bedrooms.

An example of private housing

An aerial view of Athlone

Suburbanisation and industrialisation

As a result of developments like these, Irish towns have changed a great deal since the 1930s.

- They have expanded in area, as new housing estates were built in **suburbs** on the edges of towns.

- They have become **quieter** at night. In 1900, the centres of towns and cities were full of people, with shopkeepers living over their shops and workers staying near their jobs. Now, many people live in the suburbs and travel into the towns to work or to shop. At night, town centres are often deserted when people go home.

- Today, many towns have **industries**. Electric power has made it possible to set up a factory anywhere, so there are now modern factories near most towns. These factories employ some of the people who had to leave the farms as electric power and modern machinery reduced the need for farm workers.

- Up to the end of World War II, Ireland was unusual in Western Europe because more people lived in the country than in towns. Since the 1960s, this had changed, as this table shows.

PERCENTAGE OF POPULATION LIVING IN TOWNS IN THE REPUBLIC	
1926	32.27%
1936	35.55%
1951	41.44%
1961	46.10%
1966	49.20%
1971	52.25%

◢ QUESTIONS ◢

1. List some of the solutions by which councils tried to improve housing.
2. Not all housing estates were built by councils. Who built the others? What kind of people lived in these estates?
3. Look up the word "suburb" and explain it in your own words. Using what you know about your own district as evidence, discuss the opinion that "today, most Irish people live in the suburbs".

Activity

USING THE INFORMATION IN CHAPTERS 3 AND 4 OF THIS SECTION, WRITE A SHORT ESSAY WITH THE TITLE "IRISH TOWNS (OR CITIES) SINCE 1900".

BE SURE TO USE PLENTY OF FACTS. YOU MAY WISH TO INCLUDE INFORMATION WHICH YOU HAVE RESEARCHED ABOUT YOUR OWN TOWN OR CITY. YOU COULD FIND THIS BY INTERVIEWING OLDER PEOPLE, BY LOOKING AT OLD MAPS OR PHOTOGRAPHS OR BY CONSULTING OLD NEWSPAPERS.

Looking at the evidence

THIS PICTURE SHOWS PATRICK STREET IN CORK. (A) LIST 3 TYPES OF TRANSPORT SHOWN HERE. (B) WAS THIS PHOTO TAKEN IN 1900, 1930 OR 1960? GIVE 2 REASONS FOR YOUR CHOICE. (C) IN WHICH COLLECTION OF OLD PHOTOGRAPHS WOULD YOU FIND THIS? GIVE A REASON FOR YOUR ANSWER.

Changes in Transport in Ireland since 1900

In the nineteenth century, the development of railways and steamships had speeded up travel. But it was the **petrol engine** which produced the main transport developments of the twentieth century.

Steam engines were big and heavy and required a large amount of coal to run. Petrol-driven engines were small enough to fit in individual carriages and so replace the horse. They were also light enough to defy gravity and power aeroplanes.

Horses

In the early years of the twentieth century, horses were everywhere. In cities and towns, they provided the main means of transport. Goods of all kinds were moved in horse-drawn carts, and bakers, butchers and grocers delivered their goods in horse-drawn vans. Wealthy people had their own carriages, while the less well-off hired side-cars as taxis. In country areas, "long-cars" like those invented by Bianconi a century earlier still provided a bus-type service between towns which did not have rail links.

This remained the situation right up to the 1930s, as Paddy Crosbie remembered.

▽ *Travelling by side-car*

SOURCE A

"Although the bicycle was coming into general use, the horse was still king of the roads – the smell of horses was strong up to the '30s ... There were many different types of horse-drawn vehicle – drays, landaus, lorries, traps, hackney or side-cars, long-cars, cabs, brakes and floats ..."
Paddy Crosbie, *Your Dinner's Poured Out*

The coming of the motor car

It was the motor car, along with the motor bus and the motor lorry, which ended the horse's role in transport. The petrol engine was invented in Germany in the 1880s. It was then fitted into a carriage to produce a "horseless carriage". You can see this if you compare the shape of early cars with a carriage.

Early cars were very expensive, so only wealthy people could afford them. In 1904, when a new car cost over £400, there were only 38 cars registered in Dublin. Today, this does not seem expensive, but remember how little workers earned at the time (page 64).

Cars also broke down often and there were few garages, so most owners employed a chauffeur who would also act as a mechanic.

The spread of motor transport

Lorries and buses became common before cars did. Transport firms bought buses because they carried more people and were quicker than the old long-cars. By the 1920s, the long-cars were gone. By the 1940s, when **Coras Iompair Éireann (CIE)** was set up as the national transport authority, even railways were under threat. In the 1960s, railway branch-lines were closed, leaving only the main-line routes running.

Before 1914, only the rich could afford cars. Usually they employed a chauffeur to drive them around.

After World War I, motor cars became cheaper. This was due mainly to the mass-production techniques pioneered in America by **Henry Ford**. This brought the price of cars down, within the reach of middle-class people like teachers, lawyers and shopkeepers. After the war, cars continued to increase in popularity until by the 1980s, a majority of families had one.

Traffic jams began to happen in the 1970s and are a continuing problem.

THE IMPACT OF THE CAR

From the 1890s, bicycles had allowed more people to move around than ever before. But most bicycles were only for one person and anyway, there was a limit to how far a cyclist could travel.

Cars had no such limitations. When they became common, people could travel long distances to work and the word **commuter** entered the language. Roads improved and towns spread out into the suburbs. Some people chose to stay on farms while earning their livings by working in a town.

Traffic jams appeared as people in cars went to shop in the town centre. This in turn led to the building of out-of-town shopping centres and the decay of town centres.

But many people could not afford cars to get to the new shopping centres. This was especially true of mothers with young children and old people. They suffered as it became more difficult to find all the shops and services they needed locally.

Henry Ford, the son of an Irish emigrant, who made the first cars on a production line rather than one by one. This greatly reduced their cost.

Air travel

Balloons which were invented in the eighteenth century were the first form of air travel. But in 1903, two Americans, the **Wright brothers**, succeeded in inventing a "heavier than air" flying machine.

The plane in which the Wright brothers first flew. Do you think this is a real photograph or an imaginary reconstruction?

World War I gave a boost to the development of aircraft and longer flights became possible. Because of its position on the western edge of Europe, Ireland was an obvious starting or ending place for those trying to fly across the Atlantic.

The first west-to-east trans-Atlantic flight landed near Clifden, Co. Galway, in 1919.

The east-to-west crossing, against the prevailing winds, was much more difficult. An Irish Air Corps officer, **James Fitzmaurice**, tried to do this in 1927 but was forced to return. In April 1928, he set out again, accompanied by two German flyers. They left from Baldonnell and landed in Newfoundland in Canada 36 hours later.

AIRPORTS ON THE SHANNON

These flights showed that trans-Atlantic air travel was possible. In the 1930s, airlines from America chose the sheltered waters of Foynes in Co. Limerick as the best European site to land their **flying boats**. An airport opened at Foynes in 1937. Throughout World War II, planes flying between Britain, Europe and America landed there on a regular basis, carrying generals, politicians and film stars.

A "flying boat" of the type that landed at Foynes. This one carried between 100 and 150 passengers.

The war led to the development of bigger, land-based planes and Foynes airport moved to its present site at Shannon in 1945. To make it more attractive to travellers, the government created the world's first **duty free zone** at Shannon, an idea later copied by airports around the world.

However, the development of long-range jets in the 1950s meant that trans-Atlantic planes could now fly directly to Britain and Europe. By the 1960s, Shannon had lost its role as a centre for European flights.

AER LINGUS

Meanwhile, the government decided to set up an Irish-owned airline, **Aer Lingus**. Its first route was between Baldonnell and Bristol. Flights to London, Liverpool and the Isle of Man were added later. The present Dublin Airport opened in 1940 but the war slowed development until the 1950s, when routes to continental Europe and America were opened up.

Dublin airport in the 1950s, before jet planes became common.

The development of air travel changed Irish people's views of the world. Since the 1960s, foreign travel has become common. In 1900, it was a big adventure to take a train or spend a day at the seaside. Today it is not uncommon for people to go to Spain or Florida for a summer break or to visit relatives in Australia. In 1900, emigrants who left Ireland did not usually expect to see their families again. Today they can come home for a week at Christmas.

Activity

SELECT ONE OF THE FOLLOWING TOPICS AND WRITE AN ESSAY ON IT.

"CHANGES IN ROAD TRANSPORT IN IRELAND IN THE TWENTIETH CENTURY"

OR

"CHANGES IN AIR TRANSPORT IN IRELAND IN THE TWENTIETH CENTURY"

YOU SHOULD INCLUDE AN ACCOUNT OF THE SITUATION AROUND THE START OF THE CENTURY, THE REASONS FOR CHANGE, SOME OF THE SOURCES OF CHANGE AND THE SITUATION AT PRESENT.

Changes in Entertainment in Ireland since 1900

Entertaining themselves

In 1900, most people provided their own entertainment. In the countryside, neighbours gathered in each others' houses to sing, tell stories and dance. In towns, families gathered around the piano in the parlour and played and sang together.

Dancing was a popular form of entertainment. A girl performs at an early "feis". Traditional costume has not yet been introduced.

Theatres

Townspeople also had access to organised entertainment. In Dublin, there were several theatres. Most of them regularly put on concerts and operas or plays by foreign playwrights. In 1904, Lady Gregory and W. B. Yeats set up the **Abbey Theatre** to put on plays by Irish writers (page 6).

There were theatres and playhouses in other towns too. Even small villages had halls which were visited by groups of travelling actors who put on plays

by Shakespeare and others. People also enjoyed "lantern shows" which were still pictures projected onto a screen, usually accompanied by a lecture.

Cinema

In 1895, moving pictures were invented by the **Lumière brothers** in Paris. The first Irish film show was held in the Olympia Theatre in April 1896. People came in their thousands to see live movement on the screen and soon short pictures which told a story were being made. These were very popular and moving picture shows were quickly organised in halls around the country.

The brothers, Augusta and Louis Lumiere, who first made moving pictures in 1895.

The first purpose-built Irish cinema opened in 1909 under the management of the writer **James Joyce**. Films were made in Ireland as early as 1910, many of them showing episodes from Irish history, like the story of Robert Emmet.

THE CHILDREN'S MATINEE

Right up to the 1960s, children usually went to the matinees on Saturday or Sunday afternoon. Admission cost a penny and the seats were soon filled. Paddy Crosbie recalled what it was like in the 1920s before talking pictures appeared.

> *"Those were the days when kids really lived the stories. They never sat quiet through a screen fight. Each boy dug into his neighbour and synchronised his blows with that of the 'chap's'. In every film there was always a 'chap', a 'girl' and a 'villyun' ...*

The sight of the 'villyun' creeping up behind the 'chap' or the 'girl' brought frenzied cries of 'Look behind!' One thing that makes me smile when I look back at silent films, and that is the reading of the captions and the dialogue. Everybody read the printed words aloud, and I mean everybody. The pictures were very real to us because they were a new thing in our lives and Hooded Terrors were to be found in every school playground."

Paddy Crosbie, *Your Dinner's Poured Out*

Hero and heroine together at the end! A still from the kind of cowboy film that the kids loved.

"Talking pictures" appeared in the 1930s and this helped to make Hollywood the movie capital of the world. Young Irish people learned to use American slang like "OK!" and "So long!" – to the dismay of their elders who thought they should be learning Irish instead. **Censorship** was introduced in the 1920s to prevent nasty foreign ideas from damaging Irish innocence. The film censor banned or cut many of the best films of the day.

Radio

Radio was invented by **Guglielmo Marconi**, an Italian whose mother was Irish. He made several early broadcasts from the west of Ireland as he tried to send radio messages across the Atlantic. A trans-Atlantic radio-telegraphic station was established on Valentia, Co. Kerry.

Broadcasting

At first, radio was used to send direct messages, mainly at sea. When the Volunteers took over the GPO in 1916, they sent one of the world's first "broadcast" messages (i.e. to anyone who might happen to be listening), announcing the establishment of the Irish republic.

By the 1920s, radio stations broadcasting music and news were common. After the Irish Free State was set up, the Irish government established a national broadcasting service. It was called **2RN** (which sounded like "Éireann") and began broadcasting on 1 January 1926. In 1932, the name was changed to **Radio Éireann**.

Radio Éireann was part of the civil service. The people who ran it had a hard time persuading the government to spend money on broadcasting. The early broadcasts were mainly music, which was cheap (one man and a few records!). Slowly, news, sport, drama and talks were added throughout the 1930s.

But radios were too expensive for many people. They also had to pay for an annual licence, so the numbers listening to radio only grew slowly, as these figures show.

NUMBER OF RADIO LICENCES SOLD	
1926	5,000
1933	33,000
1937	100,000
1961	500,000

Television

The first television broadcasts were made by the BBC in Britain just before World War II but were then suspended until the war was over. By the 1950s, British television could be received by homes on Ireland's east coast which were equipped with a tall aerial tied to the chimney. Pictures were very poor but people were fascinated by the blurry images.

The demand for an Irish TV station grew, and RTÉ television began broadcasting in 1961. It was an instant success. By the late 1960s, most homes in the country had a TV.

The impact of new forms of entertainment

Film, radio and television all had an enormous effect on Irish life. Through them, people were introduced to new worlds. They saw different lifestyles, different houses and different values. Accents changed as people adapted to British and American ways of speaking and the Irish language, which was little used in these **media**, declined even more.

Of the three, television probably made the most difference to people's lives. It was in people's homes and was watched daily. On RTÉ, young presenters such as Gay Byrne on the "Late Late Show" encouraged the discussion of issues like contraception or divorce which had never been mentioned in public before. News reporters dug up stories that political leaders would have preferred to keep quiet and challenged the leaders of Church and State to justify their behaviour. This kind of thing opened up Irish society and made it more varied and tolerant.

Activity

WRITE AN ESSAY WITH THE TITLE: "CHANGES IN POPULAR ENTERTAINMENT IN TWENTIETH-CENTURY IRELAND".

BE SURE TO INCLUDE A DESCRIPTION OF POPULAR ENTERTAINMENT BEFORE THE ARRIVAL OF FILM, RADIO AND TELEVISION, AS WELL AS SOME COMMENTS ON HOW THESE CHANGES CAME ABOUT.

IF YOU WISH, YOU COULD DO SOME RESEARCH BY ASKING OLDER PEOPLE WHAT LIFE WAS LIKE IN THE DAYS BEFORE TELEVISION AND INCLUDE THESE FINDINGS IN YOUR ESSAY.

CHAPTER 7

The Changing Status of Irish Women since 1900

A woman's place

Up to the middle of the nineteenth century, women in the United Kingdom (which then included Ireland) had very few rights. Women from poor families got almost no schooling. Even when families could afford to send their daughters to school, they were only taught "ladylike" skills such as sewing or playing musical instruments.

No woman could become a doctor, a lawyer or get any kind of professional qualification. In fact, there were many men – as well as some women – who argued that studying science or maths would be bad for women and damage their ability to have babies. People who held this view believed that a woman's main aim in life should be to please a man who would marry her and look after her.

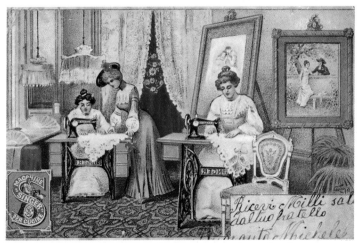
Many 19th century women had to support themselves by dressmaking. This advertisement for a sewing machine glamorises their living and working conditions.

In reality, of course, many women had to earn their keep, but the only jobs open to them were badly paid. Poor women worked in shops or factories, earning half as much as the men. Women with some education could work as nurses or governesses, jobs which were also poorly paid. While a woman was still single, she could own property but if she married, her property and even the wages she earned belonged to her husband.

Women and education

From about 1870, this situation began to change. Some fathers provided their daughters with a good education and these women worked for equal rights with men.

▸ They got the law changed to allow women to keep control of their property after marriage.

▸ When school examinations began in Ireland in 1878, they persuaded the politicians to let girls enter on the same terms as boys. To everyone's surprise, girls did as well as the boys.

▸ This made it difficult for the universities and the professions to bar women. By 1900, women could become doctors and get university degrees.

Hanna Sheehy-Skeffington and "Votes for women"

Hanna Sheehy-Skeffington

By this time, only one big barrier remained. Women could not vote or take a seat in parliament, although any man over twenty-one could do so, even if he was illiterate.

Educated women bitterly resented their second-class status. In 1900, Hanna Sheehy was a young university student. She wrote:

"I ... was amazed and disgusted to learn that I was classed among criminals, infants and lunatics – in fact, my status as a woman was worse than any of these."

Hanna joined a group that was demanding women's **suffrage** (the right to vote). They wrote letters and signed petitions. They even managed to win the support of some men. One of them was Frank Skeffington, whom Hanna married. They used both their surnames to stress the equality between them.

But many men did not approve of giving women the vote. One Home Rule leader said:

"Women's suffrage will, I believe, be the ruin of our western civilisation."

It was this attitude which led Hanna and a few other women to set up the **Irish Women's Franchise League**. Members held demonstrations and attacked politicians. The police arrested them and several, including Hanna, went on hunger strike. When World War I began in 1914, the "votes for women" campaign was called off and Hanna and her husband began to work for peace.

DISCUSS THE STATEMENT OF THE HOME RULE LEADER ABOUT WOMEN'S SUFFRAGE. WHAT IS YOUR OPINION OF HIS ATTITUDE?

Activity

Constance Markievicz

Another woman who worked for women's rights was Constance Markievicz. Her family were landlords in Co. Sligo and she had married a Polish count.

Constance worked among the poor in Dublin and was a friend of the socialist leader, James Connolly (page 11). He supported women's rights and made sure that they were mentioned in equal terms with men in the 1916 Proclamation of the Republic. It begins: "Irishmen and Irishwomen ...".

Constance Markievicz

CUMANN NA MBAN AND THE 1916 RISING

Women played an important part in the struggle for Irish independence. In 1914, they set up **Cumann na mBan**, the women's version of the Irish Volunteers.

In the 1916 Rising, *Cumann na mBan* served alongside the Volunteers in the GPO and other places. Constance Markievicz was in command of the garrison at Stephen's Green. At the end of the Rising, she was arrested and sentenced to death by the British army. But the British called off the executions before she was shot and set her free in 1917.

Meanwhile, Frank Sheehy-Skeffington, who was trying to stop the fighting, was murdered by a British officer. After that, Hanna became an ardent supporter of Sinn Féin's campaign for an Irish republic.

Another republican activist, Mary McSwiney, sister of Terence McSwiney. She was a member of Cumann na mBan and of Sinn Féin, was later elected to Dáil Éireann and opposed the Treaty in 1922.

Votes at last!

When the war ended in 1918, the British government finally gave women the vote. But men and women were still not equal. Although any man over twenty-one could vote, a woman could only vote if she was over thirty and owned property.

THE ELECTION OF CONSTANCE MARKIEVICZ

Women could now stand for parliament. Sinn Féin put forward two women candidates in the 1918 election and one of them, Constance Markievicz, was elected.

She was the first woman MP in either Britain or Ireland. Following Sinn Féin's policy, however, she did not go to Westminster but took her place in Dáil Éireann in 1919. When the first independent Irish government was elected, de Valera made her Minister for Labour.

Full equality

Cumann na mBan played a big part in the War of Independence which followed. As a result, when the first Irish constitution was made in 1922, women at last got equal rights with men. They could vote at twenty-one and hold any office in the government.

Maud Gonne McBride was another woman who combined the demand for women's rights with support for an independent Irish Republic.

Reducing women's rights

But there is a big difference between having a right and being able to use it. Women might have had the vote, but few of them would vote for a woman. After 1922, very few women went into politics or were elected to the Dáil.

This situation allowed various governments to whittle away the principle of equality between the sexes. Between 1922 and the 1950s:

- Women were barred from working after marriage (the **marriage bar**). This made it difficult for them to reach the top jobs.
- Women's right to serve on juries was limited.
- Contraception was completely outlawed.
- When de Valera brought in a new constitution in 1937, it said that a woman's place was in the home. A few women protested, but de Valera paid no attention to them.

A new women's movement

In the 1960s, a new women's movement began. It demanded real equality, not just equality on paper. The number of women TDs gradually increased and the laws which discriminated against women were withdrawn. The marriage bar was dropped and the right of women to equal pay for equal work was established. The laws on contraception were changed so that women could decide for themselves how many children to have.

Women and the Court of Human Rights

The women's cause was helped by Ireland's membership of the European Union. Several women brought cases to the European Court and won, forcing the Irish government to give them justice. Among the lawyers who took these cases was **Mary Robinson**.

Women leaders since the 1970s

Since the 1970s, women have played a bigger part in the Dáil. Three women, Máire Geoghegan-Quinn, Gemma Hussey and Mary O'Rourke became cabinet ministers in the 1980s. In 1990, Mary Robinson was elected to the highest post in the land, that of President of Ireland.

Mary Robinson, elected President of Ireland in 1990.

Máire Geoghegan-Quinn

▲ *Gemma Hussey*

▲ *Mary O'Rourke*

Activity

WRITE AN ESSAY DESCRIBING THE CHANGES WHICH HAVE OCCURRED IN THE STATUS OF IRISH WOMEN SINCE 1900. YOU SHOULD ORGANISE YOUR ESSAY UNDER THE FOLLOWING HEADINGS:
- WHAT WOMEN COULD AND COULD NOT DO IN 1900
- TWO WOMEN WHO WERE INVOLVED IN THE CAMPAIGN FOR EQUALITY AND WHAT THEY DID
- THE PART WOMEN PLAYED IN THE STRUGGLE FOR IRISH INDEPENDENCE
- HOW THE STATUS OF WOMEN CHANGED AFTER INDEPENDENCE
- THE NEW WOMEN'S MOVEMENT SINCE THE 1960S AND SOME OF THE CHANGES IT HAS BROUGHT ABOUT

Looking at the evidence

ARE IRISH WOMEN BETTER OFF TODAY THAN THEY WERE IN 1900? HERE ARE SOME FACTS TO HELP YOU FORM AN OPINION.
- UNTIL THE 1970S, WOMEN IN MOST JOBS HAD TO RETIRE WHEN THEY GOT MARRIED. NOW THEY MAY CONTINUE WORKING.
- IN 1926, A WOMAN'S AVERAGE WAGE WAS 70% OF A MAN'S. BY 1990, THIS HAD NOT CHANGED.
- UP TO 1960, THE AVERAGE IRISH WOMAN HAD OVER FOUR CHILDREN. BY 1990 SHE HAD TWO.
- IN 1926, 328 MOTHERS DIED IN CHILDBIRTH. IN 1990, FIVE MOTHERS DIED IN CHILDBIRTH.
- IN 1900, WOMEN COULD NOT BECOME LAWYERS. TODAY, A WOMAN IS A MEMBER OF THE SUPREME COURT (ALONGSIDE FOUR MEN).

Finding Out

TO FIND OUT HOW THE ROLE OF WOMEN HAS CHANGED IN THE LAST FIFTY YEARS, TALK TO SOME OLDER WOMEN ABOUT WHETHER THEY THINK WOMEN ARE BETTER OFF NOW THAN WHEN THEY WERE YOUNG.
- HAVE THEY EVER BEEN DISCRIMINATED AGAINST? HOW? BY WHOM?
- DO GIRLS HAVE A BETTER EDUCATION AND MORE CAREER OPPORTUNITIES TODAY THAN WHEN THEY WERE YOUNG?
- ARE MODERN WOMEN FORCED TO WORK AGAINST THEIR WILL WHEN THEY MIGHT PREFER TO BE AT HOME WITH THEIR CHILDREN?
- DO WOMEN TODAY HAVE MORE INFLUENCE ON GOVERNMENTS?

YOU MIGHT WANT TO THINK OF SOME QUESTIONS OF YOUR OWN FOR THE INTERVIEW. THEN WRITE A REPORT ON YOUR FINDINGS.

PART 3

INTERNATIONAL RELATIONS IN THE TWENTIETH CENTURY

The Effects of World War I

When World War I ended in 1918, old empires collapsed and new countries appeared on the map of Europe. Treaties were signed between the defeated powers and those who had won the war. The **League of Nations** was set up and there was great hope for world peace.

But the war had caused terrible damage. Before the war, Europe had been the richest place on earth. But after four years of war, Europe's economy was in ruins. Production levels were down because men had been fighting in the war instead of working on farms and in factories.

During World War I, large areas of agricultural land had been destroyed. Even after the fighting ended, a great deal of land remained useless because of unexploded mines and shells. Thousands of kilometres of railway lines and roads had also been destroyed.

Trade with the rest of the world had been affected by the **submarine warfare** which had destroyed hundreds of cargo ships. Countries like Britain and France had borrowed heavily to finance the war. Now, they had to pay back this money.

The people of Europe faced many other problems. More than fifteen million soldiers and civilians had been killed. For every individual killed, two more had been crippled and would have to be looked after for as long as they lived. There were many widows and orphans, prisoners of war and refugees. To make matters worse, an influenza epidemic broke out just as the war ended, and millions more died as a result.

World War I also changed the attitudes of ordinary men and women all over Europe. Although there was some bitterness and a desire for revenge, most people wanted to live in harmony with each other. Poets and novelists wrote great works about their experiences of war. All of them said "Never again".

But their hopes for peace were soon disappointed. During the next twenty years, European countries adopted different forms of government. Some were **democracies** while others were **fascist dictatorships**. One country, the Soviet Union, had a **communist dictatorship**. A struggle between democracy, fascism and communism developed which led to the outbreak of World War II in 1939.

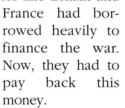

British soldiers survey the scene after a battle in 1915. Note the waterlogged trenches, the duck boards and the mud.

---

1. MANY BOOKS, PLAYS AND POEMS HAVE BEEN WRITTEN ABOUT WORLD WAR I. VISIT YOUR LOCAL LIBRARY AND FIND OUT MORE ABOUT WHAT THESE PEOPLE WROTE TO DESCRIBE THE EFFECTS OF THE WAR ON THE PEOPLE OF EUROPE.
2. DO YOU KNOW ANY FAMOUS IRISH OR BRITISH POETS WHO SERVED IN THE WAR AND THEN WROTE POEMS ABOUT IT? READ SOME OF THEIR POEMS. TALK ABOUT HOW THEY FELT ABOUT THE WAR.

Finding Out

 ## The Paris Peace Conference: 1919

Britain, France and the United States had won World War I. Their leaders were determined that such a war must never happen again. They believed that a better future could only come about if everyone worked together for peace. It was only in this way that the horrors of another war could be prevented.

Lloyd George of Britain, Vittorio Orlando of Italy, Georges Clemenceau of France and Woodrow Wilson of the USA meet at Versailles in 1919.

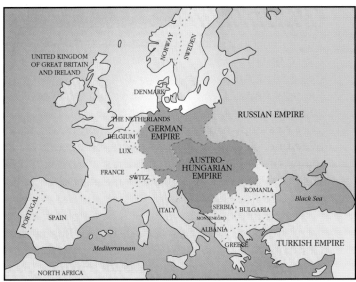

Europe before the First World War (1914)

In January 1919, the leaders of the victorious countries met in Paris to try and solve the problems caused by World War I. The most important decisions were taken by the leaders of Britain, France and the USA. Separate treaties were signed with each of the defeated powers. The most important one was the **Treaty of Versailles** which dealt with Germany.

Delegates gather in the Great Hall of Mirrors at Versailles to witness the Germans signing the Treaty.

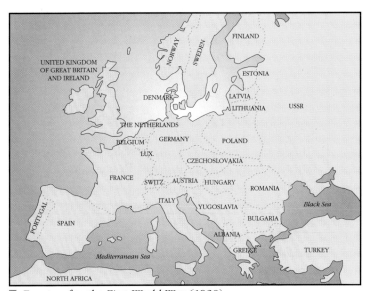

Europe after the First World War (1920)

🏛 Self-determination

Before the war, many people had lived in the old German, Russian, Austro-Hungarian and Turkish empires. The delegates at the Paris Peace Conference believed that these people had the right to **self-determination**. This meant that people could choose the state they wished to belong to. Poles, Czechs, Slavs and others began to set up states of their own.

The Paris Peace Conference helped to draw up the borders between the new states. As a result, the map of Europe in 1920 looked very different from Europe in 1914.

LOOK AT THE TWO MAPS. ONE SHOWS EUROPE IN 1914. THE OTHER SHOWS EUROPE IN 1920.
1. LIST THE SEVEN NEW COUNTRIES WHICH HAD APPEARED BY 1920.
2. LIST THOSE COUNTRIES WHICH HAD REMAINED THE SAME AS IN 1914.
3. LIST THOSE COUNTRIES WHICH WERE SMALLER IN 1920 THAN IN 1914.

Looking at the evidence

Minorities

The Paris Peace Conference recognised the wishes of the **majorities** in most areas of Eastern Europe. But dissatisfied **minorities** were left behind in many of the new states. These minorities would be a constant source of trouble in the years ahead.

It was impossible for the peace treaties to please everyone. So when borders were being drawn in many of the newly-created states, particularly in Eastern Europe, there were still minorities who wanted to live elsewhere.

For example, in the new state of Poland, there were Russians who wanted to be in Russia and Germans who wanted to be in Germany. In that part of Czechoslovakia called the **Sudetenland**, there were three million Germans who would have preferred to be in Germany. There were also many Poles and Hungarians living in Czechoslovakia who were not happy to live under Czech rule.

THE PROBLEM OF EUROPEAN MINORITIES IS STILL WITH US TODAY. FIND OUT ABOUT THE CAUSES OF THE PRESENT CONFLICT IN BOSNIA AND SERBIA. BOTH OF THESE WERE PART OF THE FORMER YUGOSLAVIA, ONE OF THE NEW COUNTRIES CREATED BY THE PARIS PEACE CONFERENCE IN 1919.

Finding Out

QUESTIONS

1. Make a list of the problems facing Europe after World War I ended. Can you think of any others which are not mentioned in the text?

2. In your opinion, which was the hardest problem to solve? Give reasons for your answer.

3. What do you understand by the term "self-determination"? Do you think it was a good idea? Give reasons for your answer.

4. Why do you think it would have been impossible to satisfy every minority in Europe after World War I? What problems do you think would have arisen if this had been tried?

5. In 1920, the new president of Czechoslovakia said: "The peace treaty has created more just conditions throughout Europe. We are entitled to expect that the tensions between states and races will decrease." Do you think he was right or wrong? Give reasons for your answer.

The League of Nations

For everyone at the Paris Peace Conference in 1919, perhaps the most important question was: how can we stop war from breaking out again? **President Woodrow Wilson** of the United States suggested one answer.

> *"Merely to win the war is not enough. It must be won in such a way as to ensure the future peace of the world. This could be achieved though a League of Nations where the peoples of the world could act together to solve the problems of the nations around the conference table rather than on the battlefields."*

Woodrow Wilson, President of the USA 1913-1921. He was disappointed that America voted against joining the League of Nations. In 1919, he was awarded the Nobel prize for peace.

President Wilson persuaded the other leaders in Paris to accept his idea, and so the **League of Nations** was born. Its headquarters was in Geneva in Switzerland. By 1923, fifty-four countries had joined the League, including Ireland.

The aims of the League of Nations were:

☑ to find a **peaceful settlement** to disputes between states

☑ to **prevent war** by getting all countries to join together to stop any aggressors. This was called **collective security**.

☑ to encourage **disarmament** (to end the production and use of weapons)

☑ to protect the **rights of minorities**

☑ to deal with **social, economic, health and labour problems**.

A meeting of the General Assembly of the League of Nations in 1921. In the early days there were great hopes for the League, but it failed to prevent the outbreak of World War Two.

How the League worked

COUNCIL

It had four permanent members – Britain, France, Italy and Japan – and eleven other rotating member states which were elected for a fixed number of years. The Council met four times a year, as well as during emergencies. All votes had to be unanimous, which made it difficult for the League to take strong action.

PERMANENT COURT OF JUSTICE

It consisted of fifteen judges from various member states. It met at the Hague in the Netherlands and gave legal judgments on disputes between member states.

SECRETARIAT

This was the civil service of the League. The civil servants came from all member states. They owed their allegiance to the League itself, not to their own countries.

ASSEMBLY

It represented all the member states. It met once a year, in autumn, and dealt with relations between member states. Each country, regardless of size, had only one vote. All major decisions had to be unanimous.

INTERNATIONAL LABOUR ORGANISATION

It tried to improve working conditions for people in the member states – rates of pay, hours of work, annual holidays and workers' compensation.

COMMISSIONS AND COMMITTEES

Special bodies were set up to deal with particular problems such as refugees, prisoners of war, the slave and drug trades, disarmament and minorities.

Weaknesses of the League

The League had a number of serious weaknesses.

ABSENT STATES

When he returned to the United States after Versailles, President Wilson campaigned to win support for the League. He said:

"The League of Nations is a definite guarantee of peace. If the United States does not join the League, I can predict with absolute certainty that within another generation, there will be another world war."

But his party was defeated in an election and the American Senate voted against joining the League. It seemed that Americans preferred a policy of **isolation**. Their absence greatly weakened the League.

This cartoon shows how people felt at the time about the failure of the USA to join the League of Nations. Explain the cartoon's message in your own words.

The League was also weakened because Germany was not allowed to join until 1926. Russia was not invited to join until 1934 because of its communist government. So three world powers were absent from the League of Nations from the beginning.

LACK OF POWER

The League did not have its own army or police force, so how could it enforce its rules? It had to rely on the willingness of its members to protect smaller states by guaranteeing to help them if a bigger neighbour invaded. This was called **collective security**. Many large states, however, were not prepared to go to war in defence of smaller states.

This left the League with only one weapon to enforce its decisions – **economic sanctions**. If a member state disobeyed the rules or attacked another state, the League could impose economic sanctions on it. This meant that other member states would agree not to trade with the offending state.

However, economic sanctions could only be effective if all the member states were prepared to impose them. Many countries preferred to follow their own interests, so sanctions either did not work or were not applied at all.

The League of Nations: a success or a failure?

In 1931, a British politician called Lord Grey wrote this about the arms race before World War I.

"If there are armaments on one side, then there must be armaments on the other side. Every measure taken by one nation is noted and leads to counter-measures by others. The enormous growth of arms in Europe, the sense of insecurity and fear caused by them – it was these that made war inevitable."

The League of Nations encouraged member states to disarm, but few of them did so. Throughout the 1920s and 1930s, world armies grew larger. More destructive weapons were invented. Just as before World War I, another **arms race** began. In Chapter 7 in this section, you will read how Hitler rearmed Germany. The League of Nations was powerless to do anything about it.

During the 1920s, the League solved about twenty small disputes between member states. Many of these disputes were settled by the Permanent Court of Justice in the Hague. For example, Finland and Sweden agreed to accept the League's decision over rival claims to islands in the Baltic.

However, during the 1930s, Japan invaded Manchuria, Italy invaded Abyssinia and Hitler took over Czechoslovakia. When the League tried to impose economic sanctions on them, other member states failed to co-operate and the League was shown to be powerless.

SOCIAL PROBLEMS AND THE LEAGUE OF NATIONS

The League of Nations was also concerned with social problems. It met with more success in this area. For example, it set up a **World Health Service** to give medical aid to countries which suffered from famine and disease.

In 1919, a special committee was also set up by the League to send home 400,000 prisoners of war and to find new homes for millions of refugees. Other special committees were set up by the League which successfully tackled the international trade in slaves and drugs.

One of the most important commissions of the League of Nations was the **Mandates Commission**. It looked after all the former colonies of Germany and Turkey which had been taken away by the Treaty of Versailles. The Mandates Commission was to control these colonies until they were ready for independence.

Ireland joined the League of Nations in 1923. For a time, Éamon de Valera was president of the Assembly. He spoke on issues of international importance on many occasions.

In 1932, Eamon de Valera, while addressing the General Assembly, criticised the structure of the League of Nations when he said: "In the final analysis, the League has no sanctions but the force of world opinion". Do you think he was right?

The end of the League of Nations

By 1939, ten countries, including Japan, Italy, Germany and the USSR, had either left the League or had been expelled. In the long term, the League was unable to enforce its own rules, to prevent rearmament and to keep the peace by preventing the outbreak of World War II.

The League of Nations met for the last time in April 1945. Within a year, it was replaced by a new international organisation called the **United Nations**. (See also page 136.)

(See also page 136.)

Activities

1. MAKE YOUR OWN DIAGRAM OF HOW THE LEAGUE OF NATIONS WORKED. WRITE DOWN IN YOUR OWN WORDS WHAT EACH OF THE FOLLOWING DID: (A) THE ASSEMBLY; (B) THE COUNCIL: (C) THE SECRETARIAT; (D) THE PERMANENT COURT OF JUSTICE.
2. DO YOU THINK IT WAS A GOOD OR A BAD IDEA THAT A UNANIMOUS VOTE WAS NEEDED FOR ALL IMPORTANT DECISIONS? HAVE A CLASS DISCUSSION ON THIS. GIVE REASONS FOR YOUR ANSWER.

◢ QUESTIONS ◢

1. In your own words, describe the main aims of the League of Nations.
2. Which of these aims do you think was the most important? Give reasons for your answer.
3. Explain each of the following terms: economic sanctions, collective security, Mandates Commission.
4. Make two separate lists, one showing the strengths and successes of the League, and the other showing its weaknesses and failures.

Looking at the evidence

HERE IS WHAT A BRITISH DELEGATE AT THE LEAGUE OF NATIONS ONCE SAID.

"BEFORE I CAME TO GENEVA, I ALWAYS VOTED FOR WHAT I THOUGHT WAS BEST FOR MY OWN COUNTRY. BUT NOW I TRY TO VOTE FOR WHAT IS BEST FOR MANKIND SINCE I REALISE THAT THIS WILL BE BEST FOR MY OWN COUNTRY IN THE END."

USING THE EVIDENCE IN THIS CHAPTER, DO YOU THINK HIS VIEWS WERE THOSE OF ALL THE OTHER DELEGATES AT THE LEAGUE OF NATIONS?

Democracy, Fascism and Communism in Europe: 1920-45

What is a democracy?

The countries which won World War I claimed they were fighting for democracy. In 1917, President Woodrow Wilson of the USA said:

> *"The world must be made **safe for democracy**. We shall fight for democracy, for the right of those who submit to authority to have a voice in their own governments."*

The word "democracy" comes from two Greek words which mean "people power". In a democracy, all adults have the **right to vote**. They **elect representatives** to sit in a parliament which makes laws and approves taxes for the country.

In a democracy, people also have the right to join or set up **political parties** of their own. These parties can put forward policies and the voters can choose the policies they prefer at election time.

Democratic countries also allow **freedom of speech** and of **information**. They can criticise the government and put forward alternative policies. A democracy gives people **personal freedom** against wrongful arrest or imprisonment.

When World War I ended, most countries in Europe, with the exception of Russia (the Soviet Union), adopted a democratic system of government. Britain, France and the Irish Free State were examples of democratic countries with parliaments elected by the people.

A party which won a majority of the seats in an election formed a government. Sometimes, two or more parties joined together to form a government. This is called a **coalition government**.

Women and the right to vote

Of course, some countries were more democratic than others. Before the war, women in Britain, Ireland and most other countries could not vote in general elections. So a small number of them began a campaign for women's right to vote. In Britain, they were known as **Suffragettes**. ("Suffrage" means "the right to vote".) Before 1918, only four countries had given women the right to vote.

Emmeline Pankhurst 1858-1928 was a famous British suffragette. She once went on hunger strike to gain support for her cause. In 1918 the right to vote was granted to women over thirty in both Britain and Ireland.

Emmeline Pankhurst is supported by her female bodyguards in 1905, as their campaign for votes for women becomes more violent.

As a result of World War I, attitudes towards women changed dramatically. Governments now acknowledged the vital role women had played throughout the war. They had worked in factories and on the land. They had driven trams and buses and had served as doctors and nurses at the front.

By 1920, the number of countries which had granted women the right to vote had increased to twenty-eight. For the first time in most of Europe, both women and men had an equal say in who should govern them.

While the men fought in the trenches, their wives, girlfriends and mothers took over their jobs at home. Here we see a wartime bus conductress collect fares. She was known as a "clippie".

Threats to democracy

Most people believed that democratic governments would bring stability and prosperity to Europe. But in some European countries after the war, the democratic system of government was not strong enough to survive the challenges it faced.

These are some of the problems democratic governments had to deal with.

- **high unemployment**
- **widespread poverty**
- **demobilised soldiers**
- **an economic depression**
- **a breakdown of law and order**

In many countries, people were not used to the ways in which a democracy works. They saw the different political parties, the debates in parliament and the complicated systems of voting as a weak system of government. Democracies seemed unable to solve the post-war problems. As a result, two other systems of government were put forward as alternatives to democracy. They were **communism** and **fascism**.

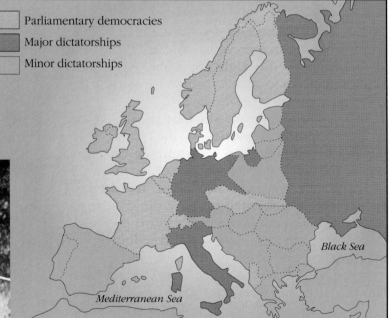

Parliamentary democracies
Major dictatorships
Minor dictatorships

Black Sea

Mediterranean Sea

Dictatorships and democracies in Europe: 1919-39.
Name each of the countries on the map and say whether it was a democracy or dictatorship.

What is communism?

Karl Marx was a nineteenth-century German writer who set down his ideas in a book called **The Communist Manifesto**. He believed that society was controlled by rich men who owned the land, the factories, the mines, the banks and all other sources of wealth. Marx called these people **capitalists**. He believed that capitalists controlled the government and had the support of the police and the army to keep the workers under control.

Karl Marx 1818-1883. Although born in Germany, he was exiled for his revolutionary ideas. He lived in England between 1850-83, where he wrote and developed his theories. He is regarded by many as the founder of modern socialism.

Marx argued that, one day, the workers would revolt against this unfair treatment. They would overthrow the capitalists and set up a "classless society" in which there would be no private property. From then on, everything – including land, industries and businesses – would be owned **in common** by all the workers.

Everyone would get a fair share and people would work together for the good of all, not just for themselves. Marx called this **communism**.

Lenin and the Russian Revolution

In October 1917, a communist revolution took place in Russia. It was led by **Vladimir Illych Lenin**, who believed in communism. He renamed the country the **Union of Soviet Socialist Republics (USSR)** and set out to destroy capitalism and create a classless, communist society according to the teachings of Karl Marx. Communist officials took over factories, banks, railways and businesses. The government now controlled all means of production and distribution. Churches were closed down and their lands were confiscated.

Lenin did not believe in democracy. All political parties, except the Communist Party, were banned. Lenin became a **dictator**, which means he had complete power to make the laws. Anyone who opposed him was executed.

Nicholas II, the last Czar of Russia, with his wife Alexandra and five children. In July 1918, the whole family was executed by the Communists.

An artist's impression of Lenin addressing a meeting of Russian workers in 1917.

A recruitment poster for the Soviet Army. The caption reads: "Volunteers for the Red Army." Note the red star on the soldier's cap. By 1920, the Red Army was five million strong.

Stalin in power: 1927-53

After Lenin died in 1924, he was succeeded by **Joseph Stalin**. He believed that the USSR was weak and feared that anti-communist countries would try to attack it.

Joseph Stalin as a young political activist. He ruled the USSR from 1927-1953.

"Do you want our socialist fatherland" he told his people "to be beaten and to lose its independence? We are fifty to a hundred years behind the advanced countries. We must make up this distance in ten years. Either we do it or they will crush us."

To make the USSR a great industrial power, Stalin launched a series of **Five Year Plans**. These set down targets to be achieved in heavy industries such as coal, iron, steel, oil, railways, canals and energy.

As a result of Stalin's plans, the USSR had become the third most powerful industrialised country in the world by 1939, just behind the USA and Germany.

Collectivisation

Stalin also tried to improve the old-fashioned and inefficient farming methods in the USSR. His answer to this problem was **collectivisation**. This meant that the government would take over the peasants' farms and **collect** thousands of them together to form huge, state-owned collective farms. Through collectivisation, Stalin hoped that surplus grain would be produced. This could be sold abroad to raise money for new industries. The peasants who no longer lived on the land would be sent to the cities to work in the new industries.

Most peasants, however, were opposed to collectivisation. They took pride in owning their own land. They did not wish to give it up or go to live in cities.

Since they would not co-operate with Stalin, peasants' land, cattle and crops were taken from them by force. Millions of them were killed and millions more were exiled to remote regions. By the early 1930s, famine had broken out in the countryside. The government kept the famine a secret from foreigners.

The banner says: "We demand collectivisation and the liquidisation of the kulaks (the wealthier peasants) as a class". Why do you think that some peasants supported collectivisation?

In 1931, when a government official entered a small village, this is what the peasants told him.

"All the dogs have been eaten. We've eaten everything we could lay our hands on: cats, dogs, field mice and birds. When it's light tomorrow you will see that the trees have been stripped of their bark, for that too has been eaten."

Despite the famine conditions and opposition from the peasants, Stalin had his way. By 1939, all farming land in the USSR had been collectivised. But it was a failure. After ten years of collectivisation, there were fewer farm animals, and less grain produced than before.

USING WHAT YOU HAVE JUST READ ABOUT COLLECTIVISATION, TALK ABOUT WHY YOU THINK THIS SYSTEM WAS SUCH A FAILURE. WHY MIGHT THERE HAVE BEEN FEWER FARM ANIMALS AND LESS GRAIN AFTER TEN YEARS OF COLLECTIVISATION?

Looking at the evidence

Communist terror

Stalin's reforms in the USSR were achieved at a great price. He used fear and terror to achieve his aims. Millions of Russians were sent to special labour camps where they were forced to work as slaves, building canals and working in mines. Millions more were executed for criticising the system. It is estimated that during his lifetime, Stalin was responsible for the deaths of more than forty million Russians.

Stalin's propaganda

Stalin used clever **propaganda** to lie about the achievements of the USSR under communism. He also portrayed himself as a much-loved and popular leader. Thousands of public buildings were covered with his portrait. There were statues of him in every city and town. A large city, Stalingrad, as well as mountains, lakes and rivers were named after him. Hundreds of plays and books were also written in praise of him.

An artist's impression of Stalin speaking at a Congress of the Russian Communist Party. Note the bust of Lenin in the background.

Communism spreads in Europe

Outside the USSR, many people were fooled by Stalin's propaganda and the apparent success of communism. They were told how powerful the Soviet Union had become and that the workers there had jobs, houses, free education and free medical care. But they knew little about the terror, the executions and the terrible methods which Stalin had used to achieve his aims.

During the 1920s and 1930s, many people in western Europe regarded communism as better than their own weak systems of parliamentary democracy. Famous writers like George Bernard Shaw and H.G. Wells visited the USSR and returned full of praise for the communist system. But they were not shown the suffering and hardship which so many people had to endure.

George Bernard Shaw, the Irish born writer, visited the USSR during the 1930s and was impressed by what he saw.

After World War I, communist parties were founded in many other European countries, including Italy and Germany. They won seats in parliament and enjoyed considerable support. They wanted to set up Soviet-style systems of government and some even tried to stage communist revolutions like the one which had occurred in Russia in 1917.

What is fascism?

As communist ideas spread throughout Europe in the 1920s, people who owned property were terrified. They feared that, if the communists came to power, they would lose everything. They thought that the democratic system was too weak to protect them from communism, so they looked for an alternative. They found it in the **fascist** parties which emerged in the 1920s.

Fascists were very patriotic. They had exaggerated beliefs in the greatness of their own country. They wanted a strong leader to restore law and order, to improve the economy and to protect them from a communist revolution. Unlike communists, fascists believed in the **capitalist system**. But like the communists, they were prepared to destroy democracy to achieve their aims.

Wherever fascists gained power, the freedom of the individual suffered. The rights of other political parties were destroyed and the power of trade unions was overturned. Like communist dictators, fascist dictators also had complete control over the lives of their people and the destiny of their country.

Between 1918 and 1945, there was a struggle in Europe between democratic governments and communist and fascist dictatorships. Fascism first began in Italy. The idea later spread to Germany where it was known as **nazism**. In the following chapters, you will read about fascist dictatorships in Italy and Germany.

◼ QUESTIONS ◼

1. Make a list of the political, social and economic problems facing Europe after 1920. Which problems do you think governments would find the most difficult to solve? Give reasons for your answer.
2. (a) Explain in your own words what you think a democratic government means. (b) Why did some people think democratic governments were ineffective?
3. Why did many westerners find communism under Stalin so attractive?
4. (a) What kind of people feared communism? Why? (b) What parties did many of them join?
5. (a) Set out three ideas that fascist parties put forward. (b) Set out two differences and two similarities between fascism and communism.

VISIT YOUR SCHOOL OR LOCAL LIBRARY AND FIND OUT MORE ABOUT COMMUNISM IN THE USSR DURING THE 1920s AND 1930s.

Finding Out

CHAPTER 4

Mussolini and Fascism in Italy

🏛 Italy in 1920

Italy faced many problems after World War I. The Italian government had to raise taxes in order to pay its war debts. To make matters worse, the Italian currency lost its value. By 1920, the annual rate of **inflation** was 600%. This meant that prices were so high that many people could not afford to buy food or clothing. Jobs were impossible to find.

In 1920 alone, almost one million Italians emigrated, mostly to America. Many of them were poor peasants from southern Italy who could not make a living from the land and could not pay their rents to wealthy landlords.

Some Italian workers were impressed by Lenin's communist revolution in Russia in 1917. They founded their own communist party, organised strikes and tried to take over the factories. Many of them wanted a communist revolution in Italy as well.

The Italian communists were opposed by property owners and by groups of ex-soldiers. These former soldiers disliked communism because they thought it was foreign and unpatriotic. One of their leaders was **Benito Mussolini**.

Benito Mussolini 1883-1945. He is wearing a black shirt, part of the fascist uniform. The medals are those he got for serving in the First World War.

Note the fascist symbol on the drape in front of the stand. "Fascist" comes from the Latin word "fasces" which was a bundle of sticks bound by a rope with an axe attached to it. It was used in ancient Rome as a symbol of authority.

manufacturer, supported Mussolini. Even shop-keepers with small businesses and farmers who owned a few acres of land turned to the fascists to protect them from communism.

Mussolini and the Fascist Party

Mussolini was born in 1883. As a young man, he had worked as a teacher and a newspaper editor. During World War I, he served in the Italian army. He was later discharged when he suffered leg wounds as a result of an explosion. After the war, Mussolini condemned Italy's weak democratic government. He said:

> "The present government in Italy has failed. We must be ready to take its place. For this reason, we are establishing the Fascist Party."

In 1919, Mussolini set up the Fascist Party. He dressed his fascists in a uniform of black shirts and black berets and encouraged them to use a straight-armed salute. The fascists, or **Blackshirts** as they were often called, were very **nationalistic**. They considered Italy to be the greatest country in the world. When men joined the fascists, they took this oath:

> "I swear to defend Italy. For her, I am prepared to kill and to die."

Many of those who joined Mussolini's fascists did so because they were afraid of what might happen in Italy if the communists came to power. Wealthy landlords, bankers and the owners of large industries like Agnelli, who built Fiat cars, and Pirelli, the tyre

QUESTIONS

1. Do you think that communist strikes, demonstrations and factory take-overs might have encouraged people to support Mussolini's fascists? Explain your answer.
2. Look back to pages 90-91 about Stalin. Then say whether each of the following people might or might not have supported the Italian Communist Party: (a) an industrialist; (b) a landlord; (c) a shopkeeper; (d) a soldier who had fought in World War I. Give reasons for your answers.

Fascists and Communists clash

Between 1919 and 1922, Italy was almost in a state of civil war. Hundreds of people were killed in riots between fascists and communists on the streets of Italian cities and towns.

This is how a young fascist described the burning of a Communist Party building in Ravenna in northern Italy in 1922.

> "We risk our lives every day, for the final aim is the salvation of our country. The flames from the great burning building rose into the night. The whole town was illuminated by the glare. We had to strike terror into the heart of our enemies."

A squad of young fascists. Note that many of them are wearing World War I medals.

Young fascist supporters campaigning in Naples in 1920. Many of them are former soldiers who have just returned from the war.

Mussolini becomes prime minister of Italy

Italy's democratically-elected government seemed unable to stop this political and social unrest. Support for the fascists grew and in 1921, they won thirty-five seats in parliament.

A year later, in October 1922, Mussolini told 25,000 armed Blackshirts to march on Rome. They demanded that the Fascist Party be included in a coalition government. The prime minister of Italy tried to persuade the king, Victor Emmanuel, to call out the army and arrest the Blackshirts. The king refused. Like many Italians, he feared communism more than fascism. Instead, he sacked the prime minister and sent the following telegram to Mussolini.

"His majesty begs you to come to Rome as soon as possible as he wants you to form a government."

On 30 October 1922, Mussolini became prime minister of Italy. The following day, fascists gathered in Rome for a great victory parade. This is what a British journalist wrote in the *Daily Telegraph* at the time.

"The fascist revolution is triumphant today all over Italy. The fascists this morning, when marching in Rome, were acclaimed by tens of thousands of people. Italy is on the threshold of a new period in her history which it is hoped will lead her on to greater destinies."

Mussolini the dictator

Within a very short time, Mussolini had changed Italy from a democracy into a fascist dictatorship. He enrolled his Blackshirts in the police. They ruthlessly put down strikes and beat up communists. When the leader of the Italian socialist party protested at the behaviour of the fascists, the Blackshirts murdered him.

Because other parties in the Italian parliament were afraid of the fascists, they let Mussolini change the way in which Italy was governed. Here are some of the things he did.

- He banned all political parties except the fascists.
- He banned all trade unions and made strikes illegal.
- He made laws without consulting anyone.
- He set up a secret police to arrest his opponents.
- He ended freedom of speech.
- He imposed strict censorship on books, magazines and newspapers.
- He demanded the complete loyalty and obedience of every Italian.

Fascist propaganda

Like all dictators, Mussolini used propaganda to convince Italians that he was a great leader and that all important decisions could be left to him. The fascists controlled the radio and cinema and used these to glorify Mussolini.

A young girl kisses the Italian flag which from 1926 included the fascist emblem. This poster was used to recruit young people into Italian fascist youth movements.

Italian newspapers reported all of his speeches and carried pictures of him helping farmers, advising soldiers or teaching children. Huge posters of Mussolini hung on public buildings with such slogans as:

"One leader, one voice."
"Believe, Fight, Obey!"
"Mussolini is always right. He is ours."

Fascist organisations were even set up for boys and girls. In schools, pupils were taught that Mussolini was their great leader. Italian school children recited the following prayer.

"I believe in the genius of Mussolini and in the conversion of Italians to fascism."

The corporate state

For over twenty years, Mussolini ruled Italy. He set up special corporations to run the economy. Each corporation represented the employers and workers in a different industry. For example, there were corporations for transport, banking, the timber industry, the clothing industry and so on.

Each corporation decided on such things as wages, prices and production methods in their own sector. Corporations were a special feature of Mussolini's Italy. Because of this, it was sometimes called a **corporate state**.

Other reforms

Under Mussolini, many new railway lines were built and trains ran on time. The first motorway in Europe, from Milan to the Alps, was constructed. The Pontine Marshes near Rome were drained and turned into fertile farmlands. He encouraged grain production and tried to end the poverty in southern Italy.

Mussolini is shown helping with the grain harvest. Why do you think he wanted to be photographed in this way?

Despite bringing about some improvements in the economy, especially an increase in the production of grain, the wages and working conditions of many Italian workers got worse rather than better under fascism.

Mussolini encouraged Italians to have larger families and set an example by having six children himself. He said:

"Italy needs sixty million inhabitants. I believe that the population of a country determines its political, economic and moral power."

The caption on this poster reads: "Benito Mussolini loves children very much. Italian children love Il Duce very much. Long live Il Duce. I salute Il Duce. To us". Do you think this kind of propaganda was effective?

Parents of large families paid no tax at all and mothers who had many children were awarded special prizes. But despite Mussolini's encouragement, Italy's birth rate did not increase.

Mussolini and the pope

Mussolini got the backing of **Pope Pius XI** who feared communism more than he valued democracy. In 1929, both men signed the **Lateran Treaty**. Mussolini agreed to recognise the Vatican State and stated that Catholicism was the official religion of Italy. The fascists also agreed to give the Church control over schools and to forbid divorce in Italy. In return, the pope agreed to recognise the fascist state and its stand against communism.

Mussolini and the representative of Pope Pius XI sign the Lateran Treaty in 1929

An Italian empire

Above all else, Mussolini wanted to create a new Italian empire. He looked back with pride to the days when the Roman empire ruled the world.

In 1935, Mussolini invaded Abyssinia in East Africa. The Abyssinian emperor asked the League of Nations for help.

The League of Nations imposed economic sanctions on Italy but they were not effective and the Italians were able to keep Abyssinia (now called Ethiopia).

The conquest of Abyssinia was a victory for fascist aggression. It also demonstrated the inability of the League of Nations to stop war.

Mussolini admired Italy's great past. Here he is shown visiting an ancient site in Rome. Do you notice the people in the background giving the fascist salute?

Mussolini supports other fascist leaders

Mussolini had such success with his Fascist Party that parties with similar ideas in other countries borrowed the name and began to call themselves "fascists" as well. Mussolini often supported them.

For example in 1936, he sent soldiers to assist the fascists under General Franco in a civil war that had broken out in Spain. In the same year, he made a treaty of friendship with Hitler who had set up a fascist dictatorship in Germany. This was known as the **Rome-Berlin Axis**.

When World War II began in 1939, Mussolini supported Hitler and the Germans. This brought about his downfall. Anti-fascist Italians, supported by British and American troops, overthrew Mussolini's government. In April 1945, Mussolini was shot dead by his opponents. His corpse was left hanging on a tree and crowds took it in turns to throw rotten fruit at it.

▲ *The corpses of Mussolini and his mistress Clara Petacci are strung up by their heels in Milan in April 1945. Both were shot by Italian resistance fighters opposed to the dictator.*

◢ QUESTIONS ◢

1. (a) What problems faced the Italian people after World War I? (b) Why do you think some Italians supported the communists, while others supported the fascists?
2. (a) In your own words, describe how Mussolini came to power. (b) Do you think what he did was legal or illegal? Give reasons for your answer.
3. Make a list of the things which Mussolini did to make Italy a fascist dictatorship.
4. How did Mussolini try to convince Italians that he was a great leader?
5. How did Mussolini's invasion of Abyssinia affect the League of Nations?
6. Give examples of how Mussolini supported other fascist leaders in Europe.

Activities

1. MUSSOLINI SAID THAT FASCISM WAS A BETTER FORM OF GOVERNMENT THAN DEMOCRACY. SET OUT THREE POINTS IN FAVOUR OF THIS VIEW AND THREE POINTS AGAINST IT.
2. DRAW A POSTER WHICH MUSSOLINI MIGHT HAVE USED TO PROMOTE HIS FASCIST IDEAS. USE THE INFORMATION IN THIS CHAPTER TO HELP YOU.

Looking at the evidence

LOOK AGAIN AT WHAT YOU HAVE READ ABOUT STALIN'S COMMUNIST STATE AND MUSSOLINI'S FASCIST STATE. HOW WERE THEY DIFFERENT? HOW WERE THEY SIMILAR? COMPARE THE SUCCESSES AND FAILURES OF EACH.

Germany between the Wars: 1918-33

The Weimar Republic

When it became clear in November 1918 that Germany had lost World War I, the German emperor **abdicated** (stood down) and Germany became a republic. The government of the new republic first met in the town of Weimar. As a result, this period in Germany's history (1918-33) has always been known as the **Weimar Republic**.

⚑ *A French caricature of Emperor Wilhelm II of Germany who abdicated in 1918. The caption reads: "A great poker-faced prince". What message is the picture trying to convey?*

Losing the war came as a great shock to most Germans. As a result, the new Weimar Republic got off to a bad start. First, it had to order the army to surrender and later, it was forced to sign the humiliating Treaty of Versailles. Many Germans felt betrayed by this. They were suspicious of the new republic from the start.

The treatment of Germany

In January 1919, the leaders of the victorious countries met at the Paris Peace Conference. The German people hoped that they would be fairly treated, because the American president, Woodrow Wilson, said he wanted a "just peace". But Britain and France blamed Germany for starting the war and wanted to make her pay for it. They imposed harsh and humiliating conditions on Germany.

Germany's representatives were not let into the conference until the other leaders had decided on Germany's fate. Then they were told that they had to accept the Treaty of Versailles without discussion. In other words, it was a **dictated peace**.

⚑ THE TREATY OF VERSAILLES: JUNE 1919

On 28 June 1919, in the Hall of Mirrors at Versailles on the outskirts of Paris, the German delegates signed the treaty. This is what a German newspaper said on the same day.

"Today in Versailles, the disgraceful treaty is being signed. Do not forget it. The German people will increasingly press forward to reconquer the place to which it is entitled among nations. Then will come vengeance for the shame of 1919."

Now read what an English diplomat who was at the peace conference wrote.

"The historian, with every justification, will come to the conclusion that we are very stupid men. We arrived at Versailles determined that a peace of justice and wisdom would be negotiated. However, we left conscious that the treaties imposed upon our enemies were neither just nor wise."

Looking at the evidence

THE MAIN TERMS OF THE TREATY

THESE ARE SOME OF THE TERMS OF THE TREATY OF VERSAILLES. READ THEM CAREFULLY. THEN DECIDE IF YOU TOO THINK THEY WERE "NEITHER JUST NOR WISE". GIVE REASONS FOR YOUR ANSWERS.

- GERMANY HAD TO ACCEPT THE BLAME FOR STARTING THE WAR. THIS WAS CALLED THE **WAR GUILT CLAUSE**.
- GERMANY HAD TO PAY **REPARATIONS** (COMPENSATION) FOR THE DAMAGE CAUSED BY THE WAR. THIS WAS FIXED AT £6.6 BILLION.
- GERMANY WAS FORCED TO **DISARM**. ITS ARMY WAS REDUCED TO 100,000 MEN. ITS NAVY WAS ALSO REDUCED IN SIZE AND NO SUBMARINES WERE ALLOWED. NOR WAS GERMANY PERMITTED TO HAVE AN AIR FORCE.
- GERMANY **LOST TERRITORIES** IN EUROPE AMOUNTING TO 13% OF HER LAND. SOME OF THIS LAND BECAME PART OF NEWLY-CREATED COUNTRIES SUCH AS POLAND. GERMAN LAND WAS ALSO GIVEN TO FRANCE, DENMARK AND BELGIUM. ALTOGETHER, GERMANY LOST SIX MILLION INHABITANTS OR 12% OF HER POPULATION AND 48% OF HER COAL AND IRON PRODUCTION.
- GERMANY HAD TO GIVE UP ALL HER **OVERSEAS COLONIES**.
- GERMANY COULD NOT STATION ITS ARMY IN THE RHINELAND ALONG ITS BORDER WITH FRANCE. THIS WAS CALLED THE **DEMILITARISATION OF THE RHINELAND**.
- GERMANY AND AUSTRIA WERE **FORBIDDEN TO JOIN** TOGETHER IN ANY KIND OF ALLIANCE.

Germany's problems

In the years after the war, there was great instability in Germany. There were many weak coalition governments and no effective leaders. Strikes and demonstrations occurred throughout the country. The German Communist Party tried to stage a communist revolution, but it was crushed.

Germany's loss of territories under the Treaty of Versailles.

An unemployed soldier in Weimar Germany in 1920. His placard reads: "I will take on any work of any kind immediately." This was a common sight during the early years of the Weimar Republic.

Thousands of demobilised soldiers roamed the streets of German cities, causing trouble. To make matters worse, fuel was scarce and food was in short supply. Some people actually died of hunger. This is what a German minister said in 1923.

"For many people, meat has become a rarity. A million and a half German families are inadequately provided with fuel. Thousands upon thousands of people spend their lives jammed together in the most primitive dwellings and must wait for years before they can be given quarters which satisfy even the most elementary hygienic requirements."

German inflation: 1920-23

To add to the country's problems, the German government found it difficult to pay the £6.6 billion in reparations forced upon them at Versailles. To meet its debts, it printed more and more paper money. But this made the German mark (its unit of currency) lose its value and caused **inflation**. Prices soared and people's savings became worthless.

People who were no longer able to pay the rent were evicted from their homes. They needed a barrow-full of notes just to buy a loaf of bread.

Factory owners load up baskets and cases full of German banknotes outside a bank in Berlin in 1923. These were then brought to factories and businesses to pay the workers.

Here are two pieces of written evidence that tell us about the effects of inflation on people's lives. The first is from a teacher. The second is from a newspaper report.

A TEACHER'S REPORT

"A friend of mine, a clergyman, came to Berlin from a suburb with his monthly salary to buy a pair of shoes for his baby, but he could only afford to buy a cup of coffee."

A NEWSPAPER REPORT

"Two women went to a bank with a washing basket filled with notes. They passed a shop and saw a crowd standing round the window. They put down the basket for a moment and hurried forward to see if there was anything that could be bought. Then they turned around and found that all the notes were there, untouched. But the basket had gone."

These figures show the exchange rate for the US dollar and the German mark between January 1920 and October 1923.

	1 US DOLLAR =
JANUARY 1920	64 MARKS
JANUARY 1922	191 MARKS
JANUARY 1923	17,972 MARKS
JULY 1923	353,412 MARKS
OCTOBER 1923	25,260,208,000 MARKS

STUDY THE INFORMATION IN THE BOX, IN THE PHOTOGRAPHS AND IN THE TWO PIECES OF WRITTEN EVIDENCE. DESCRIBE HOW THESE SHOW THAT INFLATION AFFECTED THE LIVES OF ORDINARY GERMANS IN 1923.

Looking at the evidence

Germany's economic recovery: 1924-29

The situation in Germany became so bad that Britain, France and the USA realised they would have to help. They also felt guilty over their harsh treatment of Germany in the Treaty of Versailles. In 1924, it was agreed that:

- Germany could pay the war reparations over a longer period of time.
- The USA would lend Germany 800 million dollars to develop her industries and agriculture.
- In return, the German government would bring in a new currency, the **rentenmark**.

A dole queue in Berlin. By 1932, more than 30% of the German workforce were unemployed.

GERMANY BETWEEN THE WARS: 1918-33

As a result of these measures, the German economy recovered. Industries started up again and people were able to get work.

Between 1924 and 1929, a German politician called **Gustav Stresemann** helped restore stability and economic prosperity to the country. At long last, it seemed as if Germany was overcoming the effects of World War I.

▲ *Elderly people having lost all their savings due to inflation gather in the snow outside a soup kitchen in Berlin in 1930.*

THE GREAT DEPRESSION IN GERMANY: 1929-33

However, in October 1929, the American Stock Market crashed. American banks which had loaned money to Germany now asked to be repaid. Once again, the German economy went into a depression. Factories were forced to close down and by 1932, nearly one-third of all German workers had lost their jobs. In German cities, people were starving to death.

GERMAN UNEMPLOYMENT FIGURES	
1928	1,862,000
1929	2,850,000
1930	3,217,000
1931	4,886,000
1932	6,042,000

Germans were in despair. Their government was weak and divided and it seemed unable to solve the country's problems. Some Germans turned to the communists and hoped for a communist revolution. Others supported a German fascist party called the **Nazis** which was led by **Adolf Hitler**.

Adolf Hitler

Adolf Hitler was born in Austria in 1889. As a young man he went to Vienna to become an artist, but had little success. Later he joined the German army, fought in World War I and was awarded the Iron Cross for bravery.

Like many others, Hitler was shocked by Germany's defeat in World War I and the harsh terms of the Treaty of Versailles. He blamed the leaders of the Weimar Republic for this humiliation.

▲ *Adolf Hitler (right) as a soldier in 1916. In November 1918, while recovering in hospital from a gas attack, he cried when he learned of Germany's surrender.*

101

The Nazi Party

In 1919, Hitler joined the **Nationalist Socialist German Worker's Party** and soon became its leader. It was a small fascist group which had been set up in Munich. It soon became known as the **Nazi Party**. Its emblem was a black **swastika** in a white circle on a red background.

Hitler's *Mein Kampf*

The Nazis wanted to overthrow the Weimar Republic and seize power. They staged an unsuccessful *putsch* (an attempted seizure of power) in Munich in 1923. Hitler and other leading Nazis were arrested. Hitler spent more than a year in jail where he wrote a book called *Mein Kampf* ("My Struggle"). In it, he set out his aims for the Nazis.

- DESTROY THE WEIMAR REPUBLIC.
- GIVE GERMANY A STRONG GOVERNMENT (I.E. A FASCIST DICTATORSHIP).
- UNDO THE TREATY OF VERSAILLES.
- REBUILD THE GERMAN ARMY.
- SET UP A NEW GERMAN EMPIRE (A THIRD REICH) IN EASTERN EUROPE.
- DESTROY COMMUNISM.
- DESTROY THE JEWISH PEOPLE.

This last idea was called **anti-Semitism** (a hatred of Jewish people). It would have a terrible outcome for European Jews in the coming years (page 106-8).

Building up the Nazi Party

A 1932 election poster. The caption reads "Our Last Hope". How do you think this poster might have influenced German voters?

When he was released from prison in 1924, Hitler began to build up the Nazi Party. He admired Mussolini's success in Italy and copied some of his tactics. He organised his followers into a private army, the **Stormtroopers (SA)**, and dressed them in brown shirts. Many of them were former German soldiers who had served in World War I. Hitler travelled all over Germany making speeches, holding huge demonstrations and torch-light processions.

A Nazi rally shortly after Hitler came to power in 1933. The slogan reads: "Work and Freedom."

Germany listens to Hitler

At first, only a minority of Germans took Hitler seriously. After all, between 1924 and 1929, the German economy had improved and the country seemed prosperous again. But when this prosperity ended suddenly after the crash of the American Stock Market in 1929, more and more people listened to what Hitler had to say.

A colour portrait of Adolf Hitler taken at the height of his power.

He told them that their troubles were caused by the weakness of the Weimar government. He also blamed the Treaty of Versailles and the communists for Germany's problems. He assured the German people that only the Nazis could deal with the crises facing their country.

As unemployment got worse, many desperate Germans started to believe what Hitler and the Nazis said. They had heard of what Stalin was doing in the USSR and feared that the same thing might happen to them if the German Communist Party came to power. This is how one German who joined the Nazi Party described his feelings.

"When Hitler spoke of the disgrace of Germany, I felt ready to attack any enemy. The intense will of the man, the passion of his sincerity, seemed to flow from him into me. I experienced a feeling like that of a religious conversion. I gave Hitler my heart."

Hitler takes the salute at a rally in Nuremberg in 1932. Note the brownshirted uniforms and the flowers strewn on the streets.

HITLER IS CHANCELLOR OF GERMANY: JANUARY 1933

In July 1932, there was a general election in Germany. More than 13 million Germans voted for the Nazis. This made them the largest party in Germany. In January 1933, the president of Germany asked Hitler to become **chancellor** (prime minister).

Hitler with President Hindenburg and a young boy. In 1934, following Hindenburg's death, Hitler combined the offices of chancellor and president and called himself "Der Fuhrer".

Hitler's fascist dictatorship

Hitler now set out to destroy the Weimar Republic. In February 1933, the **Reichstag** (parliament) building was burned down. Hitler blamed the communists and immediately banned their party. He also got the Reichstag to pass the **Enabling Act**. This act "enabled" Hitler to pass any laws he wished.

Hitler then banned all other political parties except the Nazis. When Germany's elderly President Hindenburg died in 1934, Hitler combined the offices of chancellor and president and called himself **Der Führer** ("the leader"). He promised that Nazi rule would last one thousand years and would be known as the **Third Reich**. In less than a year, Hitler had become a dictator. Democracy in Germany was dead.

Berliners watch the Reichstag Building go up in flames in February 1933.

✎ QUESTIONS ✎

1. (a) What problems faced Germany after World War I? (b) In your opinion, which problem was the most serious? Explain your answer.
2. (a) How did the German economy improve between 1924 and 1929? (b) Why do you think the Allies agreed to help Germany?
3. (a) Write a short paragraph on the early life of Adolf Hitler. (b) What was the name of the book he wrote? Set out four ideas it contained.
4. Why do you think Hitler's speeches are an important source of evidence for historians?
5. (a) Why did the Great Depression begin in Europe in 1929? (b) How did it affect Germany?
6. After he became chancellor, Hitler quickly made himself dictator of Germany. Write a short paragraph describing the steps by which he came to such power.

Germany under Hitler: 1933-39

🏛 A Nazi dictatorship

All fascist dictators behave in a similar way. You have already read how Mussolini imposed his rule on Italy. His tactics influenced Hitler.

Once Hitler came to power in Germany in 1933, he also set about destroying democracy. Here is what this meant.

- ALL POLITICAL PARTIES EXCEPT THE NAZIS WERE BANNED.
- NO TRADE UNIONS WERE ALLOWED, EXCEPT THE NAZI-CONTROLLED "LABOUR FRONT".
- NEWSPAPERS, RADIO PROGRAMMES AND FILMS COULD ONLY GIVE THE NAZI POINT OF VIEW.
- A SECRET POLICE CALLED THE GESTAPO ROUNDED UP ANYONE WHO OPPOSED THE NAZIS AND PUT THEM IN CONCENTRATION CAMPS.
- CIVIL LIBERTIES AND FREEDOM OF SPEECH WERE ENDED.
- THE ARMED FORCES SWORE AN OATH OF LOYALTY TO HITLER AND NOT TO THE STATE.

▲ *Hitler believed in great theatrical displays as this torchlight parade in Berlin in 1938 shows.*

▲ *Nazi Storm Troopers march at a rally with Nazi banners proclaiming "Germany Awake". What do you think was meant by this?*

🏛 The German army

Hitler quickly gained the support of the German army. Many of his policies appealed to army officers. After all, he had promised a strong government, the re-armament of Germany and a revision of the Treaty of Versailles. Under Hitler, every army officer swore the following oath of loyalty to their leader and not to the state.

> *"I swear by God this holy oath, that I will render to Adolf Hitler, leader of the German nation, unconditional obedience and I am ready as a brave soldier to risk my life at any time for this oath."*

Nazi propaganda

The Nazis put a lot of effort into telling the Germans that Nazi rule was good for them. They used newspapers, films and radio to spread the Nazi message. They also organised huge rallies with military bands, banners, speeches and songs to give Germans a sense of pride in themselves after the humiliations of the past. Hitler said:

"All effective propaganda must be limited to a very few facts and must harp on these in slogans until the very last member of the public understands what you want him to understand by your slogan."

THE NAZIS AND GERMAN YOUTH

Like Mussolini in Italy, Hitler paid particular attention to young people. He told German parents:

"We will train and educate your children to become new Germans. We will not allow them to lapse into the old ways of thinking. They shall not escape us."

A poster with a typical member of the League of German Maidens collecting money. The caption reads "Build youth hostels and homes".

German boys between the ages of fourteen and eighteen had to join the **Hitler Youth Movement**. They were trained to obey and carry out orders. There was also a special movement for girls called the **League of German Maidens**.

In schools, history textbooks were rewritten to inform students about Germany's great past and to encourage them to imitate it. This is how one German remembered his schooldays under Nazi rule.

"Every subject in school was now presented from the Nazi point of view. Hitler's **Mein Kampf** became the textbook for our history lessons. We read and discussed it with our teacher, chapter by chapter. And when we had finished, we started again from the beginning."

Hitler speaks to a group of girls. He always stressed the importance of good health and motherhood for young German women.

Young Nazis at a summer camp giving Nazi salute. By 1939, membership of the Nazi Youth Movement was compulsory for every German.

USE YOUR LOCAL OR SCHOOL LIBRARY TO FIND OUT MORE ABOUT THE HITLER YOUTH MOVEMENT AND THE LEAGUE OF GERMAN MAIDENS. WRITE A REPORT ABOUT YOUR FINDINGS.

Finding Out

The Nazis end unemployment

- Between 1933 and 1939, more than 200,000 Germans worked on the building of new roads and motorways.
- Slums were cleared and new houses were built.
- The Nazis encouraged factories to make cars (like the Volkswagen) and heavy machinery. Later on, these same factories made guns, aircraft and tanks for Hitler's new army.
- By 1939 unemployment had ended. Workers' wages also increased and they were better off than before.

Hitler's anti-Semitism

The Nazis' greatest crime was their treatment of the Jewish people. Hitler was a **racist** who believed that the German people (**Aryans**) belonged to a **master race** which was destined to rule the world. He also believed that the Jews (**Semites**) had caused many of Germany's problems.

Hitler said that Jews were inferior to Germans and blamed them for Germany's defeat in World War I. He also thought that Jewish businessmen were plotting to take control of the world. This hatred of the Jewish people is called **anti-Semitism**.

Hitler's anti-Semitism was quite illogical. Out of a population of 60 million, only 500,000 Jewish people lived in Germany when Hitler came to power. Apart from their religion, they were the same as other Germans and wanted nothing more than to live in peace with their neighbours as they had done for centuries.

A Nazi propaganda poster from 1937 advertising a film and exhibition entitled "The Eternal Jew". Describe how the Jew is depicted.

A public notice, published in 1942 which states: "Whoever wears this sign is an enemy of our people".

NAZI ATTACKS ON JEWISH PEOPLE

When the Nazis came to power in 1933, they made anti-Semitism the official policy of the Third Reich. The Nazis organised a boycott of Jewish shops and businesses. Jewish civil servants lost their jobs and Jewish doctors were forbidden to work in hospitals. In 1935, the Nazis passed the **Nuremberg Laws** which stated that:

"A Jew may not be a citizen of Germany. Marriages between Germans and Jews are forbidden. A Jew has no vote. He may not fill any public office."

On 9 November 1938, Hitler's Stormtroopers organised attacks on Jewish shops and synagogues throughout Germany. Thirty-six Jews were killed and 7000 Jewish businesses and hundreds of synagogues were set on fire. This became known as "Kristalnacht" or the **Night of Broken Glass**.

A Jewish shopkeeper sweeps up outside his business after the Night of Broken Glass. Later, to add insult to injury, a fine of one and a half billion marks was imposed on the Jewish people.

Some Jews decided to leave Germany, but they were not allowed to take any money with them. For those who remained, daily life became almost impossible. This is how a foreign journalist described their conditions.

"In many towns, over the doors of the grocery and butcher shops, the bakeries and the dairies were signs, 'Jews not admitted'. Pharmacies would not sell them drugs or medicines. Hotels would not give them a night's lodging. And always, wherever they went, were the taunting signs, 'Jews strictly forbidden in this town' or 'Jews enter this place at their own risk'."

The deportation of German Jews. Note the Star of David they were forced to wear and the few belongings they have.

The word "Jew" is daubed on the windows of a Jewish department store in Berlin in 1933, encouraging shoppers to boycott it.

The extermination of the Jews

When World War II began (see Chapter 8 in this section), the Germans took over Austria, Poland, Czechoslovakia, the Netherlands, France and other parts of Europe. Many more Jewish people lived in these countries. At first, Hitler's special military unit, the **SS**, rounded them up and killed them. But in 1941, Hitler decided on a terrible **final solution** to deal with all the Jews in Europe.

Special **concentration camps** were built. They were surrounded by barbed wire fences and patrolled day and night by the SS. Inside many of the camps, there were factories where Jews who were fit to work were forced to make weapons and other war materials. Appalling medical experiments were also carried out on many of these Jews.

The old, the young and those unfit to work were sent to gas chambers which were disguised as shower rooms. In many camps, the corpses were then burned in specially constructed cremation ovens.

No one knows for certain how many Jews were killed in these camps, but it was probably about six million. This extermination of the Jews is called the **Holocaust**. Besides Jews, other groups such as gypsies, disabled people, communists, homosexuals and resistance fighters were also exterminated.

After the camps were liberated in 1945, thousands of Jews who had been killed were buried in mass graves like this one.

REPORTING THE HOLOCAUST

WHEN REPORTS OF WHAT WAS HAPPENING IN THE CAMPS REACHED THE OUTSIDE WORLD, FEW BELIEVED THEM. PEOPLE COULD NOT ACCEPT THAT CIVILISED EUROPEANS WOULD TREAT THEIR FELLOW HUMAN BEINGS IN SUCH A DREADFUL WAY. THEY THOUGHT THAT THE REPORTS WERE JUST ANTI-GERMAN PROPAGANDA.

IN 1945, WHEN THE WAR WAS DRAWING TO AN END, ALLIED FORCES AT LAST ENTERED THE CONCENTRATION CAMPS. THIS IS WHAT A BRITISH ARMY OFFICER SAW AT BELSEN IN GERMANY.

"Piles of corpses were lying all over the camp, outside and inside the huts, some of them in the same bunks as the living. Near the crematorium were massed graves which had been filled in, and there was one open pit full of corpses.

The huts were filled to overflowing with prisoners in every stage of emaciation and disease. In some, which were only suitable to house a hundred people, there were as many as a thousand."

REPORTS LIKE THIS AND FILMS WHICH THE ALLIES ALSO MADE OF WHAT THEY SAW AT LAST SHOWED THE WORLD WHAT HITLER HAD MEANT BY THE "FINAL SOLUTION".

Young children are liberated from the camp at Auschwitz in Poland in 1945. Most German civilians denied they knew about the gas chambers.

Two young survivors from the concentration camp at Bergen-Belsen in Germany. Most of those who survived never recovered from the dreadful treatment they had received in the camps.

◢ QUESTIONS ◣

1. List the different ways in which Hitler changed Germany from a democracy to a dictatorship. Compare his methods with those of Mussolini.
2. What forms did Nazi propaganda take? Were they effective? Give reasons for your answer.
3. Why do you think the Nazis had a particular interest in the youth of Germany? List as many reasons as you can.
4. Although Hitler destroyed democracy in Germany, he was still popular with most Germans. How do you explain this fact?
5. In your own words, explain the terms "racist" and "anti-Semitic". In what way was Hitler both racist and anti-Semitic?
6. Why were many people slow to believe the reports of the extermination camps? How was this disbelief overcome?

Activity

MANY BOOKS HAVE BEEN WRITTEN ABOUT THE SUFFERING OF THE JEWISH PEOPLE UNDER NAZI RULE. ONE OF THE MOST MOVING IS *THE DIARY OF ANNE FRANK*, KEPT BY A JEWISH GIRL IN THE NETHERLANDS WHILE SHE WAS HIDING FROM THE NAZIS. READ IT (OR SOME OTHER SIMILAR BOOK) AND THEN WRITE A REPORT ON THE NAZIS' TREATMENT OF THE JEWS.

The Drift towards World War II

Hitler plans a German empire

When Hitler came to power, he wanted to make Germany into a great empire. To achieve this, he planned to conquer the countries of eastern Europe to create more **living space (lebensraum)** for the German people. He wanted to expel the Poles, the Czechs, the Russians and others who lived there and to replace them with Germans. Only then would they become Europe's master race. In *Mein Kampf* Hitler wrote:

> "We the Nazis must hold steadfastly to our aims in foreign policy, namely to secure for the German people the land and soil to which they are entitled on this earth."

GERMANY REARMS

Hitler knew that his plan to create a new German empire would mean another war, but this did not worry him. Ever since 1933, he had been rearming Germany. At first, he did this secretly because of the Treaty of Versailles. But from 1935, he rearmed openly. He also withdrew from the League of Nations which forbade rearmament. Hitler said:

> "If we do not succeed in making the German army the best army in the world, then Germany will be lost."

Appeasement

Britain and France were alarmed at what Hitler was doing. Unlike him, however, they were afraid of another war. They hoped that if they gave Hitler what he wanted, he would be satisfied and not start one. Between 1933 and 1938, the British and the French did their best not to anger Hitler. They let him:

- build up the German army, air force and navy.
- send the German army into the demilitarised Rhineland in 1936.
- take over Austria in March 1938. Austria, Hitler's homeland, was a German-speaking country, but the Treaty of Versailles forbade it to unite with Germany.

All of these acts were strictly forbidden by the Treaty of Versailles but Hitler kept arguing that all Germany wanted was justice. He blamed the Treaty of Versailles for taking land belonging to Germany which the German people now wanted back. The British and the French kept hoping that Hitler would be satisfied and that Europe would remain at peace. This attitude on the part of the British and the French is called **appeasement**.

Hitler and the Sudetenland

In 1937, **Neville Chamberlain** became prime minister of Britain. He was in favour of appeasing Hitler, but when Hitler turned his attention to Czechoslovakia, Chamberlain became concerned.

Three million Germans lived in the **Sudetenland**. This was an area in northern Czechoslovakia, one of the new countries created in 1919 by the Treaty of Versailles. Hitler accused the Czech government of treating these Germans badly and demanded that they be allowed to unite with Germany. When the Czech government refused, Hitler threatened to go to war unless he got his own way.

Cartoons like this one appeared in the Evening Standard between 1934 and 1939. Explain in your own words what the cartoon means.

The Munich Conference: 1938

This would mean Germany conquering Czechoslovakia, and that was too much, even for Chamberlain. In September 1938, he flew to Munich where he tried to persuade Hitler not to attack the Czechs.

Mussolini and the French and Czech prime ministers were also present at the conference. In the end, Britain and France agreed to let Hitler take over the Sudetenland if he promised not to touch the rest of Czechoslovakia.

Chamberlain returned to Britain and announced to waiting journalists: "I believe it is peace for our time." This belief lasted only six months. In March 1939, Hitler broke his promise and sent German troops to conquer all of Czechoslovakia. It was now clear to everyone that appeasing Hitler had not worked.

Chamberlain speaks to waiting journalists after his return from Munich in 1938. He holds Hitler's so called "guarantee of peace" in his hands.

Chamberlain meets Mussolini in 1938, hoping he can persuade him to influence Hitler to leave the Sudetenland alone.

The threat to Poland: 1939

Look at Poland and Germany on the map. You can see that part of Germany called **East Prussia** is cut off from the rest of the country by a narrow strip of land called the **Polish corridor**.

This territory was taken from Germany by the Treaty of Versailles in order to give Poland an outlet to the sea. However, many German people still lived there, as well as in the city of Danzig (now called Gdansk) on the coast. In 1939, Hitler said:

"We demand the return of the Polish corridor which is like a strip of flesh cut from our body. It cuts Germany in two. It is a national wound that bleeds continuously and will continue to bleed until the land is returned to us."

The two dictators, Mussolini and Hitler parade in Munich after they had formed an alliance called the Rome-Berlin Axis in 1936.

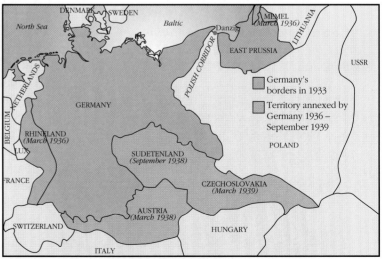

German expansion under Hitler: 1936-39

Appeasement ends

By now, Britain and France had realised that appeasing Hitler did not work. They decided to stand up to him. Chamberlain accused Hitler of trying "to dominate the world by force". Both Britain and France agreed to go to war to defend Poland if Germany invaded it.

The Soviet-German Pact: 1939

Hitler now looked for an ally to help him against Poland. Although Hitler and Stalin were bitter enemies, the two dictators astonished the world in August 1939 by announcing a **Soviet-German Pact**.

Under the terms of this pact, Hitler and Stalin promised that Germany and the USSR would not go to war against each other. They also agreed to divide up Poland between them. In spite of being enemies, this pact suited both men and gave them time to organise their own secret plans.

Hitler now felt free to attack Poland without worrying about the USSR. He still planned to invade Russia once he had defeated France and Britain.

The pact allowed Stalin to take over Latvia, Lithuania and Estonia. It also gave him more time to improve his army for a war against Hitler which he knew was sure to come.

World War II begins

On 1 September 1939, Hitler sent his planes and tanks into Poland. Britain and France kept their promise to the Poles and demanded that the Germans withdraw. When Hitler refused, they declared war on Germany on 3 September. World War II had begun.

German troops enter a Polish village in 1939 and survey the success of their blitzkrieg methods of warfare.

QUESTIONS

1. Make a list of those things which Hitler did to defy the Treaty of Versailles. Do you think he was right to do these things? Give reasons for your answer.
2. Explain in your own words what is meant by appeasement. Do you think Britain and France were right to appease Hitler? Give reasons for your answer.
3. Look at the map on page 110. (a) How do you think the German occupation of the Rhineland in 1936 might have been a threat to France? (b) How do you think the German take-over of Austria in 1938 might have been a threat to Czechoslovakia?
4. Why do you think the Soviet-German pact "astonished the world"?

FROM WHAT YOU HAVE READ SO FAR, WHICH COUNTRY DO YOU THINK WAS (A) MOST TO BLAME (B) LEAST TO BLAME FOR BRINGING ABOUT WORLD WAR II: GERMANY, THE USSR, BRITAIN OR FRANCE? GIVE REASONS FOR YOUR OPINION.

Looking at the evidence

A Nazi recruitment poster for the Luftwaffe (the German airforce). It reads "Join us! The Hermann Goring Division. Enlist voluntarily!".

CHAPTER 8

The War in Western Europe: 1939-41

Blitzkrieg

Hitler conquered Poland within a month. During the invasion, he used a new system of warfare which the Germans called **blitzkrieg** ("lightning war"). Using both aircraft and tanks, it was based on speed and surprise.

German tanks cross the plains of Poland in September 1939.

▰ German planes first attacked military targets from the air. They also bombed roads, railways, bridges and all means of communication.

▰ German tanks then swept forward on the ground, pushing their troops through the enemy's defences. The tanks were followed by troops in jeeps, motorcars and on foot.

▰ During the ground attack, the German air force continued to dive-bomb enemy targets so that their tanks and soldiers could push forward as quickly as possible.

The "phoney war"

After the Germans invaded Poland, other countries prepared for a German attack. They were especially afraid of bombing. In cities and towns throughout Britain and France, underground shelters were built, gas masks were issued and volunteer defence forces were set up. City children were **evacuated** – sent to the safety of the countryside.

However, throughout the winter of 1939 and the spring of 1940, Hitler concentrated on Poland and left Britain and France alone. There was no fighting in western Europe and people began to speak of a **phoney war**.

A British government poster advising people to carry gasmasks. Special colourful gasmasks with ears were even designed for young babies. However, throughout the war no gas was dropped in Britain.

Young evacuees leaving London in 1939. Note the cardboard boxes which contain their gas masks. During the war more than one million British children were evacuated.

Germany attacks in the west

Suddenly, in April 1940, Germany invaded **Denmark** and **Norway**. Hitler wanted to control their coastlines so that German ships and submarines could operate freely in the North Atlantic and the North Sea. A few weeks later, the German army overran the **Netherlands**, **Belgium** and **Luxembourg**.

Britain and France were taken by surprise at the speed of Hitler's campaigns. In Britain, people blamed Neville Chamberlain for not acting quickly enough. In May 1940, he was replaced as prime minister by **Winston Churchill**.

Dunkirk: May 1940

In May 1940, German planes and tanks invaded France. Within days of the invasion, British troops along the northern frontier with Germany found themselves surrounded by the enemy. Along with thousands of French soldiers, the British were forced back towards the coast near **Dunkirk**.

With no other way of escape, Churchill ordered these troops to be evacuated across the English Channel. In a huge operation involving ships and hundreds of small boats, almost 340,000 British and French soldiers were landed safely back in England.

German troops enter Paris in June 1940. Such photographs were used for propaganda purposes in German newspapers.

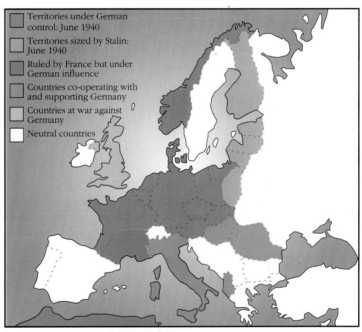

- ☐ Territories under German control: June 1940
- ☐ Territories sized by Stalin: June 1940
- ☐ Ruled by France but under German influence
- ☐ Countries co-operating with and supporting Germany
- ☐ Countries at war against Germany
- ☐ Neutral countries

Hitler's conquests by June 1940

An artist's impression of the evacuation at Dunkirk in May 1940. Note the city burning in the background.

The Nazis in Paris: June 1940

On 14 June 1940, the Germans marched into Paris. A week later, the French government surrendered. Hitler took over northern and western France. He left a French government, made up of men who had collaborated with the Nazis, in control of the south. It was based in the town of Vichy and became known as the **Vichy government**.

Britain: "We shall never surrender"

Winston Churchill, Prime Minister of Britain: 1940-1945. He convinced the British people that victory was possible if they all worked together against the Nazis.

As you can see from the map on page 113, Hitler controlled most of western Europe by the summer of 1940. He now hoped that Germany's victories would force Britain to surrender. However, Churchill promised that Britain would continue to fight. He made a famous speech in which he said:

"I have nothing to offer but blood, toil, tears and sweat. You ask 'What is our policy?' I will say it is to wage war, by sea, land and air, with all our might and with all the strength that God can give us. . . We shall fight on the beaches, we shall fight on the landing grounds, we shall fight in the fields and in the streets, we shall fight in the hills. We shall never surrender!"

Hitler was furious. In June 1940, he said:

"I have decided to prepare a landing operation against England and if necessary to carry it out."

Hitler's plan was for German troops to cross the English Channel and overrun the country. It was code-named **Operation Sealion**.

This German poster reads: "The enemy will see your light. Blackout!" Most European countries had similar type posters printed during the night-time bombing campaigns.

The Battle of Britain: July-September 1940

Before he could invade Britain, Hitler had to destroy British air power. Between July and September 1940, the **Battle of Britain** raged in the skies between the German **Luftwaffe** (air force) and Britain's **Royal Air Force** (RAF). Hundreds of German planes bombed British ships, air bases and factories while the RAF tried to defend them against attack.

The British, however, had a new secret weapon – **radar**. This helped the RAF to detect advancing German planes well in advance. As a result, the Germans lost 1400 aircraft while the British lost only 600. By October 1940, it was clear that the RAF had won. Hitler then called off "Operation Sealion".

An artist's impression of the Battle of Britain. It shows an RAF Spitfire attacking German Dorniers in a dogfight in the sky.

The Blitz

Hitler still sent German planes to bomb British cities, mostly at night. More than 200 German planes at a time dropped bombs on London, Glasgow, Coventry and Belfast. By the end of 1941, more than 50,000 Britons had been killed and three and a half million homes were destroyed. This is how a newspaper reporter described what he saw after the bombing of Coventry in 1940.

"A few miles outside Coventry, I met the first large group of refugees. There were suitcases and bundles on people's shoulders. Families trudged along hand in hand, with rugs, blankets and anything they could save from their ruined homes. I saw several people making preparations to lie down under hedgerows."

Hitler hoped that this would break the nerve of the British people and force them to surrender. But the **blitz**, as the British called the bombing, had the opposite effect. It made the British even more determined that they would never surrender to the Nazis.

Firemen try to quell the blaze in a London street at the height of the Blitz in December 1940. They often risked their own lives from bombs and burning debris.

🏛 The Battle of the Atlantic

Another of Hitler's plans was to starve Britain into submission. Britain had to import much of its food and raw materials, so Hitler used German warships and submarines (**U-boats**) to destroy British shipping.

Britain tried to defend its ships by having them sail in **convoys** protected by warships. But in the early years of the war, more than 5000 ships were sunk, as Britain did not have enough warships to protect its shipping fleet.

British merchant ships cross the Atlantic by convoy. The escort ship keeps a watchful eye on their safety.

🏛 American help for Britain

When the war began in Europe, the USA remained neutral. However, **President Roosevelt** was sympathetic to the British and condemned the attacks on them by Germany. In 1941, the USA began to supply the British with arms and ammunition which did not have to be paid for until the end of the war. These supplies made it possible for Britain to go on fighting.

✎ QUESTIONS ✎

1. Explain the following terms in your own words: Blitzkrieg, phoney war, Dunkirk evacuation, the blitz.
2. (a) Is the extract from Winston Churchill's speech on page 114 a primary source or a secondary source? Give reasons for your answer. (b) What effect do you think his speech had on (i) the Germans and (ii) the British?

The Russian Front: 1941-45

Operation Barbarossa

Despite his pact with Stalin in 1939, Hitler had always intended to conquer the USSR. He wanted to destroy communism and seize the Soviet Union's rich supplies of raw materials, particularly oil. He also wanted to settle Germans on Soviet land. He once said:

"If I had the Ural Mountains with their great store of raw materials, the Ukraine with its tremendous wheat fields and Siberia with its vast forests, Germany would swim in plenty."

After Hitler's failure to defeat Britain, he drew up plans for an invasion of the USSR. This was code-named **Operation Barbarossa**.

On 22 June 1941, Hitler launched his attack. Swarms of German planes destroyed hundreds of Soviet aircraft as they sat on the ground. At the same time, more than three million German troops and ten thousand tanks poured into Russia in a three-pronged attack which you can see on the map.

By December 1941, German soldiers were near Leningrad in the north and Moscow in the centre. They had also marched deep into the Ukraine towards Stalingrad. As they advanced on all fronts, more than three million soldiers in the Soviet Red Army were either killed or taken prisoner.

A Soviet war poster issued in Leningrad to boost the morale of the citizens against the Nazi siege. It reads: "October Victory. We will not surrender". Note the red star and the swastika on the helmets.

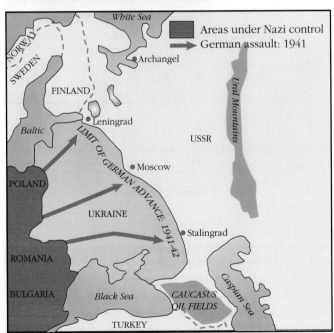

Operation Barbarossa: In 1941, Stalin ordered more than 1300 factories to be dismantled and moved east of the Urals to protect the production of vital supplies. Between 1942-45, the USA also sent food and medicine to the USSR through the port of Archangel on the White Sea.

Muscovites dig anti-tank trenches in 1942. Note the burning railway sleepers used to help thaw the ground.

The retreat from Moscow

Hitler planned to capture and destroy Moscow. However, the German soldiers were not prepared for the harsh Russian winter. As the temperature dropped to sixty degrees below freezing, the oil in their tanks froze. Many soldiers suffered from frostbite and some even froze to death. An eye-witness explains how they solved one problem.

"Some Germans hacked off the legs of dead Russian soldiers below the knee. They put the legs, with the boots still attached, into ovens. Within ten or fifteen minutes, the legs were sufficiently thawed for the German soldiers to strip off the vital boots."

German soldiers in the USSR light a fire to warm themselves against the bitter Russian winter. Unlike the Germans, the Red Army used sledges and skis when snow lay thick on the ground.

The Red Army, however, was used to sub-zero temperatures. On 6 December 1941, Soviet troops in Moscow launched a surprise counter-attack against the Germans and drove them back towards the border. Moscow was saved, which encouraged the Red Army to fight on.

Stalingrad: 1942-43

In 1942, Hitler ordered the German Sixth Army to capture the Soviet oil fields in the Caucasus and the city of Stalingrad which stood in their way. The Red Army and the people of Stalingrad fought side by side, but the Germans had taken most of the city by November 1942.

Then the Soviet army regrouped and counter-attacked, surrounding the city and trapping the Germans inside. Without ammunition or food, the German position was hopeless. On 31 January 1943, the Germans surrendered. More than 150,000 Germans were killed and over 100,000 were taken prisoner.

The Battle of Stalingrad was Hitler's first big defeat and a turning point in World War II.

A Soviet propaganda cartoon showing the Germans led by Hitler retreating through the snow in 1944 with a Red Army soldier at their back.

The siege of Leningrad

In the north, the Germans had besieged Leningrad for 900 days – nearly three years – but they could not take the city. The citizens were forced to live on rations of 120 grams of bread a day. By January 1944, when the Germans finally gave up the siege, more than one million people in Leningrad had died from starvation, disease and the cold.

A poster of Russian women working in a munitions factory. Such posters boosted the morale of the people and encouraged them to fight on.

Territories controlled by
Germany and her allies

Countries opposed to
Germany

Ruled by France but under
German influence

Neutral countries

This map shows the extent of Hitler's Third Reich when it was at its height. Compare it with the map on page 113 and list three differences you note.

The Soviet victory

By 1944, the Red Army had at last started to drive the Germans out of the Soviet Union. They pushed them back through Poland, Hungary, Romania, Bulgaria and Czechoslovakia, all of which the Germans had conquered earlier. By the spring of 1945, Soviet soldiers had reached Berlin itself.

But the USSR had paid a terrible price. More than 20 million Soviet citizens had died. Large parts of the Soviet Union had became a devastated wasteland and 25 million people were made homeless.

German soldiers, suffering from frostbite, are taken prisoner by the Red Army in 1944.

◢ QUESTIONS ◣

1. (a) Write down three reasons why Hitler wanted to conquer the USSR. (b) Draw your own map, illustrating his plan of attack.
2. Churchill once said: "It was the Red Army which tore the guts out of the German war machine." Do you agree or disagree with this statement? Give reasons for your answer.
3. Why do you think the Russians call World War II "The Great Patriotic War"?

FIND OUT MORE ABOUT THE SIEGE OF LENINGRAD AND THE BATTLE OF STALINGRAD. WRITE A SHORT ESSAY ON EACH ONE.

Finding Out

A Soviet soldier raises the red flag to celebrate the German surrender at Stalingrad in 1943.

During the war Hitler and Mussolini met several times to discuss the course of the war. Here they look at the map of the Eastern Front.

CHAPTER 10

The War in Italy and North Africa

🏛 Italy at war

Like Hitler, Mussolini also wanted to build up a great empire. He was impressed by Hitler's successes and after the fall of France in June 1940, he brought Italy into the war on the German side. Mussolini wanted to dominate the Mediterranean and to conquer more land in Africa where he already controlled Libya and Abyssinia.

An Italian propaganda poster showing Mussolini's army in North Africa with ancient legions at the rear led by the "Winged Voctory".

🏛 The Desert War

In September 1940, while Britain faced a German invasion at home, Italian troops invaded Egypt which was then under British control. But the Italians were easily defeated by a strong British force, which also included soldiers from Australia and New Zealand. Early in 1941, Hitler sent troops led by **Erwin Rommel**, one of his best generals, to North Africa to help the Italians.

Erwin Rommel in North Africa in 1942.

General Montgomery during the North African campaign.

⚖ EL ALAMEIN: 1942

At first, Rommel, who became known as the **Desert Fox**, won a number of victories against the British. But when the USA entered the war in 1941, his success ended.

In October 1942, British and American forces led by **General Montgomery**, defeated the German and Italian armies at the **Battle of El Alamein**. More than 20,000 Germans and Italians were killed or wounded and most of their tanks were destroyed.

The war in North Africa and Allied advances in Italy: 1942-45

The defeat of Italy

As more British and American troops reached North Africa, the Allies soon had twice as many soldiers and six times as many tanks as the enemy. In May 1943, the Germans and Italians were trapped in Tunisia and forced to surrender. About 250,000 were taken prisoner.

After this success, the Allies set out to invade Italy. They first captured the island of Sicily. Then, in September 1943, they crossed to the Italian mainland.

Italians were worried by this development. They overthrew Mussolini and surrendered to the Allies. Hitler, however, sent German reinforcements to defend Italy. They rescued Mussolini, who continued to rule over northern Italy. Throughout 1944, German and allied armies battled to control Italy.

On 28 April 1945, Mussolini was recaptured and hanged in Milan. A week later, the Germans surrendered and the war in Italy came to an end.

Finding Out

THE DESERT WAR PRODUCED TWO OF THE BEST-KNOWN GENERALS OF WORLD WAR II: ROMMEL AND MONTGOMERY. FIND OUT MORE ABOUT THEM AND WRITE A SHORT ACCOUNT ABOUT EACH ONE.

◪ QUESTIONS ◪

1. Why do you think some Italians wanted to overthrow Mussolini while others continued to fight for him until the very end?
2. How do you think Germany's support for Italy affected the course of World War II?

CHAPTER 11

The End of the War in Europe

United opposition to Hitler

From 1942 onwards, a strong alliance faced Hitler. Britain, the USA and the USSR were united with one common aim: the defeat of Nazi Germany. The USA was able to supply her allies with tanks, ships, planes and ammunition. America also had a large population of young soldiers who were eager to fight in the war.

Allied successes: 1943-44

By the end of 1943, Germany faced the possibility of defeat. The Soviets' Red Army had stopped Hitler at Stalingrad and the Allies had invaded Italy. That same year, German civilians also came under direct attack when the RAF and the US air force began bombing

▲ *In the last weeks of the war, German cities suffered enormous damage from allied bombings as this photograph of Berlin shows. The citizens were both terrified and helpless.*

raids on German cities. Germany soon experienced a blitz worse than that suffered by Britain. More than 600,000 civilians were killed in these raids.

A second front

As the Red Army continued to drive German troops back from the eastern front, Stalin met with Churchill and Roosevelt in November 1943. He persuaded them to invade France and attack Germany from the west. Stalin argued that this "second front" would take some of the German army away from Russia.

D-Day and the Normandy landings: June 1944

The Allies decided to invade France (code-named **Operation Overlord**) in June 1944. Their objective was to liberate France and defeat the Germans by driving them back across the River Rhine.

Five beaches along the coast of Normandy were chosen for the landings. For several weeks before the invasion, allied aircraft bombed roads and railway lines in northern France, trying to cut off German access to the coast.

France. They quickly moved inland and forced the Germans to retreat. On 25 August 1944, Paris was liberated. The Germans were driven back to their own border where they put up a last desperate resistance. It was only in March 1945 that the Allies finally crossed the Rhine into Germany.

Equipment is moved onto the beachhead at Normandy. British and Canadian troops also took part in the landings.

American soldiers wade up from the beach during the Normandy landings in June 1944. They brought with them amphibious tanks which could be used on both land and water.

The landings began soon after midnight on 6 June 1944 (called **D-Day** – "D" for "Deliverance"). On that first day alone, more than 4000 vessels and 150,000 soldiers crossed the English Channel and landed on the five beaches. The Germans had no idea where the Allies would land and they were taken by surprise.

Over the next few weeks, another 250,000 American, British and French troops arrived in

Hitler in his Berlin bunker

Refugees return to Berlin in May 1945 after the surrender of Germany.

Meanwhile, the Red Army had liberated Poland and Czechoslovakia and was advancing towards Germany from the east. On 13 April 1945, it had reached Vienna in Austria. This is what a nineteen-year-old Soviet soldier wrote in his diary at that time.

"I am proud to be one of Stalin's victorious soldiers. If I'm lucky enough, I'll be in Berlin yet. We'll get there and we deserve to get there – before our western allies do."

Hitler with Eva Braun whom he had known for fifteen years. He once said "I've told her a dozen times I won't marry her, as I can't tie any woman to my life."

On 30 April 1945, as Russian soldiers entered Berlin, Hitler married his girlfriend, **Eva Braun**. On the afternoon of the following day, they committed suicide together.

About the same time, Russian soldiers raised a flag over the Reichstag in Berlin. On 8 May 1945, known as **VE Day** ("Victory in Europe Day"), Germany finally surrendered.

◢ QUESTIONS ◣

1. Historians think that 1943 was the year in which the war turned in favour of the Allies. Give three reasons for that view.
2. (a) What kind of help did the USA give to her allies in Europe? (b) Was this help important in defeating the Nazis? Why?
3. Which of the Allies do you think contributed most to the defeat of Germany – Britain, the USA or the USSR? Give reasons for your answer.
4. Do you think that Hitler himself may have been one of the causes of Germany's defeat? Give reasons for your answer.

From his headquarters in an underground bunker in Berlin, Hitler issued his last order on 16 April 1945.

"He who at this moment does not do his duty is a traitor to the German nation. The regiments that give up their posts are acting so disgracefully that they must hang their heads in shame before the women and children who here in our cities are braving the terror bombing."

IN YOUR LOCAL LIBRARY, FIND OUT MORE ABOUT D-DAY AND THE NORMANDY LANDINGS. THEN, IMAGINE THAT YOU WERE A REPORTER WHO ACTUALLY WITNESSED THE EVENTS. WRITE A NEWSPAPER ARTICLE BASED ON YOUR EXPERIENCES. REMEMBER TO BASE YOUR REPORT ON THE EVIDENCE.

Finding Out

The War in the Pacific

🏛 Japan bombs Pearl Harbour: December 1941

While one part of World War II was being waged in Europe, a separate part was developing in Asia. It was caused by Japan, which wanted to build a great empire of its own.

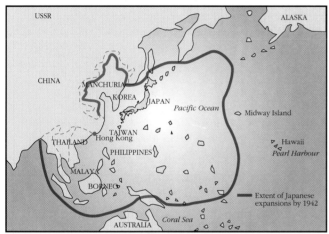

▲ *The war in the Pacific: 1941-45*

▲ *A US battleship engulfed in flames. On the left, the crew of a small boat look vainly for survivors.*

On 7 December 1941, the Japanese launched a surprise attack on America's Pacific Fleet which was stationed at **Pearl Harbour** in Hawaii. Within two hours on a quiet Sunday morning, they had destroyed 120 American aircraft and fourteen warships. More than 2000 people were killed. Only twenty-nine Japanese planes were lost.

The attack on Pearl Harbour was a stunning blow for the Americans. They immediately declared war on Japan. A few days later, Britain also declared war on Japan. In return, Germany and Italy, who had earlier made a treaty of friendship with Japan, declared war on the USA. With every great power in the world now involved, the war had become a world war in every sense.

🏛 The atomic bomb

After Pearl Harbour, the Japanese conquered much of eastern Asia. The Americans quickly rebuilt their fleet and were soon advancing on Japan. They ignored the Japanese conquests and concentrated on bombing Japan itself. Tokyo and other cities were destroyed and hundreds of thousands of Japanese civilians were killed.

◄ *The lethal mushroom cloud which resulted from the dropping of the atomic bomb on Nagasaki.*

This photograph was taken from a US plane a few days after the atomic bomb was dropped on Hiroshima. Few buildings remain standing and nowhere is there any sign of human life.

When the Japanese government still refused to surrender, President **Harry S. Truman** decided to use the **atomic bomb** which the Americans had just developed. He later said:

"I regarded the bomb as a military weapon and never had any doubt that it should be used. The top military advisors recommended its use."

President Harry Truman: 1945-52. The Russians were angry that he did not inform them of his intentions to drop the atomic bomb on Japan.

HIROSHIMA AND NAGASAKI

On 6 August 1945, an American plane called the *Enola Gay* dropped an atomic bomb on the Japanese city of Hiroshima. The bomb floated down on its parachute until it was about 450 metres above the ground. Then, in a blinding flash, it exploded. The city centre burst into flames and thousands of people were vaporised in the 100 million degree heat.

A huge fireball rose in the air. The atomic blast was followed by a great gust of wind which levelled the entire city centre. About 80,000 people were killed. Many more died later from radiation sickness.

Two days later, another atomic bomb was dropped on Nagasaki. This time, more than 40,000 people were killed.

Fifty years later, Japanese people are still dying from the effects of these bombs.

The Japanese knew they had no answer to the atomic bomb. On 14 August 1945, the Japanese emperor surrendered. On **VJ Day** ("Victory in Japan Day"), World War II was over at last.

The US General Douglas Mac Arthur reads the surrender terms to the Japanese onboard the USS Missouri in Tokyo Harbour in September 1945.

◢ QUESTION ◣

How do you think the war in the Pacific might have affected the war in Europe?

READ THE ACCOUNT OF THE BOMBING OF HIROSHIMA AND NAGASAKI CAREFULLY. FIND OUT MORE ABOUT THE BOMBINGS, IF YOU WISH. WERE THE AMERICANS RIGHT TO USE THE ATOM BOMB AGAINST THESE TWO CITIES? HOLD A CLASS DISCUSSION OR DEBATE ABOUT THIS.

Activity

American warship in the Pacific

CHAPTER 13

Europe in 1945

Counting the cost

America's President Woodrow Wilson had described World War I as "the war to end all wars". However, little did he and others realise at the time that just twenty years later, a much greater and more destructive world war would take place.

Between September 1939 and August 1945, the peoples of fifty-seven nations were involved in fighting World War II. Only a small number of countries, including Ireland, were able to remain **neutral**.

LOSS OF LIFE

During the course of the war, at least 20 million soldiers died, including six million Russians and three million Germans. These were two of the countries which suffered the greatest loss of human life.

But it was not just members of the armed forces who died. Civilians also suffered. It is estimated that civilian deaths from bombing, starvation and policies of deliberate extermination numbered at least 25 million. The exact death toll will never be known.

A father says goodbye to his son as he sets off to war in September 1939. Over the next six years an estimated twenty million young soldiers died in the fighting.

DEVASTATION AND RECONSTRUCTION

At the end of the war, much of Europe and Asia lay in ruins. Whole cities and towns were reduced to rubble. There were millions of refugees and homeless people. The widespread destruction of property, industries and businesses also meant the loss of livelihoods for millions of people. Over the next twenty years, reconstruction would cost billions of pounds.

Berliners return to their city shocked by the devastation of war. The problems of refugees, homelessness and rebuilding their lives would take many years to solve.

The war also saw the disappearance of some national frontiers and the creation of new ones. Germany and Japan, both ruined by the war, were occupied by the armies of the victorious countries. Western Europe no longer led the world. Its place was soon taken by the USSR and the USA. These countries emerged from the war as the **superpowers** of the future.

"Man's inhumanity to man"

The end of the war also revealed the horrors of the concentration camps and the extent of "man's inhumanity to man". Before the end of 1945, leading

Nazis were put on trial in Nuremberg for **crimes against humanity**.

🔲 *Some people, like these elderly men, grieved at "man's inhumanity to man".*

The start of the nuclear age

The development of the atomic bomb and its use against Japan during the war marked the beginning of a new age in human history – the **nuclear age**. Men and women now had to face the reality that they had the power to destroy the world.

A NEW START

The statesmen of the victorious powers met in 1945 to plan a better future for all people. Once again, they resolved to set up an organisation which would keep order in the world and prevent a major war from breaking out again. It was called the **United Nations**.

QUESTIONS

1. Compare the effects of World War I (pages 80-82) with the effects of World War II. Make a list of the similarities and differences.
2. Do you think that the victors of World War II had any lessons to learn from the victorious powers in World War I? Make a list of your suggestions.
3. How do you think the development of the atomic bomb would change people's attitudes towards future wars?

CHAPTER

Origins of the Cold War

World War II brought ruin to Britain, France, Germany and Japan. Only the United States and the Soviet Union (USSR) emerged in strong positions. Because of their large populations, strong economies and vast armies, these two countries had become the world's **superpowers** by 1945.

During the war, the United States and the USSR had been allies against Hitler. After the defeat of Germany, however, serious differences arose between them. Within three years, the two superpowers were involved in a struggle for power which dragged on for more than forty years. Since the two sides never actually came to blows, the struggle between them is called the **cold war**.

Why was there a cold war between the superpowers?

 END OF THE ALLIANCE

On 26 April 1945, American and Soviet troops met along the banks of the River Elbe in Germany. Yet shortly after these soldiers celebrated their victory, relations between their governments became strained. There were two reasons for this.

1. As soon as World War II ended, the US halted the aid which it had been giving to the USSR

An American soldier shaking hands with a Russian soldier in the town of Torgau. He was one of the first four Americans to meet the Russians. Do you think this was a spontaneous meeting or one carefully arranged for its propaganda value?

during the war. This consisted of tools, food and raw materials as well as arms and ammunition. The withdrawal of this aid caused great problems for the USSR, which had suffered badly in the war.

2. During the Potsdam Conference between the Soviet, American and British leaders, the Americans had dropped the first **atomic bomb** on Japan. Under wartime agreements, the Allies were supposed to share their technological developments, but the Americans refused to tell the Soviets the secrets of this terrible new weapon. The USSR immediately began to develop their own atomic weapons. These factors explain why the alliance between the superpowers began to fall apart as soon as the war ended.

DIFFERENT IDEOLOGIES: COMMUNISM VERSUS CAPITALISM

The distrust between the US and the USSR dated back to before the war. It was based on their different views of the way governments should work. Here are some of those differences.

THE UNITED STATES WAS

- a **democracy** where the government was freely elected by the people.
- a **free society** where people could express any opinions they wished.
- a **capitalist** state where farms, shops, factories etc. belonged to private individuals or companies.

THE SOVIET UNION WAS

- a **one-party state** where only Communist Party members were allowed to hold government positions.
- controlled by Stalin's **secret police**. Anyone who criticised him could end up in a concentration camp.
- a **communist** state where all shops, farms etc. had been taken over by the state.

Post-war disagreements between the superpowers

THE FATE OF EASTERN EUROPE

After the war, the two superpowers disagreed over what should happen to Europe. Stalin was afraid that the capitalist countries might attack the USSR. For protection, he decided to create a **buffer zone** of "sympathetic" states in Eastern Europe. By "sympathetic", Stalin meant communist dictatorships. Since Stalin's army occupied Eastern Europe, he was able to have his way.

The states of Eastern Europe

THE TRUMAN DOCTRINE

The Americans were alarmed by this. They feared that the Russians were planning to set up communist governments all over Europe.

In 1946, a civil war broke out in Greece between the government and communist guerrillas. Believing that the Russians were helping the communists, the American president, **Harry S. Truman**, sent help to the Greek

Harry Truman, President of the USA, 1945-1952

government. He also promised that the United States would help anyone else who was fighting against communism. This promise was called the **Truman Doctrine**. It became the basis of American policy during the cold war.

▲ *Russian reaction to the Truman Doctrine. What point is the cartoonist trying to make?*

🏛 THE MARSHALL PLAN

Europe was in ruins after the war. People were homeless, hungry and unemployed. In despair, many began to support communist parties. To stop this, **George Marshall**, the US Secretary of State, announced a plan to give billions of dollars to the countries of Europe to help them rebuild their economies.

Aid under the **Marshall Plan** was offered to the countries of Eastern Europe but Stalin would not allow them to accept it. Instead, he set up a new body called **Cominform** to bind the countries of Eastern Europe more closely to the USSR.

By the summer of 1948, relations between the superpowers had become quite hostile. For the next forty years, they would take opposite sides in almost every diplomatic problem around the world. The most serious division, however, remained the problem of what to do with Germany.

▲ *West German poster welcoming Marshall Aid. What is the significance of (a) the flags, (b) the lorry and (c) the customs barrier?*

◤ QUESTIONS ◥

1. When World War II ended, two American decisions made the Russians deeply suspicious of them. What were these decisions?
2. "One reason why the superpowers were suspicious of each other was the difference between the communist and the capitalist systems of government." Explain this statement.
3. Write a paragraph on the Truman Doctrine. Explain: (a) why it was introduced; (b) what it was; (c) what effect it had on the Russians.
4. What was the Marshall Plan? What was the Russian response to it?

CHAPTER 2

The Berlin Crisis

What to do with Germany?

The Soviet Union, Britain, France and the US had joined forces to defeat Nazi Germany. But once they had won, they disagreed about what to do next. Should they punish Germany by making her pay for starting the war? Should they split up Germany into several parts?

As a temporary arrangement, they agreed on the following points.

- Nazi leaders would be punished for the evil things they did during the war. This led to the **Nuremberg trials** where Nazi leaders were tried for war crimes (crimes against humanity) such as the killing of six million Jews and other groups in the concentration camps.

- Germany would be divided into four **zones of occupation** in which the armies of each of the Allies would be in control.

- The German capital, Berlin, which was deep inside the Russian zone, should also be divided into four zones.

- A joint **Allied Control Commission** would be set up to ensure co-operation among the four occupying powers.

▲ Berliners digging potatoes in front of the ruins of the Reichstag building.

Refugees and the food problem

The biggest problem which the Allied Control Commission had to deal with was the food supply. In 1945, Germany was in ruins. Millions of Germans were homeless and hungry. To make matters worse, the country had been flooded by 15 million refugees from Eastern Europe. Most of them brought no more than their clothes with them. By 1947, nearly two million people had died in Germany from disease or starvation.

At first, the Allies refused to let Germany rebuild its industries. Since great firms like Krupps had helped Hitler rise to power, the Allies felt that this was the only way to guarantee the security of Europe. But in 1946, they had to start sending food to feed the starving people.

Map labels:
Hamburg
BRITISN ZONE
Hanover
Berlin
Oder-Neisse Line
SOVIET ZONE
Frankfurt
Berlin: Military sectors and air corridors
AMERICAN ZONE
Hamburg Air Corridor
FRENCH ZONE
French Sector
Soviet Sector
British Sector
American Sector
Hanover Air Corridor
Frankfurt Air Corridor

— 1937: German border
— 1945: Zones of Occupation
◄·– Air corridors to Berlin
▢ German land lost to Poland
▢ German land lost to USSR

Germany after the war
Inset: Military zones in Berlin and approved air routes to Berlin from the western military zones

"If we don't let him work, who's going to keep him?" What is the cartoonist trying to say?

Berliners watching the approach of an American plane carrying supplies.

People in Britain soon began to question the wisdom of the Allied policy towards German industries. In America, too, opinions were changing. This is what George Marshall had to say in 1946.

"Germany is part of Europe, and recovery in Europe, particularly in the states adjoining Germany, will be slow indeed if Germany, with her great resources of iron and coal, is turned into a poorhouse."

George Marshall, US Secretary of State for Foreign Affairs

The division of Germany begins

When the Americans announced that they would give Marshall Aid to Europe, they decided to give aid to Germany as well. They wanted to unite the four military zones, encourage the German economy to start up again and bring in a new German currency, the deutschmark. The three western Allies – Britain, France and the US – agreed. But the Russians refused to let their zone take part in these proposals.

The Berlin Blockade: 24 June 1948- 12 May 1949

The new German currency, the deutschmark, was introduced in 1948. However, the Russians tried to stop it from being used in the western zones of Berlin. They closed all road and rail links between Berlin and the west of Germany. They also cut off supplies of food, coal, gas and electricity. Within a few days, the Soviet blockade of Berlin was complete.

The western powers thought that Stalin wanted to force the whole of Berlin into the Soviet zone. They were determined to foil his plans. Although the land routes to Berlin were closed, Stalin had agreed to leave the air routes open. He did not think the western Allies could possibly keep Berlin supplied by air. But he was wrong.

For eleven months, one and a half million tonnes of food, fuel and other supplies were airlifted to the beleaguered people of Berlin. At the height of the blockade, a plane was landing in Berlin every forty seconds. Russian planes frequently buzzed them in flight, but they made no attempt to shoot them down.

These months were bleak times for Berliners, as this report shows.

"She (Mother) queued at one shop for two hours. There was no meat on sale. Shopping consisted of dried beans, dried carrots, dried potatoes, powdered soup, powdered egg, dried plums, Canadian flour and synthetic coffee made from corn. She met a friend who had tried to go

shopping in the Soviet sector ... The friend was caught by an East Berlin policeman at the border ... He confiscated the four pounds of potatoes and the flower-pot that she had with her. On the way home, Mother swopped a soap ration card for one for fat. She had had a successful day."

Although food and other essentials were scarce, the Berliners held out. In May 1949, Stalin realised that the western powers would not abandon the city and called off the blockade.

Results of the Berlin Blockade

The Berlin Blockade is usually seen as the start of the cold war. It showed that the United States and the Soviet Union were no longer allies but enemies. Many people were afraid that a third world war was about to break out between them.

The Berlin Blockade had several other results.

■ It led to the **division of Germany**. In May 1949, the three western Allies agreed to let their

zones unite to form the **Federal Republic of Germany** (West Germany). In October, the Soviets formed their zone into the **German Democratic Republic** (East Germany). Germany remained divided into a communist East Germany and a capitalist West Germany until the cold war ended in 1990. Then, the two parts were re-united.

■ After the Berlin Blockade, each superpower formed a military alliance against the other. In 1949, the **North Atlantic Treaty Organisation** (**NATO**) was set up by the United States, Canada, France, Britain and other western European countries who felt threatened by the Soviet Union. When West Germany was allowed to have an army in 1955, it joined NATO as well.

The Soviets were frightened when West Germany joined NATO. So, in 1955, they set up a military alliance with the communist states of Eastern Europe. This alliance was known as the **Warsaw Pact**.

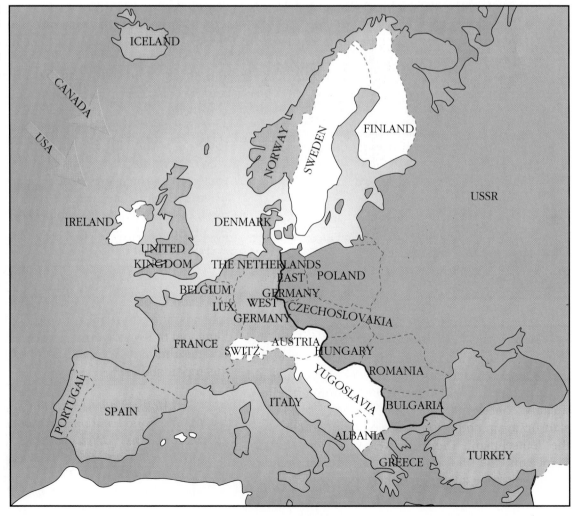

NATO and Warsaw Pact countries. Unshaded countries were neutral.

The Berlin Wall: 1961

In the 1950s, Marshall Aid helped West Germany to prosper. East Germany did less well, however. Many East Germans decided to flee to the west to share in its prosperity. In 1952, the East German government closed its border with the west to stop them from leaving.

But Berlin, which was deep inside East Germany, was also divided into a communist East Berlin and a capitalist West Berlin. East Germans could still escape to the west by going to West Berlin.

In 1961, the East German government decided to solve this problem by building a wall between the two parts of the city.

On 13 August 1961, East German troops used barbed wire to close the border with West Berlin. Work began immediately on building a wall between the Soviet and Allied sectors of the city. America protested to Russia although it took no further action. It was not prepared to go to war over Berlin.

The Berlin Wall soon became a symbol of Europe's division between the free west and the unfree east. Relations between the superpowers had never been worse. Within a year, a new crisis would bring them to the brink of a nuclear war over Cuba (pages 139-142).

West Berliners, some of them smiling, look on as East German troops erect a barbed wire barricade along the border between East and West Berlin on August 13, 1961.

Looking at the evidence

IN 1963, THE AMERICAN PRESIDENT, JOHN F. KENNEDY, VISITED BERLIN AND MADE A FAMOUS SPEECH. IN IT, HE SAID:

"ALL FREE MEN, WHEREVER THEY MAY BE, ARE CITIZENS OF BERLIN, AND THUS I TAKE PRIDE IN SAYING 'ICH BIN EIN BERLINER' (I AM A BERLINER)."

WRITE A PARAGRAPH EXPLAINING WHAT HE MEANT.

◢ QUESTIONS ◣

1. How did the Allies deal with Germany in 1945?
2. Why did the Americans offer Marshall Aid to Germany in 1948?
3. Write an account of the Berlin Blockade. Refer to: (a) reasons for the crisis; (b) actions taken by the Russians; (c) how the Allies supplied Berlin; (d) how it affected Berliners; and (e) the results of the blockade.

CHAPTER 3

The Korean War

In 1949, just as the Berlin Blockade was coming to an end, an even more dangerous conflict between the superpowers was beginning in eastern Asia. It concerned Korea, a peninsula stretching southwards from Manchuria towards the Japanese islands.

Korea occupies a strategic location between Russia, China and Japan. The Chinese viewed it as "a hammer ready to strike at the head of China". To the Japanese, Korea was a "dagger pointed at the heart of Japan".

Find Korea on the map. Then find Russia, China and Japan. Can you see why each of these countries was concerned about Korea?

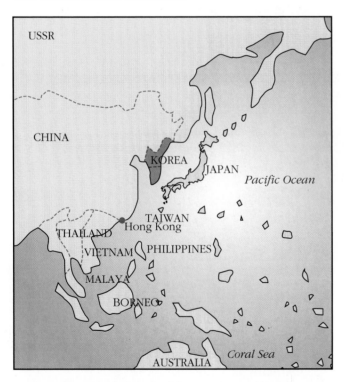

Korea divided

Since 1910, Korea had been a colony of Japan. At the end of World War II, it was invaded by the Soviets from the north and the Americans from the south.

They divided the country along the **38th parallel** of latitude. Both sides agreed that free elections should be held and Korea re-united. But as relations between the superpowers got worse, this did not happen.

In 1947, the South elected Dr **Syngman Rhee** as its leader. He had American support. In the North, **Kim Il Sung**, a communist, became leader with Stalin's support.

The Americans and Soviets then withdrew their armies, leaving behind a divided country. Both Syngman Rhee and Kim Il Sung claimed authority over all of Korea and both threatened to unite the country by force.

China becomes communist: 1949

In 1949, **Mao Tse Tung** led the communists to victory in the Chinese civil war. This was dangerous for South Korea. It was now surrounded by communist countries and was open to attack from the North.

◢ QUESTIONS ◢

Write a paragraph explaining how Korea had became a divided country by 1949.

North Korea invades the South: June 1950

On 25 June 1950, the North Koreans invaded the South. Their Soviet tanks easily smashed through the border defences. Within three days, they had captured **Seoul**, the capital of South Korea.

KIM IL SUNG CLAIMED THAT HIS INVASION WAS A RESPONSE TO AN ATTACK ON THE NORTH BY THE ARMY OF SOUTH KOREA. THE AMERICANS, HOWEVER, BELIEVED THAT THIS WAS PART OF A PLAN BY STALIN TO EXPAND SOVIET POWER. STUDY THIS EVIDENCE AND MAKE UP YOUR OWN MIND. CAN YOU SAY WHO IS TELLING THE TRUTH?

▲ *Kim Il Sung, President of North Korea, 1948-1994.*

SOURCE A

VALENTINE PAK, TRANSLATOR AND AIDE TO KIM IL SUNG, 1948-56, ON WHETHER THE ATTACK WAS THE IDEA OF THE SOVIET UNION:

> *"DID STALIN DIRECTLY ENCOURAGE KIM IL SUNG TO ATTACK THE SOUTH? I'M HIS FORMER ASSISTANT AND TRANSLATOR, AND I AND MY COMRADES SAW MANY OF THE DOCUMENTS ADDRESSED TO HIM, AND I CAN ABSOLUTELY CONFIRM THAT STALIN DID NOT ENCOURAGE KIM."*

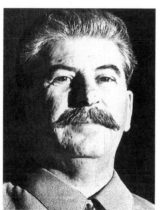

▲ *Joseph Stalin, who became supreme leader of the USSR in 1928.*

SOURCE B

A TELEGRAM FROM STALIN TO KIM IN JANUARY 1950:

> *"I UNDERSTAND THE DISSATISFACTION OF COMRADE KIM IL SUNG. BUT HE SHOULD REALISE THAT SUCH AN IMMENSE OPERATION OF THE SORT HE WANTS TO UNDERTAKE IN RELATION TO SOUTH KOREA REQUIRES MUCH PREPARATION. THE OPERATION SHOULD BE ORGANISED IN SUCH A WAY THAT RISK IS MINIMISED."*

SOURCE C

VALENTINE PAK ON THE SOVIET ROLE IN PLANNING THE INVASION:

> *"THE INVASION OPERATION WAS DEVISED BY THE SOVIET ADVISORS TO THE NORTH KOREAN ARMY. THE PLAN WAS HANDED TO US ON TRACING PAPER. IT WAS PUT TOGETHER BY RUSSIANS. SOVIET GENERALS AND COLONELS DREW IT UP AND THEN IT WAS TRANSLATED BY KOREAN OFFICERS ATTACHED TO THEIR STAFF. SO THIS BLITZKRIEG OPERATION WAS DRAWN UP ON A MINUTE-BY-MINUTE BASIS FOLLOWING THE SOVIET COMMAND'S PLAN."*

SOURCE D

NIKITA KHRUSHCHEV, THE SOVIET LEADER, WRITING AFTER THE DEATH OF STALIN ON THE CAUSE OF THE WAR:

> *"THE NORTH KOREANS WANTED TO GIVE A HELPING HAND TO THE BRETHREN WHO WERE UNDER THE HEEL OF SYNGMAN RHEE. STALIN PERSUADED KIM IL SUNG THAT HE SHOULD THINK IT OVER ... KIM RETURNED TO MOSCOW WHEN HE HAD WORKED EVERYTHING OUT ... STALIN WAS WORRIED THAT THE AMERICANS WOULD JUMP IN. BUT WE WERE INCLINED TO THINK THAT IF THE WAR WERE FOUGHT SWIFTLY — THEN INTERVENTION BY THE USA COULD BE AVOIDED. NEVERTHELESS, STALIN DECIDED TO ASK MAO TSE TUNG'S OPINION ... I MUST STRESS THAT THE WAR WASN'T STALIN'S IDEA BUT KIM IL SUNG'S. KIM WAS THE INITIATOR. STALIN, OF COURSE, DIDN'T TRY TO DISSUADE HIM. MAO TSE TUNG ALSO ANSWERED AFFIRMATIVELY ... AND PUT FORWARD THE OPINION THAT THE USA WOULD NOT INTERVENE SINCE THE WAR WOULD BE AN INTERNAL MATTER WHICH THE KOREAN PEOPLE WOULD DECIDE FOR THEMSELVES ..."*

▨ QUESTIONS ▨

1. Read Sources A and D. Based on this evidence, do you think Stalin encouraged Kim Il Sung to invade Korea? Explain your answer.
2. From Sources B and D, what do you think Stalin means by the phrase: the "risk is minimised"?
3. According to Source C, what part was played by the Soviet military in planning the war?

4. Read Source D carefully. Khrushchev says that Stalin thought "intervention by the USA could be avoided". Why did Stalin think this?
5. Based on these sources, do you think the invasion of South Korea was: (a) Stalin's idea; (b) Kim Il Sung's idea to which Stalin gave hesitant backing; or (c) the result of an attack by the South? Give reasons for your answer.

Truman and the United Nations

Kim Il Sung and Stalin had gambled that America would not react to the invasion of South Korea. They were wrong. The American president, **Harry S. Truman**, wrote later:

"In my generation, this was not the first occasion when the strong had attacked the weak. I recalled some earlier instances: Manchuria, Ethiopia, Austria. I remember how each time that the democracies failed to act, it had encouraged the aggressors to keep going ahead. Communism was acting in Korea, just as Hitler, Mussolini and the Japanese had acted ... years earlier. If this was allowed to go unchallenged, it would mean a third world war, just as similar incidents had brought about a second world war."

Truman acted quickly. He ordered **General MacArthur**, the American military commander in Japan, to go to Korea with military supplies. He also appealed to the United Nations for help in defending South Korea.

The United Nations had been set up in 1945 by the countries which had fought Germany and Japan in World War II. The five main countries – the US, USSR, Britain, France and China – were all on the UN's **Security Council**. Each of them could stop the UN from taking any particular action by casting a vote against it. This power was called the **veto**. As the cold war developed, different countries used their vetoes to stop the UN from intervening in various situations throughout the world.

President Truman (right) appointed General Douglas MacArthur to head the UN troops in Korea.

In 1949, when the communists won the civil war in China, America and her allies refused to let the communist government take China's seat on the Security Council. In protest, the Soviets walked out. They were therefore absent when America asked the UN to send help to South Korea. As a result, the Soviet Union could not use its veto and the UN agreed to " ... furnish such assistance to the Republic of Korea as may be necessary to repel the armed attack and to restore peace and security in the area ...". The UN appealed to its members to send troops to Korea and America's allies responded. MacArthur was now in charge of a multi-national force, although most of the troops were Americans.

The Inchon landings: 1950

The speed of the American response unnerved Stalin. He ordered all Soviet advisors to leave Korea because he did not want a war in Korea to escalate into one between the USA and the USSR.

Meanwhile, the North Korean army continued its drive southward. By early September 1950, the South Korean army and its American allies were confined to a narrow strip of land surrounding the southern port of **Pusan**.

North Korean attack, June-Sept 1950

MacArthur believed that the North Koreans could only be checked by a bold counter-stroke. He made plans for a massive **amphibious** (air and sea) landing in the heart of the peninsula which would cut off the North Korean army which was besieging Pusan.

Firemen in North Korea fighting a fire after a raid by American forces.

On 15 September, a fleet of over 200 ships landed UN troops at **Inchon**. The daring landing was successful and, after heavy fighting, Seoul was recaptured on 28 September. The North Koreans were now in disarray and by early October, MacArthur's forces had liberated all of South Korea.

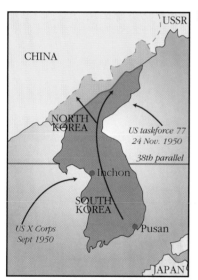

United Nations' counter attack, Sept-Nov 1950.

Chinese involvement begins

MacArthur had fulfilled his task. South Korea had been saved from communism. But he did not order his troops to stop. MacArthur thought that this was the opportunity to re-unite all of Korea under one democratic government. He ordered his troops to invade North Korea.

The Chinese government was alarmed by MacArthur's actions. Would the UN troops stop at the Chinese border, or would MacArthur try to conquer China and restore the former government which America still recognised?

China warned America to withdraw from North Korea, but they ignored the Chinese. Instead, Truman told MacArthur to continue his drive northward. The UN supported this move.

By 25 October, UN troops had reached the Yalu River. But their triumph was short-lived. That night, almost 300,000 **Chinese People's Volunteers** crossed the river and launched a fierce attack. Although the UN troops were much better equipped with tanks and planes, they were overwhelmed by the massive size of the Chinese force. They began to retreat southwards as rapidly as they had advanced.

MacArthur is dismissed: 1951

By January 1951, the Chinese and North Korean troops had pushed MacArthur's forces back south of the 38th parallel.

Chinese intervention, Oct 1950 onwards.

MacArthur wanted to contain the Chinese advance by using nuclear weapons against them. Truman refused his request, however, and he was forced to rely on conventional weapons. In February, he launched a counter-offensive and once more drove the enemy back to the 38th parallel.

MacArthur now wanted to extend the war into China and overthrow the communists. But Truman had decided that the war must be confined to Korea. He said:

"I believe we must limit the war to Korea for these vital reasons: to make sure that the precious lives of our fighting men are not wasted; to see that the security of our country and the free world is not needlessly jeopardised; and to prevent a third world war."

In April 1951, Truman dismissed MacArthur and replaced him with another general.

Stalemate in Korea

By now, the Americans had decided on a war of **containment** (i.e. they would stop the communists at the 38th parallel). Both sides dug themselves into a maze of trenches along this line.

Peace talks began at **Kaesong** in June 1951, but progress was slow and the war dragged on for another two years. There were heavy casualties on both sides as they fought for control of strategic locations. The Americans tried to break the deadlock by bombing North Korean cities and industrial sites. Near the border, in what became known as "Mig Alley", Russian and Chinese pilots flying Soviet Mig-15 jets fought with American F-86 Sabre jets for control of the sky.

Meanwhile, attempts to find a solution failed. The Chinese accused the Americans of using **germ warfare** against their troops. The Americans accused the Chinese of **brain-washing** American prisoners of war.

American bombers attacking strategic targets in North Korea. Why were they not used to bomb the Mig-15 air bases in China?

At the time, it was believed that the Soviet Union was only involved in supplying arms to the North Koreans and the Chinese. Early in 1996, a BBC "Timewatch" programme on "Russia's Secret War" suggested otherwise.

SOURCE E
Captain Boris Abakumov, a Mig-15 pilot, said:

> *"An instruction came from above to send a group of pilots to China. They dressed us in Chinese uniforms so that our Soviet uniforms wouldn't attract prying eyes. We wore reddish-brown boots, cotton trousers like workers used to wear, tucked into the boots, and green dress jackets ... So when we reached Korean airspace, we noticed that twelve Sabres were trying to catch up with us. They opened fire ... a burst hit my wings. I looked down. My hand was on the throttle and I could see the bone in my arm. It was broken. After that, the shooting stopped and I decided to eject."*

SOURCE F
Colonel Phillip Corso, US Military Intelligence, Korea:

> *"I personally sent a report to Washington that there were 22,000 Soviet troops in Korea who were actively involved in the fighting. There were also advisors ... and their tanks were run by Soviets. The Migs across the border were all Soviet, not Chinese – we picked up their voices in combat. They had 200 Migs right on the border but our policy-makers wouldn't let us bomb them."*

⬛ QUESTIONS ⬛

1. Read Source E. (a) Why was Captain Abakumov dressed as he was? (b) Did he play an active part in the Korean War? What was it?

2. Read source F. (a) How many Soviet troops did Colonel Corso say were involved in the war? (b) How did he find out about the Soviet involvement? (c) If the Americans knew that Soviet troops were fighting against them, why was America not at war with the USSR?

The Korean War ends: July 1953

In November 1952, America elected a new president, a World War II hero, General **Dwight D. Eisenhower**. He was determined to end the war but he had to get the Chinese to agree. His opportunity came on 5 March 1953 with the death of Stalin. Russia's new leaders were keen to bring the war to an end and China was forced to agree to new peace talks. Finally, on 17 July 1953, an **armistice** (ceasefire) was signed at **Panmunjom**.

The cease-fire line, July 1953.

The warring sides agreed to settle the Korean question within months. But this never happened. Now, over forty years later, the armistice is still in place. The relationship between North and South Korea remains hostile. However, in spite of many border incidents over the years, another full-scale war has not erupted.

◢ QUESTIONS ◣

1. What effect did the communist victory in China in 1949 have on the situation in Korea?
2. Read the quotation from President Truman on page 137. (a) Explain what he meant by "In my generation, this was not the first occasion when the strong had attacked the weak." (b) Why did Truman think that "If this was allowed to go unchallenged, it would mean a third world war"? (c) From this quotation, is it clear what the president intended to do? Give reasons for your answer.
3. Most of MacArthur's troops were Americans. Why did Truman feel that he needed the support of the United Nations?
4. Why did China become actively involved in the war?
5. In 1945, Truman had ordered that atomic bombs be dropped on Japan. Why do you think he rejected MacArthur's request for their use in Korea?
6. Why did Truman fire General MacArthur? What is your opinion of this?
7. Tension is still high in Korea today. Explain why this is so.
8. The Korean War can be divided into four phases. Name these four phases and write a paragraph on each one.

CHAPTER 4

The Cuban Missile Crisis

🏛 The Cuban Revolution: 1956-59

Cuba is a large island in the Caribbean just 160 kilometres from the American state of Florida. Up to the 1950s, the Americans dominated the island. The US navy had a large base at Guantanamo Bay, and Cuba's most important export, sugar, was sold to America.

Cuba had been ruled by a corrupt and ruthless dictator, **General Batista**. Under him, the country had become bankrupt. In 1956, a young lawyer called **Fidel Castro** launched a rebellion against Batista. America supported Batista with arms, but Castro had the support of the Cuban people. By 1959, Castro was victorious.

This map shows the location of Cuba in relation to the USA.

American marines on guard at Guantanamo Bay, a large US naval base in Cuba.

President Batista, the corrupt military dictator who was overthrown by Fidel Castro.

Fidel Castro (left) embraces Nikita Khrushchev at the United Nations in 1960. Why was the United States alarmed by the growing friendship between Cuba and Russia?

CASTRO'S REFORMS

Castro was a **socialist** who immediately began to introduce social reforms. He improved Cuba's health and education systems. He took the land away from the wealthy landlords and gave it to the peasants. He also took over industries owned by American companies without paying them any compensation.

The Americans were annoyed by these policies. They refused to buy Cuban sugar, hoping that this would force Castro out. Instead, he turned to America's enemy, the Soviet Union, for support. Fidel Castro formed an alliance with the Soviet leader, **Nikita Khrushchev**.

THE BAY OF PIGS: 1961

Castro's alliance with Khrushchev dismayed the Americans. They now had a communist government dangerously close to their own coast. In 1961, the Americans armed 1500 anti-Castro Cubans and helped them invade Cuba at a place called the **Bay of Pigs**. The invasion was badly planned and ended in disaster. It was a great embarrassment to America's newly-elected president, **John F. Kennedy**.

The Cuban Missile Crisis

After the Bay of Pigs, Castro turned to Khrushchev for further help. In 1962, Soviet advisors and military equipment began to arrive in Cuba. The Americans were worried that this equipment could include missiles and nuclear weapons aimed at the US. On 13 September 1962, President Kennedy warned the Russians:

"If at any time the communist build-up in Cuba were to endanger or interfere with our security in any way, or if Cuba should ever become an offensive military base for the Soviet Union, then this country will do whatever must be done to protect its own security and that of its allies."

Kennedy ordered his high-flying spy planes to keep a watch on Cuba. By 16 October, he was shown evidence that the Russians were building sites for Intermediate Range Ballistic Missiles on Cuba. When work on these sites was completed, nearly every large city in the United States would be threatened by a nuclear weapon launched from a base in Cuba. If any of these missiles were fired, the US would have only three minutes in which to respond to the attack before facing total destruction. The map below shows the extent of the problem.

Photograph of missile site in Cuba taken by an American spy plane on October 14, 1962 and released to the press.

John F Kennedy, President of the USA, 1960-63.

The Americans had to do something. But what action could they take? If they attacked the Cuban missile bases, would the Soviet Union declare war? But could they afford to do nothing?

For six days, Kennedy considered the possibilities. Finally, on 22 October 1962, he went on television to address the American nation. Kennedy told them what had been discovered and showed them the evidence. He said:

> "The urgent transformation of Cuba into an important strategic base by the presence of these large, long-range, and clearly offensive weapons of sudden mass destruction constitutes an explicit threat to the peace and security of all the Americas … All ships of any kind bound for Cuba, from whatever nation or port, will, if found to contain cargoes of offensive weapons, be turned back.
>
> It shall be the policy of this nation to regard any nuclear missile launched from Cuba against any nation in the western hemisphere as an attack by the Soviet Union on the United States, requiring a full retaliatory response upon the Soviet Union.
>
> I call upon Chairman Khrushchev to halt and eliminate this clandestine, reckless and provocative threat to world peace. He has an opportunity now to move the world back from the abyss of destruction by … withdrawing these weapons from Cuba."

President Kennedy's broadcast caused panic around the world. There were Soviet ships at sea, and low-flying American aircraft had clearly identified crated missiles on some of their decks. Would the Soviets listen to Kennedy and turn their ships back? If they did not, would the Americans open fire? America had its B-52 bombers in the air, fully loaded with atomic weapons.

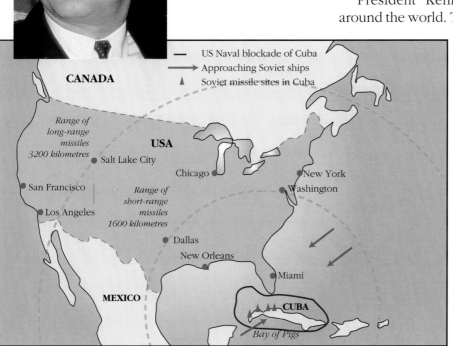

— US Naval blockade of Cuba
→ Approaching Soviet ships
▲ Soviet missile sites in Cuba

CANADA

Range of long-range missiles 3200 kilometres

USA

Salt Lake City

Chicago

San Francisco

Range of short-range missiles 1600 kilometres

Los Angeles

Dallas

New Orleans

New York

Washington

Miami

MEXICO

CUBA

Bay of Pigs

The Cuban Missile Crisis: 1962

For two days, the world teetered on the brink of a nuclear war. Then on 24 October, the Soviet ships halted. Two days later, Khrushchev offered to remove the rockets if the US promised not to invade Cuba. The Cuban Missile Crisis was over. The missiles went back to Russia, carefully watched all the way by American spy planes. The missile sites in Cuba were ploughed over.

The Russian freighter Kasimov carrying crated rockets to Cuba.

Results of the crisis

The crisis showed both the Soviets and Americans how easy it would be to slip into a nuclear war. They began to try to improve relations.

▱ Kennedy was shocked at how slow communications between the two superpowers had been during the crisis. He got Khrushchev to agree to a "Hot Line" teleprinter between Moscow and Washington which would provide a direct link between the two leaders.

▱ The superpowers also began to discuss the idea of limiting the testing of nuclear arms. In August 1963, they signed a **Test Ban Treaty**.

President Kennedy signs the Test Ban Treaty.

◿ QUESTIONS ◺

1. (a) Who became ruler of Cuba in 1959?
   (b) Why was America opposed to him?
   (c) How did America try to make him change his policies?
2. Why did the Cubans turn to the Soviets for help in 1961?
3. (a) How did America discover the Russian missile bases in Cuba?
   (b) Use the map (page 141) to explain why the Americans would have been especially worried by the presence of Soviet missiles in Cuba.
4. Read the extract from Kennedy's speech on page 141.
   (a) What did Kennedy say about the Soviet actions in Cuba?
   (b) What policy did Kennedy adopt regarding the ships carrying missiles to Cuba?
   (c) What explicit threat did Kennedy make to the USSR?
   (d) Kennedy had three options open to him.
      (i) To do nothing, but rely on negotiations with the Russians to remove the rockets.
      (ii) To attack and destroy the missile sites.
      (iii) To blockade Cuba.
      Which option did he choose? Do you think he was right? Explain your answer.
5. What lessons did the two superpowers learn from the crisis?

Activity

WRITE AN ACCOUNT OF THE CUBAN MISSILE CRISIS. SHOW HOW IT AFFECTED RELATIONS BETWEEN THE USA AND THE USSR.

Looking at the evidence

THE PHOTOGRAPH ON PAGE 141 WAS TAKEN OVER CUBA BY A USA SPY PLANE AND RELEASED TO THE PRESS. WHAT EFFECT DO YOU THINK SUCH PHOTOGRAPHS HAD ON PUBLIC OPINION AROUND THE WORLD ABOUT THE AMERICAN STAND OVER CUBA?

The End of the Cold War

Mikhail Gorbachev

No direct conflict took place between the superpowers after the Cuban Missile Crisis. But relations between them remained hostile for another twenty years. Then, in 1985, **Mikhail Gorbachev** became leader of the Soviet Union.

Mikhail Gorbachev, leader of Russia, 1985-91.

Gorbachev was determined to improve the Soviet economy. Nearly seventy years after the Russian Revolution, the Soviet Union was still unable to feed itself.

Gorbachev blamed this on too much government interference in economic decisions. He proposed to reshape the economy by cutting government subsidies which kept food prices down. He also allowed some private ownership of businesses. He called this rebuilding of the economy *perestroika* (restructuring).

For *perestroika* to work, people had to be able to discuss their problems openly. This open discussion was known as *glasnost* (openness). Soon, Russians were discussing not only their economic problems but also every aspect of their society.

To rebuild the Soviet economy, Gorbachev had to reduce military spending. This led him to negotiate a disarmament agreement with the western powers in December 1987. This removed all medium-range nuclear weapons from Europe. Relations between the superpowers now began to improve.

End of the Cold War

During 1989, demands for reform grew in the communist countries of Eastern Europe. When Gorbachev made it clear that Soviet troops would no longer be used to put down opposition to communism, communist governments were reformed or overthrown all over Eastern Europe.

On the night of 9 November 1989, thousands of East Berliners poured through the hated Berlin Wall and onto the streets of West Berlin. Some young people climbed onto the wall and began to tear it down.

The most famous symbol of the division of Europe was going, and within a year, the German people were able to celebrate the re-unification of their country. The cold war, which had begun with post-war disagreement over what to do with Germany, was over.

The Berlin Wall comes down, 9 November, 1989.

▲ *Eastern Europe in 1989.*

▲ *Eastern Europe in 1996.*

The rise of nationalism

The demand for reform now spread to the Soviet Union. The Baltic republics – Latvia, Lithuania and Estonia – demanded independence.

Gorbachev was in a quandary. If he allowed them independence, would all the other Soviet republics want the same? If he sent in the army to crush the demands for independence, would this lead to a renewal of the cold war?

Reluctantly, Gorbachev allowed them their freedom. The decision shocked hard-line communists and in 1991, they arrested Gorbachev and tried to seize control of the government. It was a gamble which backfired.

Faced with opposition from the Soviet parliament and the Red Army, the coup collapsed. Gorbachev was returned to office, but his power and that of the communist party had weakened.

In 1991 free elections were held in Russia. **Boris Yeltsin**, the man who had led the criticism of the communist party, was elected president. For the first time since 1917, the communists had lost power in Russia.

The collapse of communism led to renewed demands for independence among the peoples of Eastern Europe and the Soviet Union. Yeltsin was unable to curtail these demands and in the early 1990s, the map of Europe was reshaped by a rising tide of **nationalism**.

STUDY THE MAPS OF EUROPE IN 1989 AND 1996. (A) WHAT NEWLY INDEPENDENT COUNTRIES EMERGED FROM THE BREAK-UP OF THE SOVIET UNION? (B) WHICH NEW STATES WERE FORMED IN OTHER PARTS OF EASTERN EUROPE?

Looking at the evidence

◢ QUESTIONS ◣

1. Explain the terms *glasnost* and *perestroika*. Why were they needed in the Soviet Union in the 1980s?
2. Write an account of the part played by Mikhail Gorbachev in ending the cold war.
3. Write an account of your study of "The Rise of the Superpowers".(a) State the title of your study. (b) Write a full account of the study. (c) Show how your study helped you to understand this topic.

CHAPTER

Introduction

Ireland is a member of the **European Union** or **EU**. Until recently, this was known as the European Community (EC) or European Economic Community (EEC).

Membership of the EU now reaches into the everyday lives of people throughout the country. It has provided many opportunities for Irish citizens.

STUDY THE POSTER. WHAT IMAGE OF EUROPE IS IT TRYING TO PROJECT? WHAT DOES THE CAPTION MEAN? TRY TO IDENTIFY ALL THE FLAGS IN THE POSTER.

Looking at the evidence

· ALL OUR COLOURS TO THE MAST ·

The Beginnings of European Unity

The years of the "lost peace"

In 1918, the people of Europe had hoped there would be no more wars. Yet in the twenty years that followed, they suffered from unemployment and hunger. Some countries saw violent revolutions with ruthless dictators replacing democratic governments.

Then, in 1939 came World War II. Millions of people died during this war, either when caught up in the fighting or when sent to concentration camps. Cities were bombed, economies were destroyed and millions of people became homeless refugees. When World War II ended in 1945, Europe was even more devastated than it had been in 1918.

Berlin in 1945. Describe what you see. Comment on how you might have felt if you were one of the people in the photograph.

Searching for a better way

Even before the war ended, some people had begun to ask how they could ensure that these things would never happen again.

- How could they build up European economies to prevent the misery caused by economic depressions like the one during the 1920s and 1930s?
- How could they prevent dictatorships and guarantee that all Europeans could live under democratic governments which respected the human rights of all their citizens?
- How could they stop the countries of Europe, especially France and Germany, from fighting with one another?

HERE ARE THREE SOURCES THAT GIVE SOME OF THE IDEAS WHICH PEOPLE HAD ON THESE QUESTIONS.

SOURCE A

"... COMPELLED BY THEIR GEOGRAPHICAL POSITION TO LIVE TOGETHER, THE PEOPLES OF EUROPE, IF THEY ARE TO ENJOY SECURITY AND PROSPERITY, MUST ESTABLISH A PERMANENT SYSTEM FOR THE ORDERLY ORGANISATION OF EUROPE."

ARISTIDE BRIAND, FRENCH FOREIGN MINISTER, 1930

Looking at the evidence

SOURCE B

"THE PROBLEM WHICH MUST FIRST BE SOLVED IS THE FINAL ABOLITION OF THE DIVISION OF EUROPE INTO SEPARATE NATIONAL STATES ... PEOPLE ARE NOW MUCH MORE IN FAVOUR OF A FEDERAL REORGANISATION OF EUROPE THAN THEY WERE IN THE PAST. THE HARSH EXPERIENCES OF THE LAST TEN YEARS HAVE OPENED THE EYES OF EVEN THOSE WHO DO NOT WISH TO SEE ..."

WINSTON CHURCHILL, BRITISH PRIME MINISTER, 1941

SOURCE C

"THE PEACE OF EUROPE IS THE CORNERSTONE OF WORLD PEACE ... ONLY A FEDERAL UNION (OF EUROPEAN COUNTRIES) WILL ALLOW THE GERMAN PEOPLE TO PARTICIPATE IN THE LIFE OF EUROPE WITHOUT BEING A DANGER FOR THE REST ... ONLY A FEDERAL UNION WILL ALLOW DEMOCRATIC INSTITUTIONS TO BE SAFEGUARDED ... ONLY A FEDERAL UNION WILL ALLOW THE ECONOMIC RECONSTRUCTION OF THE CONTINENT ... "

DECLARATION OF THE EUROPEAN RESISTANCE MOVEMENTS, 1944

Finding Out

THE WORD "FEDERAL" APPEARS SEVERAL TIMES IN THESE SOURCES. USE A DICTIONARY TO FIND OUT WHAT IT MEANS. THEN WRITE AN EXPLANATION OF IT IN YOUR OWN WORDS.

Food had to be airlifted to the hungry people of Germany at the beginning of the "cold war".

◪ QUESTIONS ◪

1. What reasons are put forward in Sources A, B and C for some form of federal Europe?
2. What did Churchill mean by the "harsh experiences of the last ten years"?
3. Who were the resistance movements who made the Declaration in Source C?
4. Why did the resistance movements make the point about Germany in their Declaration of 1944?
5. Make a list of those things which already bound Europeans together and those which made them different from non-Europeans, even in 1945.
6. Can you think of any periods in the past which you have studied when some form of limited European unity existed? Explain the examples you give.

The beginnings of European unity

Much of Europe needed to be rebuilt after World War II. Economies were in ruins and people faced starvation during the very cold winter of 1946-47.

To make matters worse, relations between the Soviet Union and its former allies in the USA and western Europe were getting worse. A "cold war" was beginning (see pages 127-8).

Because of these situations, European leaders took a number of steps between 1945 and 1957 to bring about European unity. These involved setting up a number of different organisations with three main aims in mind:

- ◪ to **defend** western Europe against communist aggression
- ◪ to **protect** and strengthen democracy in Europe
- ◪ to **develop** the economies of western Europe.

⬚ THE BENELUX UNION

The first steps towards economic union were taken by three of Europe's smallest countries – Belgium, the Netherlands and Luxembourg – the **Benelux** countries. All had been over-run by Nazi Germany during the war and their governments had fled to safety in London. In 1944, these governments agreed to form an economic union as soon as peace was restored.

In 1948, they kept this agreement and formed the **Benelux Union** which removed **customs duties** between the three countries. This meant that goods could go from one country to another without paying any taxes.

THE MARSHALL PLAN AND THE OEEC: 1948-52

In 1947, America's Secretary of State (Foreign Minister) was General George Marshall (page 129). He announced that the USA was willing to give huge sums of money to help rebuild Europe after the war. He made one condition – Europeans had to co-operate and work together.

Because of this, the **Organisation for European Economic Co-operation (OEEC)** was set up. Its main job was to decide how to spend the American money.

The OEEC drew up plans which would help European countries towards economic recovery. In 1952, the OEEC was renamed the **Organisation for Economic Co-operation and Development (OECD)**. It was so successful that non-European countries like Japan and Canada joined. It still operates today.

THE COUNCIL OF EUROPE

In 1948, many leading European politicians met in the Hague in the Netherlands where they tried to set up a kind of parliament for Europe. They called this parliament the **Council of Europe**. It drew up a **Convention for the Protection of Human Rights** and discussed social and educational issues. However, politicians in different countries were not willing to give it too much power.

THE NORTH ATLANTIC TREATY ORGANISATION (NATO)

When Stalin tried to take over West Berlin in 1948-49 (page 131), the United States, Canada and many countries of western Europe joined together to form the **North Atlantic Treaty Organisation (NATO)**. It was established as a **military alliance** in which the members agreed to defend one another if attacked by the Soviet Union.

THE EUROPEAN COAL AND STEEL COMMUNITY

In 1950, many French people were still afraid of Germany. However, some of them – like the French Foreign Minister Robert Schuman, the senior French civil servant Jean Monnet and the German Chancellor Konrad Adenauer – thought that this was a foolish attitude. They realised that France and Germany

needed each other if their economies were to recover from the war.

FOLLOWING MONNET'S SUGGESTION, IN 1950 SCHUMAN PROPOSED THAT FRANCE AND GERMANY SHOULD COMBINE THEIR COAL AND STEEL INDUSTRIES. THIS IS PART OF HIS SPEECH TO THE FRENCH PARLIAMENT ON 9 MAY 1950.

"THE POOLING OF COAL AND STEEL PRODUCTION WILL IMMEDIATELY PROVIDE FOR THE ESTABLISHMENT OF COMMON BASES FOR ECONOMIC DEVELOPMENT AS A FIRST STEP IN THE FEDERATION OF EUROPE AND WILL CHANGE THE DESTINIES OF THOSE REGIONS WHICH HAVE LONG BEEN DEVOTED TO THE MANUFACTURE OF MUNITIONS OF WAR, OF WHICH THEY HAVE BEEN THE MOST CONSTANT VICTIMS."

Robert Schuman speaks to the French parliament in 1950. Although France and Germany had been enemies during World War II, why did men like Schuman feel that the two countries needed each other?

Following negotiations, Italy and the Benelux countries joined with France and Germany to set up the **European Coal and Steel Community (ECSC)** in 1951. These countries were jointly referred to as "the Six". Monnet became the ECSC's first president.

Under the ECSC, each member had to give up control of its own coal and steel industries to a "High Authority". Many people in the Six countries were suspicious of this, but when these industries prospered under the ECSC, they began to change their minds.

⌂ THE EUROPEAN DEFENCE COMMUNITY: 1952

Monnet also suggested that Europe relied too much on the USA for military protection. After the success of the ECSC, he proposed that the armies of different countries should form part of a single defence community. However, many French people still remembered their sufferings during the war and would not agree to let Germany re-arm. As a result, the idea of a European Defence Community was defeated in France.

The flag of the European Union consists of twelve stars in a circle against a blue background. The number of stars will remain constant, no matter what the number of EU members.

The Founding Fathers of the EU

HERE ARE SOME OF THE MEN WHO HELPED TO START THE MOVE TOWARDS EUROPEAN UNITY. EXAMINE THESE SHORT BIOGRAPHIES CAREFULLY. THEN DO THE FOLLOWING.

1. LIST THE THINGS WHICH THESE PROMINENT EUROPEANS HAD IN COMMON.
2. CAN YOU SUGGEST ANY REASONS WHY THESE MEN WOULD HAVE SUPPORTED THE IDEA OF EUROPEAN UNITY?

ROBERT SCHUMAN (1886-1963)

SCHUMAN WAS A DEVOUT FRENCH CATHOLIC POLITICIAN. WHEN HE WAS BORN IN THE PROVINCE OF LORRAINE, IT WAS STILL PART OF GERMANY. DURING WORLD WAR II, HE HAD OPPOSED THE NAZI OCCUPATION AND SPENT SOME TIME IN EXILE. FROM 1946 ONWARDS, HE SERVED IN SEVERAL SENIOR GOVERNMENT POSTS, INCLUDING FINANCE MINISTER, FOREIGN MINISTER AND PRIME MINISTER.

JEAN MONNET (1888-1990)

MONNET WAS A FRENCH ECONOMIST AND CIVIL SERVANT. LIKE CHARLES DE GAULLE, HE HAD FLED FRANCE DURING THE WAR. IN THE UNITED STATES, HE HELPED RAISE MONEY AND SUPPORT FOR DE GAULLE'S FREE FRENCH FORCES. AFTER THE WAR, HE ADVISED AND WORKED WITH GOVERNMENTS IN FRANCE TO RECONSTRUCT HIS COUNTRY AFTER THE MASSIVE DESTRUCTION OF THE PRECEDING YEARS.

ALCIDE DE GASPARI (1881-1954)

GASPARI WAS AN ITALIAN POLITICIAN AND JOURNALIST. IMPRISONED BY MUSSOLINI IN 1926-27, HE LATER BECAME LEADER OF ITALY'S CHRISTIAN DEMOCRAT PARTY. HE WAS PRIME MINISTER BETWEEN 1945-52 AND FOREIGN MINISTER FROM 1951-53.

PAUL-HENRI SPAAK (1899-1972)

SPAAK WAS A BELGIAN POLITICIAN. HE HAD BEEN PRIME MINISTER OF HIS COUNTRY IN THE LATE 1930s, BUT THE NAZI OCCUPATION FORCED HIM TO SPEND THE WAR YEARS IN EXILE IN LONDON. AFTER THE WAR, HE RETURNED TO HELP REBUILD BELGIUM AND WAS AGAIN PRIME MINISTER FROM 1947-49. HIS LATER YEARS WERE SPENT AS SECRETARY GENERAL OF NATO.

KONRAD ADENAUER (1876-1967)

ADENAUER WAS A GERMAN POLITICIAN. HE WAS MAYOR OF COLOGNE FROM 1917-33 AND AGAIN IN 1945, JUST AFTER THE END OF THE WAR. HE WAS ARRESTED BY THE NAZIS IN 1934. IN 1944, HE WAS RE-ARRESTED AND IMPRISONED. IN 1949, HE BECAME THE FIRST CHANCELLOR OF THE FEDERAL REPUBLIC OF GERMANY AND REMAINED IN OFFICE UNTIL 1963.

Looking at the evidence

A further step towards union

The European Coal and Steel Community was a success. The governments of the Six were so pleased that they decided to draw up common policies on transport, atomic energy and trade. A scheme was suggested by Jean Monnet and discussed at the Messina Conference in 1955. The result was the **Messina Resolution**.

THE MESSINA RESOLUTION

The Messina Resolution stated that it was time "to initiate a new phase on the path to reconstructing Europe". This was necessary in order "to preserve for Europe its place in the world, to restore its influence and to improve steadily the living standard of its population".

Paul-Henri Spaak was chosen to head the committee which drew up the detailed proposals. Spaak's report was presented to the leaders of the Six in 1956. He proposed that the ECSC be expanded to take in other matters and be renamed the **European Economic Community (EEC)**. This proposal was accepted when the **Treaty of Rome** was signed in March 1957.

◪ QUESTIONS ◪

1. What reasons did the Messina Resolution give for further moves towards European unity? Do you think these were good reasons? Give reasons for your answer.
2. The Messina Resolution talked of restoring Europe's position in the world. How had this position been lost?

The Treaty of Rome: 25 March 1957

In this photograph, representatives from each of the Six sign the Treaty of Rome which set up the EEC. They also signed a separate treaty to establish the **European Atomic Energy Community (Euratom)**. These treaties dealt with trade, labour, atomic energy and other issues.

◪ *The Treaty of Rome is signed on 25 March 1957. Name the six countries which signed this treaty.*

☖ TRADE

The **free movement of goods** was a key point of the Treaty of Rome. One of its articles declared:

"The Community shall be based on a customs union which shall cover all trade in goods and which shall involve the prohibition between member states of customs duties on imports and exports... and the adoption of a common customs tariff in their relations with third countries ..."

This diagram illustrates the EEC's trade policy.

☖ LABOUR

Workers from any of the Six could move freely to seek work in any of the member countries.

☖ ATOMIC ENERGY

In the Euratom Treaty, the Six agreed to adopt a common policy on the peaceful use of atomic power.

☖ OTHER ISSUES

Article 3 of the Treaty of Rome set out ambitious plans for the EEC.
◪ the adoption of common policies in the spheres of agriculture and transport.

▰ the creation of a European Social Fund to contribute to the raising of workers' standards of living.

▰ the establishment of a European Investment Bank to help the economic expansion of the community.

▰ the association of overseas countries to the EEC to increase trade.

Looking at the evidence

1. Read the headings from Article 3 of the Treaty of Rome. Do you think these were ambitious aims? Give reasons for you answer.
2. The EEC came into being on 1 January 1958. Based on what you have learned, can you predict any problems which this organisation was going to have?

▰ QUESTIONS ▰

1. The first moves towards European unity were caused by conditions in Europe in the late 1940s. List three of the main reasons which persuaded some Europeans that unity was necessary.
2. In your own words, tell what the article dealing with trade meant. The diagram will help you with your answer.
3. Why was the free movement of workers within the EEC an important part of the Treaty of Rome?
4. In 1957, why was it necessary to have a treaty dealing especially with the nuclear issue?

CHAPTER 3

The EEC: 1957-86

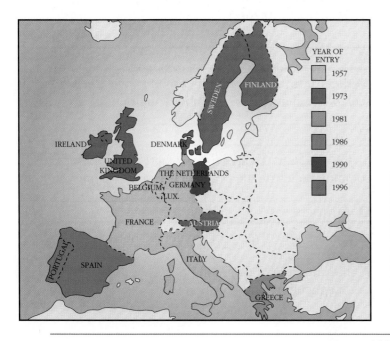

YEAR OF ENTRY
- 1957
- 1973
- 1981
- 1986
- 1990
- 1996

🏛 The growth of the European Union

The EEC grew considerably after it was set up by the Six in 1957. This map shows the fifteen member states in 1996 of what is now called the **European Union** (**EU**). Study the map carefully and then answer the questions.

▰ QUESTIONS ▰

1. Name the original Six who set up the EEC in 1957.
2. There are now fifteen members in the EU. Make a time chart to show the dates at which the other states joined.

FOUR STATES SIGNED TREATIES TO ENTER
THE EU IN 1994, BUT ONLY THREE OF
THEM JOINED THE FOLLOWING YEAR. FIND
OUT WHICH APPLICANT DROPPED OUT AND
THE REASON WHY.

Finding Out

Ireland, Britain and the EEC

Ireland and Britain were involved in some of the early moves towards European unity. Both were founder-members of the Council of Europe and Britain had been involved with NATO from the beginning. Britain was also invited to join the EEC but refused. The British had a "special relationship" with the United States and with their Commonwealth and they felt that these were more important than a European union.

Edward Heath tried to negotiate Britain's entry into the EEC in 1961. Why was he unsuccessful?

But after the EEC proved so successful, the British changed their minds.

In 1961, the British Conservative politician, **Edward Heath**, was put in charge of negotiating Britain's entry into the EEC. The Irish government applied at the same time. Five of the original six members were happy to see Britain join. But the French leader, General **Charles de Gaulle**, objected and Britain was turned down. Since Ireland had such close economic links with Britain, she withdrew her application.

In 1967, the British Labour government applied again, but de Gaulle blocked Britain's entry once more.

De Gaulle was no longer in power in France when Britain and Ireland next applied in 1971. This time, their applications were successful, and in 1973, the two countries joined the community, along with Denmark.

▨ QUESTION ▨

When Britain failed to gain entry in 1961 and 1967, there was no hope that Ireland could enter on its own. Why do you think this was so?

LOOK CLOSELY AT THE CARTOON. THE TWO
CHARACTERS ARE THE IRISH TAOISEACH, **SEÁN
LEMASS** (RIGHT), AND THE BRITISH PRIME
MINISTER, **HAROLD MACMILLAN** (LEFT). THE
YEAR WAS 1961. WHAT POINT IS BEING MADE
BY THIS CARTOON?

Looking at the evidence

"You go first, Macmillan, and see how deep it is."

The Institutions of the European Union

There are four main institutions of the European Union.

THE COMMISSION

The Commission is made up of men and women (known as **commissioners**) who are appointed for a five-year term by their own member state governments. Large states have two commissioners, while smaller states have one. Commissioners swear to serve the community as a whole and not their own countries. A **president** is appointed by the agreement of the member states.

The job of the Commission is to make proposals for EU laws and carry out EU policy. Because it represents the general interests of the EU, the Commission has been described as "the guardian of the treaties". The Commission is based in Brussels and has a staff of about 15,000. One-third of them are employed in the language service.

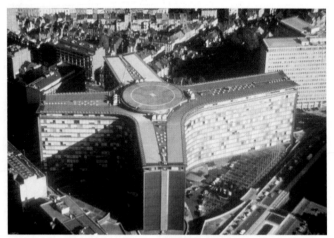

The Berlaymont Building in Brussels is the headquarters of the EU.

THE COUNCIL

The Council is made up of one representative from each EU government. The government ministers who attend Council meetings determine the topics discussed. For example, one Council meeting might be of agriculture ministers. The next could be a Council meeting of finance ministers, and so on. If the meeting is between heads of government, it is called a **European Council** or **Summit**.

Each member state of the EU holds the presidency of the European Council in rotation for a period of six months. Ireland held the presidency in the second half of 1996. This meant that all meetings of EU ministers and heads of government were held in Dublin.

THE EUROPEAN PARLIAMENT

The European Parliament represents the voters of Europe. There were over 360 million of them by 1996. Members of parliament, known as **MEPs**, are elected every five years.

Ireland held the presidency of the EU in 1990. Here, EU heads of state and government pose for their photograph outside Dublin Castle. Try to identify as many people as you can.

Seats are allocated according to population. With three million people, Ireland has fifteen MEPs returned for four constituencies – Dublin (4), Leinster (4), Munster (4) and Connacht-Ulster (3). Northern Ireland forms a single constituency within the UK and returns 3 MEPs.

The powers of the parliament have increased over the years. Its main jobs are to co-operate in making laws, to supervise the work of the Commission and other institutions, and to discuss and adopt the budget for the EU.

Parliament receives regular reports from the Council. It has the power to approve or dismiss commissioners. It can accept or reject the EU budget. Parliament can debate whatever its members wish. The main parliament building is the Palais de l'Europe in Strasbourg.

The EU Parliament Building in Strasbourg. Describe the work of the Parliament.

THE COURT OF JUSTICE

The Court of Justice consists of judges drawn from the member states. Their job is to interpret EU law when requested to do so. Cases may be brought to the court by governments, organisations, companies or individuals. The court has the power to give rulings against national governments. It is based in the Hague, capital of the Netherlands

◢ QUESTIONS ◣

1. Name the four main institutions of the EU. What is the function of each?
2. Can you suggest reasons why Brussels, Strasbourg and the Hague were chosen as locations for EU institutions?

1. FIND OUT WHO THE MEPS ARE FOR YOUR AREA. TO WHICH IRISH POLITICAL PARTY DO THEY BELONG?
2. IN THE EUROPEAN PARLIAMENT, EACH MEP SITS IN A POLITICAL GROUPING WITH LIKE-MINDED MEPS FROM OTHER COUNTRIES. TO WHICH GROUPING DOES EACH OF THE IRISH POLITICAL PARTIES BELONG?
3. TRY TO FIND ANY EXAMPLE OF AN INDIVIDUAL WHO HAS BROUGHT A CASE TO THE EUROPEAN COURT OF JUSTICE. GIVE DETAILS OF THE CASE.

CHAPTER 3

The Single European Act and the Maastricht Treaty

The Single European Act: 1986

To speed up the process of European unity, the member states signed a treaty known as the **Single European Act** in 1986. This amended previous treaties in four main ways.

1. Up to 1986, a council of ministers had to vote unanimously before a decision could be taken. Now, a **majority** vote is enough in many areas.
2. Greater emphasis was put on **cohesion**. This aims to reduce the gap between the richer and poorer states. To do this, EU **Structural Funds** were increased. Money from the fund is given to poorer states to help with their development. Other policy areas given new emphasis were **research and development**, the **environment** and **social policy**.
3. The role of the **European Parliament** was increased.
4. EU states promised to work more closely on **foreign policy**.

The Maastricht Treaty: February 1992

The biggest step forward for the EU was the **Treaty on European Union** signed at Maastricht in the Netherlands in February 1992. These are the most important features of the **Maastricht Treaty**.

1. The EU wants to achieve **economic and monetary union** over the coming years. This means the introduction of a **single currency** for all EU states, a single monetary policy from a European Central Bank and co-operation between member states on economic policies and the national budget. The Madrid Summit of 1995 decided that the EU should have a single currency by 1999.

2. The EU will take steps towards a common **foreign and security policy**.

3. EU states will co-operate more in the areas of **justice and home affairs**.

4. The role of the **European Parliament** has been strengthened once again.

The term **European Union (EU)** was used officially after the Maastricht Treaty. It replaced the earlier terms, EEC and EC.

◢ QUESTIONS ◣

1. What is meant by the Single European Act?
2. Parts of the Single European Act and the Maastricht Treaty deal with foreign policy and security. What problems do these issues pose for Ireland?
3. Why do you think the EU wants a single currency? Do you think this is a good idea? Give reasons for your answer.
4. Have the Single European Act and the Maastricht Treaty pushed Europe closer to becoming a single state? Give reasons for your answer.

▲ *The former president of the European Commission, Jacques Delors, was very enthusiastic about European unity. Find out who succeeded M. Delors as president.*

▲ *Queen Beatrix of the Netherlands joins the politicians who signed the Maastricht Treaty.*

WHAT ARE STRUCTURAL FUNDS? FIND OUT HOW THEY ARE USED IN IRELAND.

Finding Out

Has the European Union been a success or failure?

Has the EU been a success or failure so far? The following lists of achievements and problems will help you form an opinion.

ACHIEVEMENTS

1. Many countries, including many former communist states in eastern Europe, have applied to join the EU. If they thought there were no advantages, they would not bother.
2. The idea of a customs union has worked quite well. Trade barriers between EU states have decreased and trade itself has increased. The EU is the largest trading market in the world and now has trade agreements with over fifty other countries.
3. At a time when food supplies in the rest of the world were not always certain, the EU's **Common Agricultural Policy** (**CAP**) has kept food supplies to Europe secure.
4. Much EU money has been spent on projects in the poorer regions of the community.
5. In 1979, the first direct elections to the European parliament were held in each member country. The parliament is elected by the largest bloc of democratic voters in the world.
6. The spending budget of the EU has increased steadily over the years.
7. The representatives of fifteen different countries now meet at regular intervals to discuss problems.
8. The way in which EU decisions are reached allows even small member states to express their views and put forward ideas.
9. The fishing waters of the EU are protected from outside interference by EU policy.

PROBLEMS

1. Some EU members don't want any new countries to be admitted. Smaller states fear that increased membership would reduce the money they receive from the EU.
2. The EU's economic growth rate has slowed down in recent years. Unemployment is a major problem throughout the entire community.
3. There have been many rows about the CAP. Some countries think it is too expensive, that it has not stopped high prices and that there is too much wastage in the form of "butter mountains" and "wine lakes".
4. There are serious differences in the wealth of different countries, e.g. Germany and Greece.
5. Some countries are not in favour of any moves towards greater political unity.
6. There is disagreement over whether there should be a common currency.
7. One-third of commission staff are kept busy producing EU documents in all the languages of the community.
8. It can often take a very long time for decisions to be made. The Council of Ministers still needs a unanimous vote on some issues.
9. Britain and Ireland have protested against EU fishing policy.

▰ QUESTIONS ▰

1. List the current member states of the EU.
2. Can you think of any points of disagreement between any two of these states? Describe these disagreements.
2. Can you find any sources already mentioned in this text which show that some EU members do not want greater political unity?

The EU now produces so much food that some of it, like these apples and tomatoes, must be put into storage.

Finding Out

1. HOW MANY MAIN LANGUAGES ARE USED BY THE EU? CAN YOU LIST ANY MINORITY LANGUAGES WHICH ARE ALSO SPOKEN IN EU COUNTRIES?
2. WHAT IS MEANT BY THE COMMON AGRICULTURAL POLICY (CAP)? DO YOU THINK IT IS A GOOD THING? GIVE REASONS FOR YOUR ANSWER.
3. THE TEXT MENTIONS "BUTTER MOUNTAINS" AND "WINE LAKES". THE PHOTOGRAPHS HIGHLIGHT OTHER "MOUNTAINS". FIND OUT WHAT THESE PHRASES MEAN. THEN SAY WHAT YOU THINK OF SUCH THINGS, USING WHAT YOU HAVE DISCOVERED.

Activity

THE "ODE TO JOY" FROM BEETHOVEN'S NINTH SYMPHONY WAS CHOSEN AS THE EUROPEAN ANTHEM. LISTEN TO THIS PART OF THE SYMPHONY (OR THE ENTIRE SYMPHONY, IF YOU WISH). WHAT FEELINGS DOES THIS PIECE CREATE? DO YOU THINK IT WAS A GOOD CHOICE FOR THE ANTHEM? EXPLAIN YOUR ANSWER.

Beethoven's "Ode to Joy" was chosen as the European Anthem.

SECTION 4

ASIAN NATIONALISM - VIETNAM: 1945-90

CHAPTER 1: THE VIETNAMESE AND THE FRENCH

CHAPTER 2: THE STRUGGLE FOR INDEPENDENCE FROM FRANCE: 1946-1954

CHAPTER 3: THE STRUGGLE FOR UNITY: 1954-75

CHAPTER 4: AN INDEPENDENT VIETNAM

Ever since the time of Christopher Columbus, Europeans had explored and conquered other parts of the world. By the time World War II began, European empires controlled Africa and much of Asia.

After the war, the people ruled by these empires began to demand the right to govern themselves. As the idea of **nationalism** gradually spread through Asia and Africa, the European empires disappeared. In this section we will look at the story of how one country, **Vietnam**, gained its independence and of the problems it faced.

CHAPTER 1

The Vietnamese and the French

As the map shows, Vietnam lies on the east coast of south-east Asia. It is a small country with a population of over 65 million who live mainly on the fertile coastal plains and river deltas. Its people are friendly, hardworking and inventive. Yet Vietnam is one of the poorest countries in the world, with an average yearly income of only $200 (about £120) per person.

To understand the reasons for its poverty, we will look at Vietnam's long struggle for independence and unity since 1945.

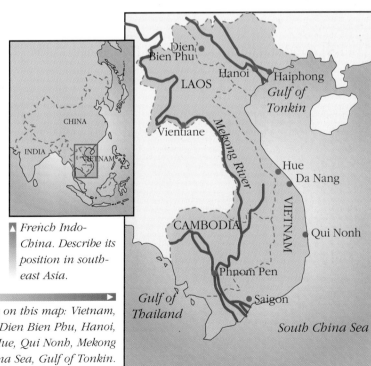

▲ *French Indo-China. Describe its position in south-east Asia.*

Locate the following on this map: Vietnam, Laos, Cambodia, Dien Bien Phu, Hanoi, Saigon, Haiphong, Hue, Qui Nonh, Mekong River, South China Sea, Gulf of Tonkin.

A French colony

Vietnam lies to the south of China, and for more than a thousand years, the Chinese dominated it. Then, between 1858 and 1885, the French took control of Vietnam and its neighbours, Cambodia and Laos. All were joined together to form the French colony of **Indo-China**.

The French were attracted to Indo-China for several reasons.

- The region's **fertile soils and warm climate** were suitable for growing rice, bananas, coconuts and natural rubber which attracted European planters and traders.

- Its large population provided a **market** in which French manufacturers could sell their goods.

A street scene in Hanoi. Why were the French attracted to a place like this?

- It had **good harbours** from which French naval vessels could protect traders in the South China Sea from pirates.

Saigon harbour. Give two reasons why natural harbours such as this were important to the French.

- French Catholic **missionaries** needed protection from hostile local rulers.

French settlers

After France took control, many French people went to live in Indo-China. Some owned rubber plantations, while others were merchants who handled the area's rich trade. Many were employed as civil servants or as policemen who helped control the colony.

These settlers brought many changes to Vietnam. The Vietnamese had to learn to speak French if they hoped to do business with the Europeans, and all newspapers were printed in French. Most Vietnamese were Buddhists, but French missionaries converted some to Catholicism. New houses were built in the same style as those in France. Soon, Vietnam's main cities, Saigon and Hanoi, began to look like French cities.

The Presidential Palace in Hanoi. Why do you think this building was built in the French style?

The growth of nationalism: 1900-1940

Many Vietnamese were unhappy at the way the French were taking over their country, but there was little they could do about it. The French secret police easily broke up nationalist movements which looked for independence. Leading nationalists were forced to leave Vietnam or face long prison sentences.

HO CHI MINH

One of these nationalists was Nguyen Tat Thanh. Born in 1890, his father was a government official who had opposed the French take-over of Vietnam.

In 1912, Nguyen Tat Thanh worked his way to France as a cook on a merchant ship. There, he made contact with other Vietnamese who were opposed to French rule.

In 1919, he presented a demand for Vietnamese independence at the Paris Peace Conference (page 81) but this was rejected. Later he joined the French Communist Party and went to Moscow where he became a teacher at a special school for revolutionaries from south-east Asia.

Ho Chi Minh (1890-1969) was the leader of the Vietnamese nationalists. He led his country to independence from the French and became president of North Vietnam until his death in 1969. Describe how Ho is shown in this poster.

In 1930, he set up the Indo-Chinese Communist Party. By now, he had changed his name to **Ho Chi Minh** ("he who brings light"). For the next ten years, the Vietnamese Communist Party remained small and Ho stayed in Russia.

The Japanese occupation: 1940-45

In 1939, World War II began in Europe. In 1940, France was defeated by Germany. The Japanese, who wanted to create their own empire, took advantage of France's weakness and occupied Vietnam. Ho Chi Minh returned to Vietnam and began to build up a new nationalist movement to resist the Japanese. It was called the **Vietminh**.

In August 1945, the Americans dropped the atomic bomb on Hiroshima and Japan surrendered (page 124). Ho Chi Minh occupied the northern city of Hanoi and declared the independence of Vietnam.

Looking at the evidence

THIS IS PART OF THE SPEECH WHICH HO CHI MINH MADE AT THE TIME.

"THE ENTIRE VIETNAMESE PEOPLE ARE DETERMINED TO MOBILISE ALL THEIR SPIRITUAL AND MATERIAL FORCES, TO SACRIFICE THEIR LIVES AND PROPERTY, IN ORDER TO SAFEGUARD THEIR RIGHT TO LIBERTY AND INDEPENDENCE ... ALL MEN ARE CREATED EQUAL. THE CREATOR HAS GIVEN US CERTAIN INVIOLABLE RIGHTS: THE RIGHT TO LIFE, THE RIGHT TO BE FREE, AND THE RIGHT TO ACHIEVE HAPPINESS."

READ HO'S WORDS CAREFULLY. DO THEY REMIND YOU OF ANYTHING? WHICH OF THE ALLIED POWERS DID HO WANT TO INFLUENCE WITH THIS SPEECH?

◢ QUESTIONS ◢

1. Give three reasons why the French wanted to take over Vietnam in the nineteenth century.
2. List three ways in which the French changed Vietnam. If you were Vietnamese, would you have welcomed these changes or resented them? Give reasons for your answer.
3. What did Vietnamese nationalists want?
4. Who were the Vietminh?

Activity

HO CHI MINH IS CALLED THE FATHER OF VIETNAMESE NATIONALISM. WRITE AN ACCOUNT OF HIS LIFE UP TO 1945. USE LIBRARY BOOKS TO GATHER MORE EVIDENCE.

The Struggle for Independence from France: 1946-1954

North and South

When Japan was defeated in 1945, Ho Chi Minh declared the independence of his country. Although this is probably what most Vietnamese wanted, the French refused to agree. Britain and America feared that Ho was a communist, so they backed the French and helped them to regain control of Saigon and the south of Vietnam.

However, Ho Chi Minh and his Vietminh still held the north around Hanoi. In November 1946, a French warship shelled the northern port of Haiphong, killing 6000 people. This was the beginning of a war between the French and the Vietminh which would drag on for eight years.

The Vietminh had neither money nor weapons. So what kind of war could they fight? Look at the following pieces of evidence which suggest an answer.

SOURCE A

"If ever the tiger (Vietminh) pauses, the elephant (France) will impale him on his mighty tusks. But the tiger will not pause and the elephant will die of exhaustion and loss of blood."

HO CHI MINH

SOURCE B

"Even in the areas under nominal French control, the Vietminh spread terror after dark, sabotaging power plants and factories, tossing grenades into cafés and theatres, and brutally assassinating French officials. 'Anyone with white skin caught outside protected areas after dark is courting horrible death,' an American correspondent reported."

G.C. HERRING, *America's Longest War*

SOURCE C

The French made frequent use of their superiority in the air to drop paratroops behind Vietminh lines.

Study these sources carefully and answer the questions.

1. Why did Ho use "the tiger" to represent Vietnam and "the elephant "to represent France?

2. What did Ho mean when he said: "If ever the tiger pauses, the elephant will impale him on his mighty tusks"?

3. (A) What do you call the type of warfare described in Source B? (B) Is the writer of Source B biased towards (in favour of) the French or the Vietminh? (C) Which words in the description show this bias?

4. Look at Source C. How did the French hope to crush the Vietminh?

French troops and supplies were often dropped by parachute.

Looking at the evidence ▼▼▼▼▼▼▼▼▼▼▼▼▼

Help from China

Up to 1950, the French had the upper hand. But from then on, the Vietminh's situation began to improve. In China, the communists won a civil war and took over the government. They supported Ho Chi Minh and sent him modern weapons.

The Vietminh now began to attack small French outposts, forcing the French to retreat to the big cities. The French still controlled the air but this was of little use against the Vietminh who operated in small guerrilla bands around the countryside.

French troops were forced to retreat to big cities like Hanoi. Explain why.

Dien Bien Phu: March 1954

The French commander decided to stop supplies from reaching the Vietminh from China. He sent his troops to occupy the town of **Dien Bien Phu** which was on the route south.

Dien Bien Phu: French troops try to locate the enemy's position. Why was this so difficult?

Dien Bien Phu was surrounded by hills covered in thick forest. The Vietminh controlled these hills, but the French commander was not worried. He believed that he could supply his men from the air. But from the hills, the Vietminh's guns were able to destroy the French airfield.

The French army was trapped and in an impossible position. After two months of heavy fighting, they were forced to surrender.

The Geneva Agreements: 1954

The loss of Dien Bien Phu was a great humiliation for the French and showed them that they would have to give up their empire in Indo-China. In 1954, at a conference in Geneva, Switzerland, they agreed to recognise the independence of Laos and Cambodia.

But Vietnam was more difficult. The North was already independent under Ho and the Vietminh. The French handed over the south to Bao Dai, a local prince. They also agreed that there would be elections within two years to unite the country under a single government.

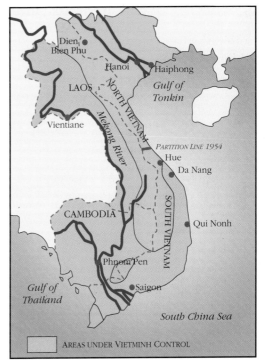

Vietnam in 1954

WRITE AN ACCOUNT OF THE WAR BETWEEN THE VIETMINH AND THE FRENCH. IN IT, REFER TO: (A) GUERRILLA WARFARE; (B) AID FROM CHINA; (C) DIEN BIEN PHU; AND (D) THE GENEVA AGREEMENTS. USE LIBRARY BOOKS TO FIND OUT MORE.

Activity

CHAPTER 3

The Struggle for Unity: 1954-75

The Americans and communism in Asia

The Geneva Agreements promised peace to the Vietnamese people, but it was not to be. Another foreign power, the United States, now intervened in the story.

After World War II, the Americans became involved in a "cold war" with the Soviet Union (pages 127-9). The Americans were convinced that the USSR planned to spread communism around the world and they were determined to stop it.

Throughout the 1950s, communism seemed to be growing in Asia. In 1949, a communist, **Mao Tse Tung**, became the ruler of China. In 1950, communists in North Korea invaded capitalist South Korea. They were only defeated after a war in which many American soldiers were killed (pages 134-9).

Mao Tse Tung. Why were the Americans concerned when he came to power in China?

THE "DOMINO THEORY"

The Americans were convinced that the Soviet Union was planning to take control of the countries of Asia, one by one. On 7 April 1954, the American president, **Dwight D. Eisenhower**, put this view very clearly.

"You have a row of dominoes set up. You knock over the first one, and what will happen to the last one is the certainty that it will go over very quickly."

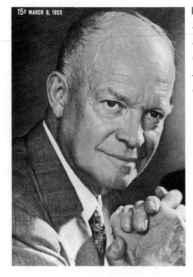

President Dwight D. Eisenhower. Why did he compare the countries of Asia to "a row of dominoes"?

This was the famous **domino theory**. It became the basis of American policy towards Vietnam.

America believed that the communist Vietminh would win any election. So they were determined that, in spite of the Geneva Agreements, no election should be held. Vietnam must remain **partitioned** into a communist (pro-Soviet) north and a capitalist (pro-American) south.

South Vietnam

When the French pulled out of Vietnam, they left the South in the hands of the local prince, **Bao Dai.** In June 1954, he appointed **Ngo Dinh Diem** as his prime minister. Diem, a Catholic, was ambitious as well as ruthless. The Americans backed him as a strong man who could stand up to the communists. Under the influence of the Americans, Diem cancelled the elections.

But Diem's government became more and more unpopular. Buddhists were upset that Diem favoured the Catholic minority. Peasants were angry when land reforms introduced by the Vietminh were overturned. Under Diem's corrupt rule, only a small number of landlords and businessmen prospered. A ruthless campaign was mounted against anyone suspected of being a communist.

The American backed the government of Ngo Dinh Diem (left). Why did Diem become more and more unpopular with the people?

North Vietnam

In North Vietnam, Ho Chi Minh's government was no more democratic than Diem's. But it was more popular. Communist party members toured the villages "educating" the people and rooting out anyone who opposed communism. But land was taken from the rich landlords and given to the peasants, and everyone had better health and education services.

The Vietcong

Ho Chi Minh was angry when the elections, promised by the Geneva Agreement, were cancelled. So he decided to support a guerrilla war against Diem's government in the South.

In 1959, Ho's communists began a terrorist campaign. They assassinated government officials, teachers and village chiefs. Soon, they controlled whole areas of the countryside. They forced villagers to supply them with food, shelter, information and recruits.

This Vietcong poster says "Better death than slavery". Describe what you see in the poster as well as the meaning of the slogan.

In 1960, the communists joined with other groups opposed to Diem. They demanded democracy, land reform and a united Vietnam. To most people, they were known as the **Vietcong** (Vietnamese communists).

America and the Vietcong

North Vietnam and the Soviet Union saw the war in Vietnam as a war of liberation. The American government had a different view.

> *"The US should realise that Vietnam is in a critical condition and should treat it as a combat area of the cold war, as an area requiring immediate treatment."*
>
> BRIGADIER-GENERAL EDWARD LANSDALE, USAF AND CIA EXPERT ON VIETNAM

In 1961, the newly-elected American president, **John F. Kennedy**, sent 3000 American officers to South Vietnam to advise and train its army. The Americans hoped to use the communists' own tactics against them. The mountainous interior of Vietnam was occupied by tribes who hated the Vietnamese from the lowlands. The Americans armed and trained many of these tribes and used them to spy on and attack the Vietcong.

President John F. Kennedy sent 3000 American troops to Vietnam in 1961. How did he hope to use the communists' own tactics against them?

To stop the Vietcong from getting help from the peasants, the Americans developed the **Strategic Hamlets Program**. Whole villages were moved to new locations where they could be protected and supervised closely. Many Vietnamese disliked these policies and support for the Vietcong continued to grow.

The fall of Diem's government

South Vietnam's Buddhists were unhappy with the restrictions placed on them by the Catholic president, Diem. They particularly hated one regulation forbidding them from carrying flags on Buddha's birthday.

In the summer of 1963, trouble flared when government troops attacked Buddhist temples. On 11 June, Quang Duc, a 73-year-old Buddhist monk, protested by setting fire to himself in a busy Saigon street. This led to protest demonstrations against the government and support for Diem collapsed. In November, he was assassinated by a successful military coup which was supported by the Americans.

Power now passed to a succession of military rulers, but none of them was able to gain widespread support or win the war against the Vietcong.

In one of the many terrible images to come out of Vietnam, an elderly Buddhist monk sets himself on fire on a busy Saigon street. Why did he do this?

QUESTIONS

1. What was the "domino theory"?
2. Who were the Vietcong? Why were they so popular with the people of South Vietnam?
3. Explain the attitudes taken towards the Vietcong by (a) the Americans and (b) the Soviet Union.
4. Explain why Vietnam's Buddhist community was unhappy with the rule of President Diem.

Activity

WRITE AN ACCOUNT OF THE RULE OF PRESIDENT DIEM IN SOUTH VIETNAM. YOU SHOULD REFER TO: (A) HOW HE CAME TO POWER; (B) WHY THE AMERICANS SUPPORTED HIM AT FIRST; AND (C) WHY HE WAS ASSASSINATED.

The Vietnam War: 1965-75

The Americans now realised that the South Vietnamese army could not win the war on its own. In 1965, the new president, **Lyndon Johnson**, had to make a decision. He could pull out of Vietnam and allow victory to the communists, or he could send in more troops to help defeat them. He made his choice clear in a speech.

"The battle against communism must be joined in south-east Asia with the strength and determination to achieve success ... We must decide to help these countries to the best of our ability or throw in the towel ... and pull back our defences to San Francisco."

Johnson ordered American troops into Vietnam. By 1967, more than half a million of them were there.

President Lyndon Johnson decided to send even more American troops to Vietnam. Why did he say that America should help the countries of south-east Asia to "the best of our ability or throw in the towel ... and pull back our defences to San Francisco"?

Vietnam and the Cold War

This American involvement turned the Vietnam War into part of the cold war (pages 127-44). When the US sent help to South Vietnam, the Soviet Union sent tanks, missiles and other war material to North Vietnam. No Soviet soldiers were involved in the fighting, but Soviet military advisors trained the North Vietnamese army.

The "Tet" offensive

After the Americans arrived, the North Vietnamese sent soldiers south to fight alongside the Vietcong. They travelled along jungle paths, known as the "Ho Chi Minh trail". With them, they brought heavy artillery and rockets, Soviet PT-76 tanks and surface-to-air (SAM) missiles.

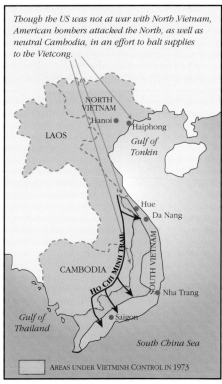

Though the US was not at war with North Vietnam, American bombers attacked the North, as well as neutral Cambodia, in an effort to halt supplies to the Vietcong.

The Ho Chi Minh Trail

AREAS UNDER VIETMINH CONTROL IN 1973

In 1968, during the Vietnamese New Year ("Tet") celebrations, the Vietcong launched a major offensive. During the **Tet offensive**, the Vietcong attacked more than thirty cities. From their bases in the nearby jungle, the Vietcong entered the southern capital, Saigon, attacking the presidential palace and the American embassy. After several days of fierce fighting, the Vietcong were driven back. But they were not defeated.

The Americans now found themselves in the same position as the French fifteen years earlier. They could use their armies to hold the large cities, but they could not stop the Vietcong from gaining control of the countryside. Waves of bombers were sent to attack North Vietnam and American troops entered neighbouring Cambodia, which was neutral.

But all of this failed to stop the flow of North Vietnamese fighters and materials along the Ho Chi Minh trail. The Americans were locked into a war which they could not win. By 1971, they were looking for a way out.

Why did the USA lose the Vietnam War?

THE AMERICANS WERE FIGHTING IN A FOREIGN LAND.

The Americans wanted to save the South Vietnamese from the Vietcong. But how could they tell one Vietnamese person from another? One American Marine captain explained the problem.

"You never knew who was the enemy and who was the friend. They all looked alike. They all dressed alike. They were all Vietnamese. Some of them were Vietcong. Here's a woman of 22 or 23. She is pregnant and she tells her interrogator that her husband works in Danang (the American air base) and isn't a Vietcong. But she watches your men walk down a trail and get killed or wounded by a booby trap. She knows the booby trap is there but she doesn't warn them. Maybe she planted it herself. The enemy was all around you."
MARINE CAPTAIN E.J. BANKS, QUOTED IN *WORLD CONFLICT IN THE 20TH CENTURY*, S.M. HARRISON

IF THE WOMAN WAS FRIENDLY TO THE AMERICANS AND KNEW THE BOOBY TRAP WAS THERE, WHY DID SHE NOT TELL THEM? DO YOU THINK THE AMERICAN SOLDIERS TRUSTED THE VIETNAMESE CIVILIANS?

Looking at the evidence

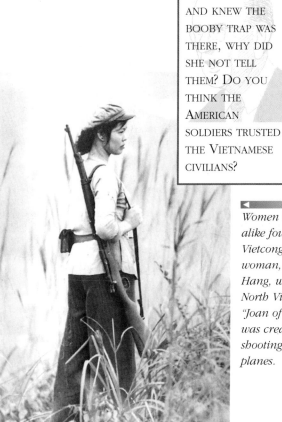

Women and men alike fought with the Vietcong. This woman, Nguyen Thi Hang, was known as North Vietnam's "Joan of Arc" and was credited with shooting down two planes.

A DIFFICULT TERRAIN

Much of Vietnam is covered in forests. The Vietcong used the cover of the jungle to frustrate and trap the Americans.

Within the jungles, the Vietcong lived in elaborate underground tunnels. Trap doors sealed off each layer to give protection against explosives, gas and water. Forcing the Vietcong out of these tunnels was a dangerous job for American soldiers since they were often booby trapped by the retreating Vietcong.

To help their soldiers, the Americans tried to destroy the forests by spraying them with **defoliants** (chemicals to kill the leaves) or burning them down with **napalm**, a jelly-like chemical which sticks to leaves or skin and burns them. But these policies were not successful and caused many civilian casualties. American soldiers were also affected by these chemicals.

A napalm attack on Danang. Comment on the use of such weapons.

Artist's lay-out of a typical Vietcong tunnel system. Tunnel systems like this were built in the jungle areas just a few kilometres outside Saigon.

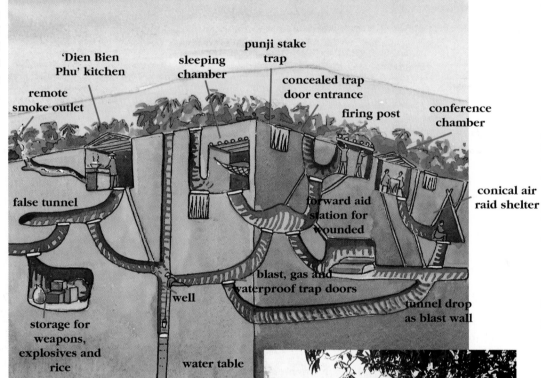

'Dien Bien Phu' kitchen

remote smoke outlet

sleeping chamber

punji stake trap

concealed trap door entrance

firing post

conference chamber

false tunnel

forward aid station for wounded

conical air raid shelter

blast, gas and waterproof trap doors

well

tunnel drop as blast wall

storage for weapons, explosives and rice

water table

A young American soldier makes his way carefully through the Vietnamese jungle. Talk about how he must have felt.

AMERICA LOSES THE PROPAGANDA WAR

Throughout the Vietnam War, the Americans let journalists and photographers move around freely. They sent back pictures and reports of what was going on. These things influenced the way in which many Americans felt about the war.

American soldiers on a "search and destroy" mission. Comment on the picture.

HERE ARE A NUMBER OF POINTS WHICH AFFECTED AMERICAN OPINION ABOUT THE VIETNAM WAR. STUDY THEM CAREFULLY AND SAY WHICH YOU THINK HAD THE MOST INFLUENCE. EXPLAIN YOUR CHOICE.

1. DURING THE TET OFFENSIVE IN 1968, A PHOTOGRAPHER CALLED EDDIE ADAMS CAPTURED THIS IMAGE OF A VIETCONG OFFICER BEING EXECUTED BY THE CHIEF OF THE SOUTH VIETNAMESE POLICE. THE COLD-BLOODED KILLING CAUSED OUTRAGE AMONG THOSE OPPOSED TO THE WAR. IT LED MANY TO DOUBT WHETHER THE SOUTH VIETNAMESE GOVERNMENT WAS WORTH SAVING.

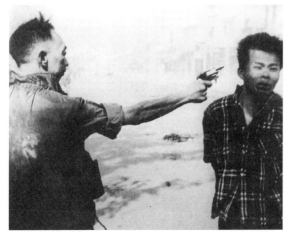

▲ *A Vietcong officer is executed by the Saigon police chief during the Tet offensive.*

2. THIS IS WHAT AN AMERICAN JOURNALIST WROTE IN 1970 ABOUT THE BOMBING AND THE USE OF DEFOLIANTS AND NAPALM.

"ONE DOES NOT USE NAPALM ON VILLAGES AND HAMLETS SHELTERING CIVILIANS … IF ONE IS ATTEMPTING TO PERSUADE THESE PEOPLE OF THE RIGHTNESS OF ONE'S CAUSE. ONE DOES NOT BLAST HAMLETS TO DUST WITH HIGH EXPLOSIVES FROM JET PLANES MILES IN THE SKY WITHOUT WARNING − IF ONE IS ATTEMPTING TO WOO THE PEOPLE LIVING THERE TO THE GOODNESS OF ONE'S CAUSE … ONE DOES NOT DEFOLIATE (DESTROY VEGETATION IN) A COUNTRY AND DEFORM ITS PEOPLE WITH CHEMICALS IF ONE IS ATTEMPTING TO PERSUADE THEM OF THE FOE'S EVIL NATURE."

3. THIS IS ONE OF THE MOST FAMOUS PICTURES OF THE VIETNAM WAR. IT SHOWS CHILDREN FLEEING FROM A MISPLACED NAPALM ATTACK. THE GIRL AT THE CENTRE, PHAN THIM KIM PHUC, SUFFERED SEVERE BURNS TO HER BACK, BUT HER LIFE WAS SAVED AND SHE WENT ON TO BECOME AN ENGLISH TEACHER IN SAIGON.

▲ *Ten-year-old Phan Thim Kim Phuc flees in terror from a napalm attack.*

4. AFTER THE TET OFFENSIVE, AN AMERICAN MILITARY PATROL ON A SEARCH-AND-DESTROY MISSION IN VIETCONG TERRITORY HAD WIPED OUT AN ENTIRE VILLAGE, KILLING MORE THAN 300, MOST OF WHOM WERE OLD PEOPLE, WOMEN AND CHILDREN. AN AMERICAN OFFICER GIVES THIS DESCRIPTION OF WHAT HAPPENED AT MY LAI.

"WITHIN MY LAI, THE KILLINGS BECAME MORE SADISTIC. SEVERAL OLD MEN WERE STABBED WITH BAYONETS, ONE WAS THROWN DOWN A WELL TO BE FOLLOWED BY A HAND GRENADE. SOME WOMEN AND CHILDREN PLAYING OUTSIDE OF THE LOCAL TEMPLE WERE KILLED BY SHOOTING THEM IN THE BACK OF THE HEAD. THE YOUNG WERE SLAUGHTERED WITH THE SAME IMPARTIALITY AS THE OLD. CHILDREN BARELY ABLE TO WALK WERE PICKED OFF AT POINT-BLANK RANGE."
LIEUTENANT-COLONEL GEORGE WALTON,
THE TARNISHED SHIELD

THE MY LAI MASSACRE RECEIVED WIDE PUBLICITY IN AMERICA AND THE OFFICER IN CHARGE WAS LATER IMPRISONED.

WHY DO YOU THINK THE AMERICAN TROOPS BEHAVED SO BADLY AT MY LAI? OTHER EVIDENCE FROM THIS SECTION MAY HELP YOU TO ANSWER THIS QUESTION.

ASIAN NATIONALISM - VIETNAM 1945-90

🏛 Americans turn against the war

The Americans, who were extremely anti-communist, had approved of their government's plan to stop the Vietcong. But as the years passed, the Vietnam War became very unpopular and opinions began to change. There were two main reasons for this.

✔ **Reports and photographs** like those you have studied made many Americans question whether they were fighting for a just cause or using the right methods.

✔ There was **conscription** in America during the 1960s. This meant most young men from the age of eighteen had to spend time in the army. Many were sent to fight in Vietnam where more Americans were killed than in either world war. As the death toll mounted, young Americans began to protest about the war. Protest marches and demonstrations were held throughout America. President Lyndon B. Johnson was greeted with shouts of: "Hey! Hey! LBJ! How many kids did you kill today?"

▲ *All over America, protest marches were held against the Vietnam War. Celebrities like actors Joanne Woodward and Paul Newman often took part.*

🏛 Moves towards peace

In 1969, Johnson did not run for a second term as president. His successor, **Richard Nixon**, began peace talks with the North Vietnamese.

▲ *President Richard Nixon. What role did he play in ending the Vietnam War?*

Eventually in 1973, a **ceasefire** was agreed. The Americans promised to withdraw their troops if the North Vietnamese withdrew theirs. The war dragged on until 1975 when the North Vietnamese broke their agreement. They attacked the southern capital, Saigon, which fell on 30 April.

Saigon was immediately renamed **Ho Chi Minh City**. After thirty years of warfare, Vietnam was at last united under communist rule.

✔ QUESTIONS ✔

1. How did the Vietnam War become part of the cold war? What was the result of this?
2. How did the Americans destroy the jungle cover? Was this policy successful against the Vietcong? What effect did these materials have on the friendly Vietnamese population?
3. Write a paragraph on the Tet offensive.

AMERICA'S ARMY IS ONE OF THE MOST ADVANCED IN THE WORLD, YET THEY LOST THE VIETNAM WAR. WRITE AN ESSAY EXPLAINING WHY AMERICA LOST THE WAR. REFER TO: (A) THE DIFFICULTIES OF FIGHTING IN A FOREIGN LAND; (B) THE VIETNAMESE COUNTRYSIDE; (C) THE EFFECT OF PROPAGANDA; AND (D) THE EFFECT OF THE ANTI-WAR MOVEMENT IN THE UNITED STATES.

Activity

An Independent Vietnam

Post-war problems

North and South Vietnam were officially united in July 1976. Now the government had to rebuild the country. Thirty years of war had left many problems.

◪ Nearly two million Vietnamese had died. Almost 300,000 were left permanently disabled.

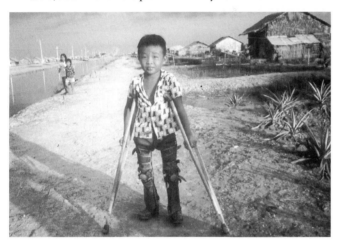

▲ Many innocent people, including children like this, were injured in the war.

◪ Much of the rich farmlands of the south had suffered major damage. The country could hardly feed its people.

▲ Bombing raids carried out by helicopter gun-ships caused a great deal of damage.

◪ American bombing had destroyed most of the country's roads, railways, bridges, water supplies and power stations.

A communist government

The new communist government took over all the country's farmland. People who had fled to the cities during the war were forced to work on the state farms. People who had supported the Americans were rounded up and sent to "re-education camps" where they too were forced to work for the state.

The "boat people"

Many of the country's small businesses were run by people of Chinese origin. When the communists took over their businesses, there was no longer a place for them in the new Vietnam. They were forced, or encouraged, to leave the country.

▲ Thousands of "boat people" tried to escape from Vietnam. Yet countries such as America and France were unwilling to give them refuge. What is your opinion of this?

Many people now fled in small boats to escape communist persecution. Soon, thousands of **boat people** were being picked up around the coast of south-east Asia. Their boats were old and over-crowded and they were often in danger of capsizing or being attacked by pirates.

None of the rich countries in the west would let them in, so most ended up in refugee camps in Hong Kong or Thailand.

The invasion of Cambodia

The Khmer Rouge said they wanted to begin again at "Year Zero". They forced millions of people to leave their homes and move to the countryside.

In 1975, a brutal communist group led by **Pol Pot**, the **Khmer Rouge**, seized control of Cambodia, Vietnam's neighbour. The Khmer Rouge forced many Cambodians to leave their homes in the cities and go to work on the land. Those who refused were slaughtered. In four years, nearly one million Cambodians, out of a total population of eight million, were killed by the Khmer Rouge.

Pol Pot then attacked Vietnam and in 1978, the Vietnamese retaliated by invading Cambodia. They defeated the Khmer Rouge and set up a pro-Vietnamese government. This made life a bit better

The brutal regime of Pol Pot and the Khmer Rouge is sometimes referred to as the "Killing Fields".

for the Cambodians, although it imposed an additional burden on the people of Vietnam.

America and Vietnam

The American government was both angry and humiliated because Vietnam had defeated them. The US refused to trade with the Vietnamese, which made it hard for them to rebuild their economy.

America also believed that the Vietnamese were allied with the Soviets. They opposed the invasion of Cambodia because they feared the growth of Soviet influence in south-east Asia.

Is this an American or Vietcong poster? Describe what you see and give reasons for your answer.

The end of the cold war

When **Mikhail Gorbachev** came to power in the USSR in 1985 (see page 143), the cold war came to an end. In Vietnam, the communist government developed a new economic policy. It allowed farmers to grow and sell what they wanted and encouraged small businesses, banks and tourism.

Ironically, the Vietnam War now became a national asset as tourists came to visit the underground tunnels of the Vietcong and the abandoned American bases. Many American soldiers returned to see the places in which they had fought and in which so many of their friends had died.

Some prosperity has finally returned to Vietnam, but this has been a very slow process. The American government still refuses to allow American firms to invest in Vietnam. Under President Clinton, some attempts have been made to improve relations. But after decades of war and occupation, it will be a long time before life returns to normal for the people of Vietnam.

▲ *Many American soldiers will never forget their time in Vietnam, as the Vietnam Memorial in Washington DC shows. "The Wall" contains the names of all American servicemen and women who died in the war. What do you think the man in the wheel chair might be doing?*

◄ *After decades of war, a couple takes a walk past a tranquil temple in Hanoi.*

◪ QUESTIONS ◪

1. What problems faced Vietnam in 1976? How did the government try to deal with these problems?
2. Write a paragraph on the "boat people". Try to find out more about them from newspapers or magazines in your school or local library.
3. Why did Vietnam invade Cambodia in 1978?
4. Why was it necessary for Vietnam to improve relations with the United States?

Activities

1. "VIETNAM HAS BEEN A PAWN IN THE POWER STRUGGLE BETWEEN THE GREAT POWERS."
   WRITE AN ESSAY DISCUSSING THE VIETNAMESE STRUGGLE FOR INDEPENDENCE SINCE 1945. INCLUDE THE PART PLAYED BY FRANCE, CHINA, THE USSR AND THE UNITED STATES.
2. WRITE AN ACCOUNT OF YOUR STUDY OF VIETNAM USING THE FOLLOWING HEADINGS: (A) COLONIAL BACKGROUND; (B) STRUGGLE FOR INDEPENDENCE; AND (C) THE POST-COLONIAL EXPERIENCE.

CHAPTER

New Arrivals in America

Introduction

When studying modern history we are constantly reminded of how important the United States of America has been in the twentieth century. This is partly because the USA has the world's most powerful economy and partly because since the end of the Second World War, it has been one of the two superpowers which have dominated the world.

But what ordinary people notice most is how the American way of life has influenced the lifestyles of people around the world. In this section we will look at three aspects of the American way of life in the twentieth century.

A nation of immigrants

The United States is a nation of immigrants. Between 1776 and 1920 about 40 million people from countries all around the world emigrated to the USA to start a new life there.

Twenty-eight million of these immigrants arrived after 1860 and by 1914 nearly 15 per cent of people living in the US had been born elsewhere. In that year New York had as many Germans as Hamburg, twice as many Irish as Dublin and half as many Italians as Naples. Over 2000 newspapers were printed in the US in languages other than English.

Arriving in America

The majority of immigrants came from Europe. The first sight that greeted many of them was the Statue of Liberty in New York harbour.

■ SOURCE A

The following words are carved on the Statue of Liberty:

> *Give me your tired, your poor,*
> *Your huddled masses yearning to breathe free,*
> *The wretched refuse of your teeming shore.*
> *Send these, the homeless, tempest-tossed to me.*
> *I lift my lamp beside the golden door.*

■ SOURCE B

▲ This is a photograph of Ellis Island in New York Harbour. It was taken about 1900. Here all new immigrants were checked by US inspectors before they were allowed to enter the USA.

■ SOURCE C

■ SOURCE D

▲ These two photographs show two different types of examination carried out at Ellis Island.

Looking at the evidence

1. IF YOU WERE AN IMMIGRANT ARRIVING IN 1900 WHAT WOULD THE INSCRIPTION IN SOURCE A LEAD YOU TO EXPECT?

2. ON ELLIS ISLAND NEW ARRIVALS WERE EXAMINED AND ABOUT 2 PER CENT OF THEM WERE TURNED BACK. USE SOURCES C AND D TO SUGGEST TWO REASONS WHY THAT MIGHT HAVE HAPPENED. DO YOU FEEL THE US AUTHORITIES WERE JUSTIFIED IN ACTING IN THIS WAY? GIVE REASONS FOR YOUR ANSWER.

3. DOES THE INFORMATION ABOUT ELLIS ISLAND MAKE YOU LOOK AT THE MOTTO ON THE STATUE OF LIBERTY IN A DIFFERENT WAY? GIVE REASONS FOR YOUR ANSWER.

Why did the immigrants come?

We have a lot of information from the immigrants themselves about why they went to the United States. The following sources illustrate some of their reasons:

■ SOURCE E

This was what an Italian immigrant who later became a successful lawyer said:

> I came to America for the sole purpose of making money. If I could have worked my way up in my chosen profession in Italy, I would have stayed. But repeated efforts showed me that I could not. America was the land of opportunity, and so I came.

■ SOURCE F

Andrew Carnegie had arrived in 1848 and became one of the richest men in the country. In his memoirs he recalled a song he had heard as a boy in his native Scotland:

> To the West, to the West, the land of the free,
> Where the mighty Missouri rolls down to the sea;
> Where a man is a man if he is willing to toil,
> And the humblest may gather the fruits of the soil.
> Where the young may be happy and the aged may rest,
> Away, far away, to the land of the West.

■ SOURCE G

A Jewish immigrant from Russia gave a different reason:

Education was free ... A little girl from across the alley came and offered to take us to school. My father was out but we five had a few words of English between us by this time. We knew the word 'school'. This child who had never seen us till yesterday, who could not pronounce our names and who was not much better dressed than we were, was able to offer us the freedom of the schools of Boston! No application made, no questions asked, no exams, rulings, exclusions, no fees. The door stood open for every one of us.

■ SOURCE H

Louis Adamic left Serbia in 1913. Twenty years later he remembered:

My notion of the United States was that it was a grand, amazing, somewhat fantastic place – the Golden Country – huge beyond conception, untellably exciting. In America one could make pots of money in a short time, acquire immense holdings, wear a white collar and have a polish on one's boots and eat white bread, soup and meat on week days as well as on Sundays ...

There were regions known as Texas and Oklahoma where single farms – ranches they were called – were larger than a whole province at home. In America even the common people were citizens, not subjects as they were in the Austrian Empire back home and in most European countries.

Looking at the evidence

1. WRITE ONE SENTENCE ON EACH OF THE SOURCES E TO H WHICH SUMS UP THEIR REASONS FOR GOING TO AMERICA.
2. WOULD YOU DESCRIBE THE AUTHOR OF SOURCE E AS A WILLING OR UNWILLING IMMIGRANT? GIVE REASONS FOR YOUR ANSWER.
3. WOULD YOU DESCRIBE THE SONG QUOTED BY CARNEGIE AS ROMANTIC OR REALISTIC OR A MIXTURE OF BOTH? EXPLAIN YOUR ANSWER.
4. WHAT POINTS DO THE SONG IN SOURCE F AND THE MEMOIRS IN SOURCE H HAVE IN COMMON?
5. (A) WHY TO YOU THINK THE FREE ACCESS TO EDUCATION SO AMAZED THE JEWISH IMMIGRANT IN SOURCE G?
   (B) WHAT DO YOU THINK HE MEANS BY HIS REFERENCE TO "NO QUESTIONS ASKED ... (NO) RULINGS, EXCLUSIONS ..."?

The immigrants settle down

Although many immigrants went to farm land in the west, most settled in the cities and looked for jobs in industry. Jobs were easy to find because the US economy was expanding fast in 1900 as the table below shows:

■ SOURCE I

THE GROWING IMPORTANCE OF THE UNITED STATES IN 1900		
	USA	**MAIN RIVALS**
COAL PRODUCTION (TONS)	262 MILLION	219 MILLION (BRITAIN)
EXPORTS (£)	311 MILLION	390 MILLION (BRITAIN)
PIG-IRON (TONS)	16 MILLION	8 MILLION (BRITAIN)
STEEL (TONS)	13 MILLION	6 MILLION (GERMANY)
SILVER (FINE OZ)	55 MILLION	57 MILLION (MEXICO)
GOLD (FINE OZ)	3.8 MILLION	3.3 MILLION (AUSTRALIA)
COTTON PRODUCTION (BALES)	10.6 MILLION	3 MILLION (INDIA)
PETROLEUM (METRIC TONS)	9.5 MILLION	11.5 MILLION (RUSSIA)
WHEAT (BUSHELS)	638 MILLION	552 MILLION (RUSSIA)
RAILWAYS (MILES)	183,000	28,000 (GERMANY)

Working conditions in industry were often harsh. In 1914 70 per cent of industrial workers worked more than ten hours a day. Some even worked a seven-day week.

Pay was usually low and living conditions for the new arrivals were often very bad. A Danish immigrant, Jacob Riis, described what conditions were like in the tenement blocks in New York:

■ SOURCE J

2781 persons on two acres of land, nearly every little bit of which was covered with buildings. There are 46 babies in the block, but not a bath tub, except one that hung in an air shaft. Of the 1538 rooms, 44 were dark with no ventilation to the outer air. In five years 32 cases of tuberculosis had been reported from that block and in that time 660 families in that block had applied for charity.

■ SOURCE K

Riis himself took many photographs to illustrate the points he made. This tenement was on New York's Lower East Side:

■ SOURCE L

◪ *An immigrant family in its new home*

■ SOURCE M

The Lower East Side was a hive of activity as Riis noted:

You are made fully aware before you have travelled the length of a single block that homes are also workshops ... It is not unusual to find a dozen people – men, women and children – at work in a single room.

■ SOURCE N

◪ *A Lower East Side workshop. These were frequently called "sweatshops".*

Looking at the evidence

1. WRITE TWO PARAGRAPHS ON LIFE OF IMMIGRANTS IN NEW YORK, USING THE SOURCES GIVEN ON P.177.
2. (A) COMPARE RIIS' DESCRIPTION OF LIVING CONDITIONS IN NEW YORK AROUND 1900 WITH LIVING CONDITIONS IN IRELAND AT THE SAME TIME AS DESCRIBED IN PAGES 52-7.
   (B) WHICH DO YOU THINK WAS WORSE? GIVE REASONS FOR YOUR ANSWER.

Making New Americans

The US authorities wanted the immigrants to become good and loyal Americans. One way to achieve this was through education. These picture sources show two ways this was achieved.

■ SOURCE O

◤ *A class of young men in the early part of the century*

■ SOURCE P

▲ *A class of junior infants in a New York school*

Looking at the evidence

1. (A) WHAT AGE ARE THE "STUDENTS" IN SOURCE O?
   (B) WHAT HAS THE TEACHER WRITTEN ON THE BLACKBOARD? WHAT IDEA IS HE TRYING TO PUT OVER?
   (C) DOES THIS RELATE IN ANY WAY WITH OTHER SOURCES YOU READ EARLIER IN THIS CHAPTER? EXPLAIN YOUR ANSWER.
2. (A) WHAT AGE ARE THE STUDENTS IN SOURCE P AND WHAT ARE THEY DOING?
   (B) WHAT DO YOU THINK WAS THE PURPOSE OF THIS RITUAL?
   (C) FIND OUT IF SUCH THINGS ARE STILL DONE IN AMERICAN SCHOOLS. DO YOU THINK IT IS A GOOD OR A BAD THING? EXPLAIN YOUR ANSWER.

Aspects of American Life

The American city

The cities the immigrants found in America were very different from the European cities they had left. For one thing, they had buildings so tall that they were called "skyscrapers".

High rise buildings became possible when iron was used to re-inforce stone and concrete in the 1860s. The first iron frame building was the Powers Block in New York. When the price of steel fell, steel replaced iron. Cheap steel frames made very tall buildings possible and the American skyscraper was born.

■ SOURCE B

▶

A Chicago skyscraper under construction in 1891. This building still stands today.

■ SOURCE A

▲ *This photo of an early twentieth-century street scene shows that skyscrapers were already common.*

Transport

American cities like New York and Chicago were very big, often spreading across many miles of countryside. They had terrible traffic problems, as you can see in Source C, p.180.

■ SOURCE C

■ SOURCE C

⬧ *A Chicago scene in 1910. How many forms of transport can you see?*

Similar problems existed in New York. There streetcars were so dangerous that pedestrians were nick-named "Trolly Dodgers". The name was later taken by the local baseball team! Source D shows a New York solution to the transport problem. Can you see what it is?

■ SOURCE D

⬧ *A New York Square at the turn of the century*

The motor car

The motor car made a huge impact on travel in America. The first American motor cars appeared in the 1890s and were an immediate success. By the 1920s cars were so popular that special outlets called filling stations had to be opened to sell petrol. Look at the one shown in Source E and compare it with its Irish equivalent.

■ SOURCE E

⬧ *Filling station in 1923*

Henry Ford

Early cars were expensive and only rich people could buy one. But just before the First World War, Henry Ford developed a new way of mass-producing cars which greatly reduced the price.

Ford used an "assembly line". A moving platform carried a car from one group of workers to the next. Each group had just one task to perform. Some fitted engines, others doors, others wheels. Far more cars could be produced on assembly lines and this greatly cut the cost of each car.

Assembly lines were soon copied, not just by other car makers but by most industrialists. It was one of the developments which pushed American industry ahead of its competitors overseas.

■ SOURCE F

⬧ *An assembly line at a Ford factory in the 1920s*

When American industry was hit by the great depression in the 1930s, many people could no longer afford cars and car factories closed. Source G is a poster published at the time. What message is it trying to put over?

New York department store in 1897

SOURCE G

SOURCE I

Commercial life

Today we are all familiar with the department stores in large towns and cities. These have their origins in the American city. As early as the 1890s New Yorkers were able to shop in large department stores like the one shown in Source H. What aspects of this shop would have been new in 1897?

Another feature we are all familiar with today is advertising in papers and magazines. This too was fully developed for the first time in the United States. Source I is a page from an American magazine from around 1910. What items is it trying to sell? Do you think it was aimed at any particular group in society? Give reasons for your answer.

QUESTION

Imagine you were an Irish person who went from Ireland to the United States around 1914. Write a letter to your family at home describing your experiences there and commenting on the differences you noticed between life in America and life at home. You should refer to arriving, work, housing, traffic, etc. Use the information in Part 2 and in this chapter as well as any information you can get from other books.

CHAPTER 3

America's Race Problem

Racial tension

Because of immigration, America by the 1920s was made up of more races, more religions and more languages than any other country in the world. This caused tension because the various races did not always like one another.

At that time white Protestants of British descent (nicknamed the WASPS for "White Anglo-Saxon Protestants") were the most powerful racial group in the country. They earned more money, owned more land and had more political power than anyone else.

They did not like the new immigrants. They regarded Jews, Catholics, and foreigners of any kind as a threat to their position and discriminated against them. But the group which suffered most from discrimination were not new immigrants but black Americans who had been there for longer than most people.

Slavery

We read above how people went to the USA looking for work, success or freedom. But black Americans had a different experience.

In the seventeenth and eighteenth centuries, their ancestors had been kidnapped in Africa, carried to America against their will and sold into slavery in the southern states. There they were forced to work without pay for white masters growing cotton and other crops.

The Civil War

By 1860, many northern Americans had grown embarrassed by the idea of slavery in the "land of the free" and wanted to abolish it. But the southerners resisted this. In 1861 some southern states broke away and set up their own government to protect slavery. This led to a civil war between the northern states and the south. Source A shows states involved.

SOURCE A

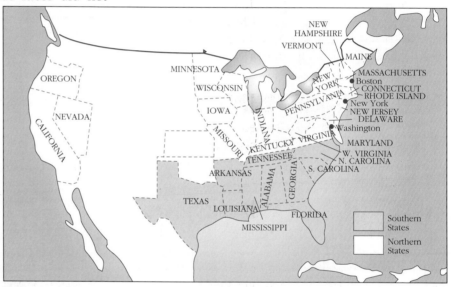

The north won the civil war and slavery was outlawed in America.

But the former slaves did not find that their lives improved as a result of being free. Interviewed in her eighties in 1937 a former slave, Martha Dixon, recalled:

SOURCE B

The masters reacted to freedom in different ways. Some said, "You all go on away ... You have to look out for yourselves now." Others said, "Go if you wants and stay if you wants." Some gave their negroes a small piece of land to work. But the mostest of 'em never give 'em nothing; a heap lot of the masters got raging mad. They shot niggers down by the hundreds. It seem like the white people can't git over us being free and they do everything to hold us down all the time ...

Activities

1. LOOK AT THE MAP (SOURCE A). MAKE A LIST OF THE SOUTHERN STATES WHICH SUPPORTED SLAVERY IN THE CIVIL WAR.
2. USING INFORMATION FROM MARTHA DIXON'S RECOLLECTIONS IN SOURCE B, WRITE A PARAGRAPH ON THE REACTIONS OF SOUTHERN LANDOWNERS TO THE FREEING OF BLACK SLAVES.

Racial discrimination

When slavery was outlawed, former slaves were supposed to become American citizens, able to get an education, to vote and to hold political office, just like white Americans. But this did not happen. White southern politicians introduced laws which made it hard for black people to enjoy their civil rights. They were prevented from getting a good education or from voting.

Education

Black students were not allowed to mix with white students, so separate "black" schools and universities were set up. But very little money was spent on them and the quality of education they gave was low.

Voting

New rules were introduced saying who could vote. In some states it was people who could read and write. But when white officials administered the test, they were easy on white applicants and hard on black ones.

In other states, only people who paid a "poll tax" could vote. But most black people were too poor to pay and so were not allowed to vote. And since there were very few black voters, no black politicians could hope to get elected.

The Ku Klux Klan

Soon after the civil war, some white men formed a secret society called the Ku Klux Klan. Its aim was to terrorise any black people who demanded their rights. As more immigrants came to the USA, the Klan spread outside the south and became very active in stirring up racial and religious hatred around the United States. Between 1920 and 1925 about 5 million white Americans joined it.

Racial tension spreads north

The spread of racial tension can be seen from a magazine report (Source C) of race riots in Chicago in 1919.

■ SOURCE C

Chicago has just finished the first week of rioting between whites and negroes. Already 33 people have lost their lives and more than 300 have been injured. During this wild, wild week mobs of whites chased and beat and killed negroes. Other mobs of negroes chased and beat and killed whites. It took about 3000 policemen and 6000 state guards to bring some kind of order back. The week ended with an attempt to set the city on fire.

Aims of the KKK

A Klan leader, Hiram Evans, explained what his organisation was about:

■ SOURCE D

The Klan has now come to speak for most Americans of the old pioneering stock. These are a blend of the peoples of the so-called Nordic race. There are three great racial instincts that must be used to build a great America: loyalty to the white race, to the traditions of America and to the spirit of Protestantism. The white race must be supreme ... The Klan believes that negroes are a special problem. The Klan wants every state to bring in laws making sex between a white and a black person a crime. Protestants must be supreme. Rome shall not rule America. The Roman Catholic Church is un-American and usually anti-American.

Terror in the south

In the southern states the Klan's favourite method of terrorising black people was lynching. Source E shows such a lynching and Source F was sung by the great black jazz singer Billie Holliday.

■ SOURCE E

▲ *Two black Americans lynched by a white mob in the southern states in the 1920s.*

SOURCE F

STRANGE FRUIT
Southern trees bear a strange fruit;
Blood on the leaves
And blood at the root;
Black bodies swinging
In the southern breeze;
Strange fruit hanging from the poplar trees.
Pastoral scene of the gallant south;
The bulging eyes and the twisted mouth;
Scent of magnolia
Sweet and fresh,
Then the sudden smell
Of burning flesh.
There is a fruit for the crows to pluck,
For the rain to gather,
For the wind to suck,
For the sun to rot,
For the tree to drop;
Here is a strange
And bitter crop.

1. WRITE A PARAGRAPH DESCRIBING THE FATE OF BLACK AMERICANS UP TO 1900.
2. WHAT WAS THE KU KLUX KLAN?
3. (A) WRITE TWO SENTENCES EXPLAINING WHAT SOURCE C SAYS HAPPENED IN CHICAGO IN 1919.
   (B) AS A PIECE OF EVIDENCE WOULD YOU DESCRIBE SOURCE C AS NEUTRAL OR BIASED? GIVE REASONS FOR YOUR ANSWER.
4. (A) IN SOURCE D, HIRAM EVANS SAID THE KLAN "HAS COME TO SPEAK FOR MOST AMERICANS". WHICH PEOPLE DID HE CONSIDER AMERICANS?
   (B) LIST THE THREE THINGS HE SAYS WILL "BUILD A GREAT AMERICA".
   (C) WHAT TWO GROUPS DOES HE ATTACK DIRECTLY?
   (D) DO HIS IDEAS REMIND YOU OF ANYTHING YOU STUDIED IN ANOTHER PART OF THIS YEAR'S COURSE? EXPLAIN YOUR ANSWER.
5. (A) USING SOURCES E AND F, EXPLAIN WHAT WAS INVOLVED IN A LYNCHING.
   (B) WHAT AUDIENCE IS BILLIE HOLLIDAY'S SONG (SOURCE F) AIMED AT?
   (C) FOR WHAT PURPOSE WAS THIS SONG WRITTEN ?

Looking at the evidence

Segregation

The Ku Klux Klan became less active after the Second World War, but discrimination against black Americans continued, especially in the south.

Segregation (that is keeping black and white apart) was an important part of this discrimination. It was used to keep black people "in their place". They could only live in certain districts, where housing and other services were poor, and go to certain schools, which were starved of resources.

On buses, blacks people had to sit at the back. They could not stay at "white" hotels, drink in "white" bars or visit "white" cinemas. Segregation gave most black people a daily dose of petty humiliation.

The Civil Rights movement

In the 1950s black Americans began to object to this discrimination and to demand their civil rights as American citizens. This led to the Civil Rights movement. One of its leaders was Martin Luther King.

Martin Luther King

In 1955 in the town of Montgomery, Alabama a black woman was imprisoned for refusing to give up her seat on a bus to a white man. A Baptist minister, Rev. Martin Luther King, organised a meeting which sent out this message to the black people of Montgomery:

SOURCE G

Don't ride the bus to work, to school, to town or any place Monday 5 December. Another negro woman has been arrested and put in jail because she refused to give up her bus seat ...

Many people joined the bus boycott. At a meeting attended by thousands, Rev. King called for a peaceful campaign:

SOURCE H

There comes a time that people get tired. We are tired of being segregated and humiliated, tired of being kicked about. We have no choice but to protest. We are protesting for the birth of justice ... There will be no threats or bullying. Love must be our ideal ... Let no man pull you so low as to make you hate him.

Although King wanted to keep the protests peaceful, violence did follow. When blacks began to run their own mini-bus service in Montgomery, King and others were arrested. Bombs were thrown into black churches and into King's home. Blacks were beaten up.

Nevertheless the boycott continued. In 1956 the Supreme Court of the United States declared that segregation on buses was illegal. After this victory King became leader of the black Civil Rights movement in America. He spent the rest of his life working for this cause.

Looking at the evidence

1. WHAT WAS THE CAUSE OF DR. KING'S APPEAL TO THE BLACK CITIZENS OF MONTGOMERY IN SOURCE G?
2. (A) WHAT WAS THE THINKING BEHIND THE BUS BOYCOTT?
   (B) DO YOU THINK IT WAS A GOOD OR BAD IDEA? EXPLAIN YOUR ANSWER.
3. IN SOURCE H KING EXPLAINS WHY THE CIVIL RIGHTS CAMPAIGN HAD TO BE STARTED.
   (A) WHAT ARE HIS ARGUMENTS?
   (B) HAVE YOU ENOUGH EVIDENCE TO KNOW IF HE WAS CORRECT?
4. WOULD A SUPREME COURT JUDGEMENT IN FAVOUR OF THE DEMANDS OF THE BLACK COMMUNITY MEAN AN END TO DISCRIMINATION? EXPLAIN YOUR ANSWER.

Ending segregation in schools

Some years before the Civil Rights movement started, a number of black people took their state governments to court to demand equality in education. In 1954 the US Supreme Court accepted their argument. It said that black students must be able to attend the same schools as whites.

At first the governments in many southern states ignored the ruling. But as the Civil Rights movement took off, President Eisenhower ordered that it must be obeyed.

The governor of Arkansas defied the president. When the day came for the first black students to enter the all-white high school in Little Rock, the governor sent state troopers to keep them out.

Source I shows Elizabeth Eckford being turned back on 4 September 1957.

☗ SOURCE I

Later Elizabeth described what happened:

☗ SOURCE J

I saw a large crowd of people standing across the street from the soldiers guarding the central high school. As I walked on, the crowd suddenly became very quiet. Then someone shouted "Here she comes, get ready" ... The crowd moved in close and then began to follow me, calling me names ... I walked up to the guard who had let the white students in. When I tried to squeeze past him, he raised his bayonet and then the other guards closed in and raised their bayonets ... Somebody started yelling "Lynch her!" They came closer shouting "No nigger bitch is going to get into our school. Get out of here!"

At first the black students were forced to go home. The local black community took the governor to court and forced him to remove state troopers. To protect black children on their way to school President Eisenhower sent 1000 federal troops to Little Rock.

☗ SOURCE K

◤ *US soldiers outside Little Rock High School*

Gradually the situation changed and by 1962 schools in most of the southern states were admitting black students. However, that same year the governor of Mississippi refused to allow black student James Meridith enter the state university. The new president, John F. Kennedy, took decisive action. A civil rights worker described what happened:

■ SOURCE L

President Kennedy made a series of phone calls to Governor Barnett. Then he called Mississippi's National Guard into federal service and sent US Army troops to Memphis to stand by for active service if needed. On 30 September Meridith was driven to the university in a convoy of army trucks. The Deputy Attorney-General of the USA went with him.

There was a riot on the campus. The 320 federal marshals who had been sent to the university were attacked by a mob of white students and townspeople. Flaming missiles, rocks, bricks and acid were thrown at them. The marshals fought back with tear gas. President Kennedy sent in the United States Army in transport planes and helicopters. When the sun rose on the littered campus the rioters retreated. Two men had been killed during the night. James Meridith stayed on at the university. He went to all his classes with federal marshals to protect him.

Looking at the evidence ▼

1. WHY DO YOU THINK WHITE SOUTHERNERS WERE SO ANXIOUS TO KEEP BLACK AND WHITE STUDENTS SEGREGATED?
2. DESCRIBE WHAT HAPPENED AT LITTLE ROCK IN 1957 USING SOURCES I AND J AS PART OF YOUR ANSWER.
3. HOW DO YOU THINK ELIZABETH ECKFORD FELT AS SHE TRIED TO ENTER LITTLE ROCK HIGH SCHOOL? USE SOURCES E AND F TO HELP YOU WITH YOUR ANSWER.
4. HOW DID PRESIDENT KENNEDY HANDLE THE CASE OF JAMES MERIDITH? DO YOU THINK HE DID IT WELL? USE SOURCE L TO BACK UP YOUR OPINION.

● Spread of the Civil Rights movement

Events like those described above attracted a great deal of media attention. Newspapers reported how peaceful protesters were attacked and television carried pictures showing white mobs howling at small black children around the world.

Because of this, many white Americans learned for the first time of the discrimination suffered by their black fellow citizens. They were horrified. Thousands of them went to join in the protest marches which Martin Luther King and others organised in the southern states.

The government in Washington wanted the marchers protected but local police chiefs often sided with the white mobs which attacked them. The Ku Klux Klan murdered some of the protesters.

● A Civil Rights bill

The violence shocked Americans. In a television address President Kennedy asked:

■ SOURCE M

If an American, because his skin is dark, cannot eat lunch in a restaurant open to the public; if he cannot send his children to the best school there is; if he cannot vote for the politicians who represent him; if he cannot enjoy the full and free life all of us want, then who among us would be content to have the colour of his skin changed and stand in his place? Are we to say to the world – and much more importantly to each other – that this is the land of the free, except for the negro?

Kennedy announced that he would present a Civil Rights bill to Congress (the American parliament). The civil rights leaders were afraid that Congress might not pass this bill so they organised a huge demonstration in Washington in August 1963.

■ SOURCE N

▲ *Civil rights meeting in Washington August 1963*

Half a million people turned up to hear Martin Luther King say:

■ SOURCE O

I have a dream that one day even the state of Mississippi will be transformed into an oasis of freedom and justice. I have a dream that one day my four little children will live in a nation where they will not be judged by the colour of their skin.

So let freedom ring from the hilltops of New Hampshire. Let freedom ring from the mighty mountains of New York. But not only that. Let freedom ring from every hill and molehill in Mississippi, from every mountainside. When we allow freedom to ring from every town and every hamlet, from every state and every city, we will be able to speed up that day when all God's children, black and white, Jews and gentiles, Protestants and Catholics, will be able to join hands and sing in the words of the old negro spiritual "Free at last! Free at last! Great God almighty, we are free at last."

Three months after King's speech President Kennedy was assassinated in Dallas, Texas. His successor Lyndon B. Johnson continued with Kennedy's policies. In 1964 the Civil Rights Act became law. Johnson explained what he had done:

■ SOURCE P

We believe that all men have a right to the blessings of liberty. Yet millions don't have these blessings because of the colour of their skin. Our constitution forbids it. The principles of our freedom forbid it. Justice forbids it. And the law I will sign tonight forbids it.

Looking at the evidence

1. (A) IN YOUR OWN WORDS, WHAT DID KENNEDY SAY TO THE AMERICAN PEOPLE IN HIS TELEVISION ADDRESS (SOURCE M)?
   (B) WHAT WAS HE TRYING TO ACHIEVE WITH THIS ADDRESS?

2. WHY DO YOU THINK MARTIN LUTHER KING AND OTHERS WERE AFRAID THAT KENNEDY'S BILL WOULD NOT BE PASSED? WHICH GROUP WAS LIKELY TO OPPOSE IT IN CONGRESS?

3. KING'S SPEECH TO THE WASHINGTON DEMONSTRATION (SOURCE O) IS A FAMOUS ONE. WHAT QUALITIES DOES THIS SPEECH HAVE THAT MAKE IT SO MEMORABLE? TRY TO SEE A VIDEO OF DR. KING DELIVERING THIS SPEECH AND YOU WILL APPRECIATE HOW MUCH MORE IMPACT IT HAS WHEN DELIVERED BY A BRILLIANT SPEAKER.

4. IN SOURCE P WHAT WAS PRESIDENT JOHNSON'S MESSAGE TO ALL AMERICANS? DO YOU THINK THAT JUST BY SIGNING A LAW, JOHNSON GUARANTEED THAT ALL BLACK AMERICANS WOULD BE "FREE AT LAST"?

Conclusion

There was a lot more violence and many more killings before black Americans had full legal equality. In April 1968 Martin Luther King was assassinated. His peaceful protests had been the main factor in changing the attitudes of millions of white Americans to their black fellow citizens.

The fruits of his work are apparent in recent years. All across America, black people have benefited from the education that was previously closed to them. Many have become lawyers and doctors or run successful businesses. Some went into politics and were elected as Congressmen, governors or mayors. In the 1980s the first black mayor of Atlanta, Georgia declared:

■ SOURCE Q

I am certain that if it had not been for Dr. King we would have looked a lot worse than Northern Ireland. We would have looked much like Beirut here in Atlanta. I mean, I was afraid for my life in this town, and now I'm the mayor.

In 1984 a black preacher, Rev. Jesse Jackson, ran a campaign to gain the Democratic Party's nomination for president. During President Clinton's visit to Ireland in 1995, he was accompanied by the Secretary of Commerce, Ron Browne, a black man who had begun his political activities as a supporter of Dr. King. Mr Browne was later killed tragically in a plane crash in Bosnia.

But the story is not all one of success. Many black people were very poor then and they have remained so. And while well-educated black people are now able to jet gobs that were previously closed to them, poor black people continue to suffer from discrimination, having higher rates of unemployment, bad housing and other social problems than any other racial group in the USA.

Looking at the evidence

1. ACCORDING TO THE MAYOR OF ATLANTA IN SOURCE Q WHAT WAS THE ACHIEVEMENT OF MARTIN LUTHER KING?
2. WHAT EVIDENCE HAVE YOU THAT THE CIVIL RIGHTS MOVEMENT IN AMERICA HAS ACHIEVED MOST OF ITS OBJECTIVES?

◢ QUESTION ◢

Write a short essay (about 6 paragraphs) on the position of black citizens in America in the twentieth century. Where you can, use the evidence presented in sources in this section.

INDEX